CONTENT OF THE
CURRICULUM

2ND EDITION

EDITED BY ALLAN A. GLATTHORN

ASCD

**ASSOCIATION FOR SUPERVISION
AND CURRICULUM DEVELOPMENT**

ALEXANDRIA, VIRGINIA

Association for Supervision and Curriculum Development
1250 N. Pitt Street, Alexandria, Virginia 22314
Telephone: 703-549-9110; Fax: 703-299-8631

ASCD publications present a variety of viewpoints. The views expressed or implied in this book should not be interpreted as official positions of the Association.

First edition 1988. Second edition 1995.

Printed in the United States of America.

Gene R. Carter, *Executive Director*
Michelle Terry, *Assistant Executive Director, Program Development*
Ronald S. Brandt, *Assistant Executive Director*
Nancy Modrak, *Managing Editor, Books and Editorial Services*
Julie Houtz, *Senior Associate Editor*
Carolyn Pool, Margaret Oosterman, and Biz McMahon, *Associate Editors*
Ginger Miller, *Copy Editor*
Gary Bloom, *Manager, Design and Production Services*
Tracey A. Smith, *Print Production Coordinator*
Valerie Sprague, *Desktop Publisher*

ASCD Stock No. 195207

$18.95

P12/95

Library of Congress Cataloging-in-Publication Data

Content of the curriculum / edited by Allan A. Glatthorn. — 2nd ed.
    p.   cm.
    Includes bibliographical references.
    ISBN 0-87120-253-0 (pbk.)
    1. Curriculum planning—United States. 2. Education—United
States—Curricula.   I. Glatthorn, Allan A., 1924-   .
II. Association for Supervision and Curriculum Development.
LB2806.15.C68 1995
375'.001—dc20   95-41749
                                          CIP

99   98   97   96   95   5   4   3   2   1

Content of the Curriculum, 2nd ed.

Preface   iv
  Allan A. Glatthorn

1. ARTS: What Students Should Learn in the Arts   1
  Paul R. Lehman

2. ENGLISH LANGUAGE ARTS: Public-Professional Tensions in the Standards Debate   23
  Miles Myers

3. ENGLISH LANGUAGE ARTS: A Mastery Curriculum for English Language Arts   61
  Allan A. Glatthorn

4. FOREIGN LANGUAGE: Foreign Language Curriculum in an Era of Educational Reform   69
  Myriam Met

5. HEALTH: Health Education: A Foundation for Learning   99
  Deborah Haber and Christine Blaber

6. HOME ECONOMICS: The Family and Consumer Sciences Curriculum   130
  Sharon S. Redick

7. MATHEMATICS: The School Mathematics Curriculum   153
  Anna O. Graeber

8. PHYSICAL EDUCATION: Physical Education Curriculum   174
  Robert P. Pangrazi and Charles B. Corbin

9. SCIENCE: Redefining the Content of the Science Curriculum   202
  Andrew Ahlgren

10. SOCIAL STUDIES: Social Studies: The Study of People in Society   225
  Donald H. Bragaw and H. Michael Hartoonian

11. TECHNOLOGY: Technology Education   252
  M. James Bensen

Conclusion   272
  Allan A. Glatthorn

About the Authors   278

Preface

Allan A. Glatthorn

This work, like much of what ASCD accomplishes, owes much to Ron Brandt, Director of Publications. Ron edited the predecessor to this work, *Content of the Curriculum*, published as the 1988 ASCD yearbook. And it was Ron who saw the need for an updated version. He and I agreed that rather than simply amending the original work, we would ask experts in each field to take a fresh look at the content of the curriculum.

It was made clear to each author that this was primarily a book for curriculum leaders at state, district, and school levels who want specific guidance about the recommended content of each field. A review of the current literature in the field and my own experience in consulting with school districts suggested that curriculum leaders have been confronted with certain recurring issues. Each author, therefore, was asked to address these issues:

- What standards for and goals of the curriculum are recommended?
- To what extent do current developments in cognitive psychology, technology, and assessment influence the content of the curriculum?
- What structure for the curriculum is recommended: What strands should be used in planning; how should the curriculum differ from level to level, and how much integration is recommended?
- What current issues divide the experts in the field and cause controversy among the public?
- What major research and evaluation studies have been carried out with respect to curriculum models?
- What major resources are available to curriculum planners?

Although we were clear about the desired content of each chapter, each author was given wide latitude in dealing with these issues and in organizing the chapter, since no uniform set of guidelines can adequately reflect the diversity of the subjects covered in this volume.

Like the original work, this book does not deal with the curriculum for all subjects within the broad area of vocational education. This omission in no way is intended to depreciate the importance of those subjects; the limitation is simply one of space availability.

The chapters are arranged alphabetically by subject name to negate the belief that some are "major" and some "minor" subjects. In the concluding chapter, I attempt to synthesize common themes from the individual chapters.

Acknowledgments

As editor of this work, I first wish to acknowledge my personal indebtedness to the individual authors who contributed chapters. In every instance they were open to my editorial guidance and feedback, submitting final drafts that I believe represent a significant contribution to the field.

I also wish to acknowledge the assistance of Valerie Branch, our departmental secretary at East Carolina University; her work in copying materials and handling the voluminous correspondence made my job much easier.

Finally, I wish to thank Nancy Modrak, project editor at ASCD, for her continued professional assistance. Every editor of a multiauthored book needs a good editor at the publisher's office—one who can note errors, polish the style, and coordinate the many complex details of publishing a professional book. Nancy and her staff did all that with a minimum of fuss.

—Allan A. Glatthorn

1

What Students Should Learn in the Arts

Paul R. Lehman

What should students learn in the arts? We can much more easily answer this question today than in 1988, when I raised it in the ASCD yearbook (Lehman 1988). During 1992–94, as a result of initiatives by the Consortium of National Arts Education Associations (CNAEA 1994), educators developed a set of national, voluntary standards for arts education. The appearance of the standards has focused attention on many issues surrounding arts education, including not only what should be taught but also why, how, and to whom.

Despite the passing years and differing contexts, the most fundamental assumptions that applied in 1988 still guide us today:

1. The arts are an essential part of the curriculum and should be an important component in the educational program of every young American. Every writer and thinker who has made a major contribution to Western educational thought since Plato has emphasized the importance of the arts in education. Today virtually all professional leaders in education and a broad segment of the public share the view that the arts belong among the basics of the curriculum. This widespread support at the leadership level, however, has not always been translated into support at the grassroots level when it is needed.

2. The arts require study. Disciplines in the arts cannot be learned through random or casual experiences any more than math or biology can. The arts require regular, systematic programs of sequential instruction leading to clearly specified outcomes. There is, indeed, content in the arts beyond superficial liking, warm feelings, and a vague belief in their inherent goodness. That content consists of skills and knowledge. The arts are enjoyable, but they are by no means merely fun and games.

3. Arts programs should be directed to all students, not only to the talented. Many professionals in the arts got their start in the schools, but that is not why the arts belong in the schools. The arts belong in the schools because they enhance the quality of life. Their importance in every society makes them legitimate subjects of study. They bring joy, enrichment, and fulfillment to every human being. They are a fundamental part of the cultural heritage of every American. They are the essence of civilization. They cannot be solely the property of an elite; everyone must have access to the arts.

4. The arts are not a single discipline, and arts education is not a single entity. Arts education is simply a convenient term for referring, collectively, to education in the disciplines of music, visual arts, theater, and dance. Although these disciplines have much in common, they are different in their media, their traditions, their means of expression, the ways they are learned, and their methods for assessment. It is important to recognize their connections and commonalities, but any instructional program based on the view that the arts are a single discipline is unlikely to be effective.

Background

Writers often refer to the problems facing the arts in the schools as though the same problems affect all the arts in the same ways. Each of the four disciplines has a different history in the schools, and the disciplines differ vastly in their current status. At another level of generalization, the problems facing theater and dance in the schools are dramatically different from the problems facing music and the visual arts. Music and the visual arts are widely accepted as part of the curriculum, and almost every school district in the United States employs teachers of music and art. Although music and visual arts programs have suffered cutbacks in some schools in recent years, and fewer children may be experiencing balanced, quality programs than were available a generation ago, in other schools they are flourishing. A vast structure is still in place for teaching music and visual arts. This structure does not yet exist for theater and dance for several reasons:

• Widespread and well-entrenched programs and procedures are in place for training music and visual arts teachers for the schools, but far fewer programs exist for training theater and dance teachers.

• Forty-nine states certify music teachers, and 42 certify visual arts teachers. Only 23 states certify theater teachers, and only 16 certify dance teachers (National Endowment for the Arts 1988, pp. 106–107).

• Many states have developed frameworks, and local school districts have curriculum guides for music and art; but far fewer such guides exist for theater and dance.

• Most important, music and visual arts education have abundant model programs in every state, traditions of excellence in instruction in many fields of specialization, and clear expectations from the community. These conditions are much more rare in theater and dance.

Although music and the visual arts may be confronted with serious problems in today's schools, theater and dance face even greater challenges. Many people consider theater as an adjunct of either the speech or English literature programs. Dance, where it exists at all, is often a division of physical education. Neither of these perceptions reflects an understanding of the aesthetic nature or the educational potential of the two disciplines. Recognizing the distinctions among the various arts disciplines is essential to any serious effort to improve the standing of the arts in the schools.

Who Determines What Is Taught?

How do we decide what is to be taught in the schools? The answer to that question may be unclear in many disciplines, but is especially confusing in the arts. Two of the most common influences are almost totally missing: textbooks and standardized tests. Textbooks are widely used in music through grade 8, but are almost nonexistent elsewhere in the arts. A few standardized tests are available in music and the visual arts, but they are much less widely used than in the other basic disciplines. Music and art test results are not featured prominently in local newspapers. Virtually no such tests exist in theater or dance. In the absence of textbooks and standardized tests, tradition exerts a particularly powerful influence.

Colleges and universities, through their teacher education programs, play a major role in determining the K–12 arts curriculum. Whatever consensus exists regarding the curriculum in the arts likely results from preservice and inservice instruction. On the other hand, whether these programs are shaping the curriculum or reacting to it is sometimes unclear.

Professional associations in the arts—at both state and national levels—also play an important role in determining what is taught. Their role is probably more critical in the arts than in other fields, and their influence extends well beyond their members. These groups provide forums for discussions of issues that continually reshape the curriculum. And they produce publications that lay the groundwork for curriculum construction and provide implicit background for many key decisions.

The public, too, plays an important role in content decisions in the arts. Public expectations have historically been more important in determining the place of the arts in schools than that of, for instance, English or history. The other disciplines tend to be far less dependent than the arts on short-term, superficial yet critical public support. Will the local high school have a marching band, and will the band perform in the community Thanksgiving parade? Will the elementary art classes take part in the exhibit at the spring art fair sponsored by the local public library? Such decisions are heavily influenced by considerations of public support. The role of public support has become even more obvious and more critical in districts using site-based management.

Most states include music and the visual arts among the subjects to be taught in elementary schools, though the language of the requirement is typically vague. No state, apparently, checks regularly to see that the requirement is met. The regional accrediting associations pay lip service to music and the visual arts in their self-study materials, but I know of no school that has lost its accreditation because of weaknesses in its arts programs.

Arts programs are disproportionately dependent on the cooperation and support of school administrators who control scheduling, funding, and facilities. A sympathetic principal is every arts teacher's greatest asset. Ultimately, however, arts teachers have traditionally been more or less free to teach whatever and however they see fit. Thus what has been taught in the arts has depended more than anything else on the whims and idiosyncrasies of individual teachers. No wonder that arts educators have no clearly defined common core of skills and knowledge of the kind taken for granted in other disciplines.

Because we lack agreement on desired outcomes, evaluating the effectiveness of particular curriculum approaches is especially difficult. Most such research consists of doctoral dissertations, and the composite results suggest that each approach tends to be successful in producing the particular outcomes it espouses.

Almost without exception, arts programs are urgently in need of greater structure and clearer sequence. They require more explicit statements of expectations at every grade level so that administrators and the public will know what outcomes to expect and will have some guidelines against which to measure progress. By providing the basis for such explicit statements of expectations, the national standards represent a uniquely important contribution to arts education.

National Standards for Arts Education

The world of arts education changed abruptly on March 11, 1994. On that date, Secretary of Education Richard Riley accepted from the Consortium of National Arts Education Associations (CNAEA) the national, voluntary standards for arts education. The Consortium, which coordinated the development of the standards, is composed of the American Alliance for Theatre and Education, the Music Educators National Conference, the National Art Education Association, and the National Dance Association.

Funding for the development of the arts standards was provided by the U.S. Department of Education, the National Endowment for the Arts, and the National Endowment for the Humanities. A National Committee for Standards in the Arts oversaw the development of the standards. Committee members included artists and representatives from professional associations, educational institutions, philanthropic organizations, government, business, and the public.

The charge to the Consortium from its funding agencies was to develop a consensus among many constituencies in society with an interest in arts education concerning what every young person should know and be able to do in dance, music, theater, and the visual arts at the end of grades 4, 8, and 12. The Consortium took its task seriously. It sought opinions from every source. It held public hearings across the United States. It sent drafts to everyone who might be interested. It did its best to reconcile the staggering diversity of opinions and suggestions it received. Because of the nature of the consensus-building process, the standards are not the work of any one group; they are the U.S. standards.

What should students know and be able to do by the time they have completed secondary school?

- They should be able to communicate at a basic level in the four arts disciplines—dance, music, theater, and the visual arts. This includes knowledge and skills in the use of the basic vocabularies, materials, tools, techniques, and intellectual methods of each arts discipline.
- They should be able to communicate proficiently in at least one art form, including the ability to define and solve artistic problems with insight, reason, and technical proficiency.
- They should be able to develop and present basic analyses of works of art from structural, historical, and cultural perspectives and from combinations of those perspectives. This includes the ability to understand and evaluate work in the various arts disciplines.
- They should have an informed acquaintance with exemplary works of art from a variety of cultures and historical periods and a basic understanding of historical development in the arts disciplines, across the arts as a whole, and within cultures.
- They should be able to relate various types of arts knowledge and skills within and across the arts disciplines. This includes mixing and matching competencies and understandings in art-making, history, and culture and analysis in any arts-related project (CNAEA 1994, pp. 18–19).

Two types of standards are provided—content standards and achievement standards. "Content standards" specify what students should know and be able to do. They identify the strands of content that are important throughout the discipline. For each content standard, typically from three to eight "achievement standards" describe the specific skills and knowledge and, when possible, the level of achievement that students are expected to attain by the end of grades 4, 8, and 12. The content standards are the same for each grade level in dance, music, and the visual arts, but different in theater. The achievement standards are different for each grade level in all four disciplines.

Because the arts are elective in most high schools, two levels of achievement standards—proficient and advanced—are provided for grades 9–12. The proficient level is intended for students who have completed courses of study involving relevant skills and knowledge in that discipline for one to two years beyond grade 8. The advanced level is intended for students who have completed courses of study involving relevant skills and knowledge in that discipline for three to four years beyond grade 8. Every student is expected to achieve at the proficient level in at least one arts discipline by the time he or she graduates from high school.

The arts standards publication (CNAEA 1994, pp. 85–127) provides an outline of the achievement standards in each discipline. As shown in Figure 1.1, the standards are arranged in four columns corresponding to the four levels, K–4, 5–8, 9–12 proficient, and 9–12 advanced. Insofar as possible, similar skills and knowledge are aligned horizontally, left to right, to illustrate sequential expectations for student learning from level to level. These outlines represent the most concise and straightforward statements of what students should know and be able to do in the arts.

The differences in the achievement standards from grade 4, to grade 8, to grade 12 reflect the fact that, while the subject matter may remain constant at all levels, increasingly mature students are able to deal with more complex stimuli; and their responses should reflect greater insight and sophistication. In dance, for example, some achievement standards are as follows:

• Students in grade 4 are expected to demonstrate nonlocomotor/axial movements, such as bend, twist, stretch, and swing.

• By grade 8, students' movement skills have developed so that they can demonstrate alignment, balance, initiation of movement, articulation of isolated body parts, weight shift, elevation and landing, and fall and recovery.

• By grade 12, students' locomotor and nonlocomotor/axial movements reflect still more highly developed skeletal alignment, body-part articulation, strength, flexibility, agility, and coordination.

The same basic movements are dealt with at all three levels, but great refinements are possible in the upper grades.

The standards describe only one level of proficiency for grades 4 and 8 and only two levels for grade 12. The National Assessment of Educational Progress (NAEP), which will include the arts in 1997, describes three levels—basic, proficient, and advanced, at all three grade levels (NAEP 1994, pp. 53–72). Similarly, the assessment standards for the arts currently under development by CNAEA are expected to identify three levels of proficiency for each achievement standard. The *proficient* level is the level sought for every student. The *basic* level reflects distinct progress toward the proficient level, but without having yet reached that level. The *advanced* level is significantly above the proficient level and normally requires either unusual talent or time for learning beyond that available to the average student.

The descriptions offered by NAEP help to clarify the relationships between the three levels of proficiency. The levels should show a clear,

Figure 1.1
Excerpt from Content Standard 1—Dance

1. Content Standard: Identifying and demonstrating movement elements and skills in performing dance

GRADES K–4	GRADES 5–8	GRADES 9–12, PROFICIENT	GRADES 9–12, ADVANCED
Achievement Standard: Students:	**Achievement Standard:** Students:	**Achievement Standard, Proficient:** Students:	**Achievement Standard:** Students:
accurately demonstrate nonlocomotor/axial movements (such as bend, twist, stretch, swing) (a)	demonstrate the following movement skills and explain the underlying principles: alignment, balance, initiation of movement, articulation of isolated body parts, weight shift, elevation and landing, fall and recovery (a)	demonstrate appropriate skeletal alignment, body-part articulation, strength, flexibility, agility, and coordination in locomotor and nonlocomotor/axial movements (a)	demonstrate a high level of consistency and reliability in performing technical skills (g)
accurately demonstrate eight basic locomotor movements (such as walk, run, hop, jump, leap, gallop, slide, and skip), traveling forward, backward, sideward, diagonally, and turning (b)	accurately identify and demonstrate basic dance steps, positions and patterns for dance from two different styles or traditions (b)	identify and demonstrate longer and more complex steps and patterns from two different dance styles/traditions (b)	
demonstrate accuracy in moving to a musical beat and responding to changes in tempo (f)	accurately transfer a rhythmic pattern from the aural to the kinesthetic (d)	demonstrate rhythmic acuity (c)	perform technical skills with artistic expression, demonstrating clarity, musicality, and stylistic nuance (h)
demonstrate kinesthetic awareness, concentration, and focus in performing movement skills (g)	demonstrate increasing kinesthetic awareness, concentration, and focus in performing movement skills (f)	demonstrate projection while performing dance skills (e)	

8

logical, and stepwise hierarchy from basic to proficient to advanced *within each grade level* for each achievement standard. A similar sequence should be evident when similar skills and knowledge are found *across the grades.*

The CNAEA (1994) standards specify that beyond grade 8, every student should elect work in at least one of the arts. Because of the elective nature of high school arts courses, many 12th graders may show the same levels of achievement in a particular art (if they have not elected to pursue this discipline) as those attained by 8th graders. The standards provide no guidelines regarding the relationship between these levels. For example, there is no indication of how or whether the basic level at grade 8 should relate to either the proficient level or the advanced level at grade 4 for a similar skill.

The standards describe the cumulative skills and knowledge expected of students for exiting grades 4, 8, and 12. What should students be doing in grades K–3, 5–7, and 9–11? They should be engaging in developmentally appropriate learning experiences to prepare them to achieve the standards at the three exit points.

The CNAEA standards are intended to apply to all students, not just to those "talented" in the arts. All students deserve access to the arts in education regardless of their background, their talents, or their disabilities. Experience has demonstrated to arts educators that all students can learn the arts if their schools provide qualified teachers and adequate time for learning.

Standards for Dance

The content standards in dance for grades K–4, 5–8, and 9–12 are as follows:

1. Identifying and demonstrating movement elements and skills in performing dance

2. Understanding choreographic principles, processes, and structures

3. Understanding dance as a way to create and communicate meaning

4. Applying and demonstrating critical and creative thinking skills in dance

5. Demonstrating and understanding dance in various cultures and historical periods

6. Making connections between dance and healthful living

7. Making connections between dance and other disciplines

Standards for Music

The content standards in music for grades K–4, 5–8, and 9–12 are as follows:

1. Singing, alone and with others, a varied repertoire of music
2. Performing on instruments, alone and with others, a varied repertoire of music
3. Improvising melodies, variations, and accompaniments
4. Composing and arranging music within specified guidelines
5. Reading and notating music
6. Listening to, analyzing, and describing music
7. Evaluating music and music performances
8. Understanding relationships between music, the other arts, and disciplines outside the arts
9. Understanding music in relation to history and culture

Standards for Visual Arts

The content standards in visual arts for grades K–4, 5–8, and 9–12 are as follows:

1. Understanding and applying media, techniques, and processes
2. Using knowledge of structures and functions
3. Choosing and evaluating a range of subject matter, symbols, and ideas
4. Understanding the visual arts in relation to history and cultures
5. Reflecting upon and assessing the characteristics and merits of their work and the work of others
6. Making connections between visual arts and other disciplines

Standards for Theater

The content standards in theater for grades K–4 are as follows:

1. Script writing by planning and recording improvisations based on personal experience and heritage, imagination, literature, and history
2. Acting by assuming roles and interacting in improvisations
3. Designing by visualizing and arranging environments for classroom dramatizations
4. Directing by planning classroom dramatizations
5. Researching by finding information to support classroom dramatizations

6. Comparing and connecting art forms by describing theater, dramatic media (such as film, television, and electronic media), and other art forms

7. Analyzing and explaining personal preferences and constructing meanings from classroom dramatizations and from theater, film, television, and electronic media productions

8. Understanding context by recognizing the role of theater, film, television, and electronic media in daily life

The content standards in theater for grades 5–8 are as follows:

1. Script writing by the creation of improvisations and scripted scenes based on personal experience and heritage, imagination, literature, and history

2. Acting by developing basic acting skills to portray characters who interact in improvised and scripted scenes

3. Designing by developing environments for improvised and scripted scenes

4. Directing by organizing rehearsals for improvised and scripted scenes

5. Researching by using cultural and historical information to support improvised and scripted scenes

6. Comparing and incorporating art forms by analyzing methods of presentation and audience response for theater, dramatic media (such as film, television, and electronic media), and other art forms

7. Analyzing, evaluating, and constructing meanings from improvised and scripted scenes and from theater, film, television, and electronic media productions

8. Understanding context by analyzing the role of theater, film, television, and electronic media in the community and in other cultures

The content standards in theater for grades 9–12 are as follows:

1. Script writing through improvisation, writing, and refining scripts based on personal experience and heritage, imagination, literature, and history

2. Acting by developing, communicating, and sustaining characters in improvisations and informal or formal productions

3. Designing and producing by conceptualizing and realizing artistic interpretations for informal or formal productions

4. Directing by interpreting dramatic texts and organizing and conducting rehearsals for informal or formal productions

5. Researching by evaluating and synthesizing cultural and historical information to support artistic choices

6. Comparing and integrating art forms by analyzing traditional theater, dance, music, visual arts, and new art forms

7. Analyzing, critiquing, and constructing meanings from informal and formal theater, film, television, and electronic media productions

8. Understanding context by analyzing the role of theater, film, television, and electronic media in the past and the present

Reaction to the Standards

In the ceaseless struggle for attention in the press, the spotlight has focused only too briefly on the national standards for arts education. Generally, however, both educators and the public have reacted positively to the standards. Many people strongly support the implementation of the arts standards—including leaders of the education reform movement and prominent organizations in both education and the arts. (See, for example, the series of brochures, *Implementing the Arts Education Standards,* published jointly by the Music Educators National Conference and the American Association of School Administrators, the National Association of Elementary School Principals, the National Association of Secondary School Principals, the National School Boards Association, the Council of Chief State School Officers, the National Association of State Boards of Education, the National PTA, the National Assembly of State Arts Agencies, and the National Assembly of Local Arts Agencies.)

A few editorial writers or columnists have argued that reforming education means spending more time on the basics (narrowly defined to exclude the arts) and less time on everything else, including the arts. This is the "When-Johnny-can't-read-who-cares-if-he-can't-draw" argument. But we don't have to choose between the arts and the other basics. That is a false dichotomy. Schools can have both, as demonstrated by many school districts every day. Education reform requires improving the quality of education in all basic disciplines across the board.

A few critics have claimed that the arts standards are unrealistically high. The task forces that developed the standards disagree. The hundreds of K–12 educators who contributed so generously to the development of the standards know very well what is realistic and what is not. Every one of the standards is being met today in schools across the

United States, though probably no single school is meeting all of them for all students, even in a single discipline.

Perhaps the standards seem unrealistic because they lack specifics in certain details. Such examples and clarifications are forthcoming in supplementary publications now being prepared. For example, music standard 2a for grade 8 says "Students perform on at least one instrument. . . ." At first glance, that may suggest playing a Beethoven violin sonata or a Mozart piano concerto. But it also means playing "Amazing Grace" on a recorder or playing an accompaniment to a folk song on a guitar. It's easy for an uninformed newspaper columnist to ridicule the idea of 8th graders composing music. The first models that come to mind may be a Brahms symphony or a Verdi opera, but the work can be an ABA[1] piece for classroom instruments. And there are 8th graders who do compose operas.

It's a familiar story. If students are not expected to achieve, they won't. If they are expected to, they will. The standards task forces set out deliberately to design high standards. Their charge was to create standards that are "world-class"—standards that represent not the status quo but a vision for the future.

Others have asked, "Where will the schools find the time to implement these standards?" One of the best answers is found in John Goodlad's (1984) landmark book, *A Place Called School*. Goodlad makes specific suggestions for time allocations in each of the various disciplines. At the elementary level, he recommends $3\frac{1}{2}$ hours per week for the arts, and at the secondary level 15 percent of every student's program (Goodlad, pp. 134, 286–287). There is still ample time, according to Goodlad, for all other disciplines.

Another answer is provided in *Prisoners of Time*, the report of the National Education Commission on Time and Learning (1994). The Commission recognizes the arts among the core disciplines every student should study. It urges a distinction between the academic day and the school day. The academic day, it says, should consist of at least $5\frac{1}{2}$ hours devoted to the core disciplines (National Education Commission on Time and Learning, pp. 30, 32). The school day may include everything else the schools want to do in addition to the academic core, of course, but that will require additional time beyond the $5\frac{1}{2}$ hours of the academic day. The Commission suggests that some of the activities schools want to offer will have to be sacrificed to maintain the academic

---

[1]ABA indicates a composition in three sections in which the third section is like the first, and the second section is different.

day. How ironic. Only a few years ago, the arts often found themselves sacrificed by local school administrators to make room for the academic core. Now, according to the Commission, they are *in the academic core,* for which other activities must be sacrificed.

Still other critics have asked what the arts standards will cost, and who will pay for them. The answer varies. Some schools already offer excellent programs (at least in music and the visual arts). In these schools there may be little or no additional cost. At the other extreme, some schools offer weak programs. In these schools, there may be significant costs. But that is what education reform is all about. It's easy to say that we want good schools, but are we willing to pay the price? That's the test of whether we're serious about education reform.

Implementation of the arts standards may have to be incremental, especially in theater and dance. Perhaps we can't afford to do everything at once. But we can't afford to do nothing.

Issues

The CNAEA standards have not resolved all the controversies surrounding arts education, of course, but they have helped clarify many issues. Discussions during the consensus-building process have raised other issues to a higher level of visibility.

Interdisciplinary Connections

One major issue is the nature of interdisciplinary relationships among the arts disciplines and between the arts and disciplines outside the arts. Such relationships are featured prominently in the standards in each of the arts disciplines. But the debate on standards revealed that many terms describing these relationships, such as *integration* and *correlation,* carry positive connotations for some participants and negative meanings for others. Because of these differences, the standards have avoided such language; they refer instead to *connections* and seek to use a more neutral and unencumbered vocabulary.

The standards clearly emphasize the importance of relationships and connections among disciplines. At the same time, students cannot understand interdisciplinary relationships until they understand something about the individual disciplines. Many people consider that a function of teaching—not a function of standards—is to help students construct interdisciplinary relationships. The same is true of integration within disciplines.

Cultural Diversity

Another important issue is cultural diversity. The cultural diversity of the United States provides a vast, readily accessible resource for arts education. No arts program can succeed if it fails to address this issue adequately. The standards have emphasized that the content of every arts program must use the art, techniques, and traditions that reflect cultural diversity—which, of course, may take different forms in different communities with different ethnic compositions. The CNAEA standards provide neither formulas nor quotas, but they clearly require that arts programs embrace the full range of our pluralistic culture and that no program that fails to recognize the need for cultural diversity is acceptable.

Technology

The issue of technology has been troublesome to many contributors to the standards. Any school or district with aspirations to be world class obviously must make generous use of technology. Some participants in the standards-development process sought to make this explicit, while others argued that any specifications regarding technology could immediately render the standards unattainable by large numbers of less affluent schools. Consequently, several of the standards clearly imply the use of technology; but by limiting themselves to what students should know and be able to do, the standards avoid specific references to delivery systems. They focus on results, but they leave to states, districts, and teachers how those results are to be achieved.

Relative Emphasis

Another issue involves the relative emphasis on various subject matters in the arts disciplines. In theater, for example, what percentage of the time should be devoted to acting, and what percentage to activities such as script writing, designing, and directing? Most people realize that some of the achievement standards require much more time to achieve than others. Determining the relative emphasis that we should place on the various skills and types of knowledge is not a matter of merely categorizing the various standards and counting the items in each category. How should we determine relative emphasis? The question remains unresolved.

At the most basic level, some people think that arts education should emphasize the performance and creation of art. Practicing artists and many arts educators tend to fall into this camp, which some refer to as the "arts approach." Other people believe that arts education should emphasize the analysis, criticism, and history of the arts. This is sometimes referred to as the "humanities approach." Many supporters of arts education who are not themselves artists tend to fall into this camp.

Of course, to say that the difference between the two approaches is the difference between *doing art* and *talking about it* is an exaggeration. This is an important distinction in arts education that is generally ignored, and it helps to explain the poor relationships between arts educators and many arts advocacy groups. Historically, the arts approach has been predominant. It has been supported by teachers not so much because of an ill-intentioned conspiracy but because it reflects what students and parents have sought in school arts programs. Recently, however, the humanities approach has gained strong supporters, led in the visual arts by the Getty Foundation for Arts Education. This view clearly deserves greater consideration. Balance between the two approaches is needed. Both are important. But to heal the rift between the two approaches, we need to better understand the basic philosophical differences they reflect.

Benefits of Art Education

Another unresolved issue concerns teaching the arts for their own sake versus teaching them for their "extra-artistic" benefits. This term refers to teaching the arts because they help students to be mentally disciplined, they aid students in learning other basic skills, and they contribute to students' self-concept and their social and emotional growth. Again, to oversimplify, arts teachers tend to teach the arts for their own sake, while other supporters of arts education often stress their extra-artistic benefits. Both emphases can be useful and can coexist without difficulty. We should avoid excessive emphasis on the extra-artistic benefits, however, because there are usually more efficient and less expensive means to achieve those goals than through the arts. Overemphasis on extra-artistic benefits can undermine the fundamental rationale for arts education.

Providers of Arts Instruction

One of the long-standing debates in arts education has focused on whether arts instruction should be provided by classroom teachers or by arts specialists. Nearly all professionals believe that arts instruction can best be provided by specialists, though classroom teachers can greatly assist by creating an atmosphere favorable to the arts and by carrying on instruction in the arts between visits by the specialists. Specialists can best teach the arts because the skills and knowledge they possess are essential in developing similar skills and knowledge in young people. Some classroom teachers have these skills, of course, but many do not. The major contribution of the classroom teacher can be to make the arts a part of the students' daily lives.

Despite the importance of specialists, some states and communities will obviously not be able to provide them in the near future. Until specialists can be made available, every school district should consider the ability to teach the arts to be a necessary condition of employment for every classroom teacher. Ultimately, however, this is one of those questions rendered exquisitely moot by the standards' focus on results rather than means. If the standards are achieved, it makes no difference how.

Next Steps

One immediate task on the arts education agenda is to reconcile the national standards with state frameworks in the arts. This alignment should not be difficult. The state frameworks served as major source materials in the development of the standards. No fundamental conflicts or inconsistencies exist between the state frameworks and the arts standards. Certain differences in vocabulary, emphasis, and organization are evident—but no significant differences in substance exist. The skills and knowledge called for in the standards are essentially congruent with the skills and knowledge called for in the state frameworks.

Because of their function, the state frameworks in the arts are more specific and more detailed than the arts standards. The standards are simply statements of what every U.S. student should know and be able to do at the end of grades 4, 8, and 12. That's all they are. The standards are not a curriculum, though they provide a basis for one. They say nothing about *how* they are to be achieved; that is left to the states, local districts, and individual teachers. The standards specify a destination but not a road map for getting there. They're like *par* in golf; they don't specify what golf club to use or how to hold it—just what to do with it.

Another immediate task is to reconcile the standards with the priorities of local school districts. District curriculum guides that are consistent with state frameworks will also be consistent with the national standards. The standards provide ample flexibility to accommodate local preferences for methodology or repertoire. The major task now is to persuade every school district to implement the arts standards. The more strongly a district aspires to excellence, the easier that task should be.

Most important of all, the standards must be reconciled with the concerns of arts educators themselves. Before the standards can be embraced by states and districts, they must be embraced by teachers. That process is well under way, but not yet complete. The general reaction of arts educators to the standards has been extremely positive. Many teachers have welcomed the standards enthusiastically. They have said, in effect, "It's about time." They have recognized that in today's climate of education reform, when standards are being developed in all the other disciplines, we must have standards in the arts as well.

On the other hand, some teachers are uncomfortable with some of the goals described in the standards. Some teachers lament the lack of explicit references to specific skills or knowledge they value. Others point to expectations they regard as unachievable within the constraints that exist in their districts. But the most serious difficulty is that the standards call for the teaching of skills and knowledge that some teachers have never before taught, and perhaps never mastered. Considerable emphasis on inservice professional development will be necessary in the arts. Indeed, if the standards movement is to achieve its potential, we must experience a new era of professional development in the various disciplines.

Opportunity-to-Learn Standards

The Goals 2000: Educate America Act provides explicit encouragement for states to develop opportunity-to-learn standards describing the resources and the learning environment necessary to give every student a fair chance to learn the content called for in the national content standards. Nowhere are opportunity-to-learn standards more important than in the arts, where there is a particularly serious imbalance between the aspirations contained in the national standards and the inadequate amounts of time and other resources devoted to instruction in some schools. Opportunity-to-learn standards have been published for music (Music Educators National Conference 1994) and are under development in the other arts.

The relationship between student learning in the arts and various characteristics of the learning environment is not easy to document, though increased research would certainly help. In the short term, the best source of guidance is the experience of teachers, who know what helps and what doesn't. Unless and until the necessary conditions can be identified through research, opportunity-to-learn standards should be based on the best practices of effective schools. That is, they should specify the conditions with respect to curriculum, scheduling, staffing, equipment, and so forth that are found in the best schools.

Evaluation

How can we evaluate learning in the arts? In the same way we evaluate learning in other disciplines:

1. Define the universe of skills and knowledge to be taught.
2. Express those skills and knowledge in terms of tasks.
3. Randomly sample from that universe to determine the extent to which the students can perform those tasks.

In practice, of course, evaluation isn't quite that simple. The universe of skills and knowledge defined by the standards may not include all of the values and appreciations that teachers seek to develop. Some of the goals of arts educators are difficult to express as tasks (e.g., appreciating good music). And sampling the tasks may not be easy because some reflect tastes that are slow to develop, insights that are highly individualized, or attitudes that are essentially nonbehavioral. The standards, which emphasize behaviors, should help immensely in evaluation. Attitudes and values tend to be regarded in the standards as byproducts of instruction. Some teachers may not view this position as optimal; but it greatly simplifies the tasks of curriculum writing, teaching, and evaluation—and it is no doubt more easily defensible in today's educational climate than a curriculum stressing attitudes and values.

Performance-based assessment is currently a topic of great interest. Music, theater, and dance educators have used performance-based assessment as long as their disciplines have been taught in the schools. Indeed, no other way to assess the essence of what they do exists. When forced to rely on less authentic means, they have resisted or ignored mandates to assess. They are delighted that their colleagues in other disciplines have finally accepted techniques they have long regarded as obvious and necessary.

Even so, we are far from doing a satisfactory job of assessment in arts education. We need much more than glib references to performance-based assessment or to portfolio assessment. These are important techniques, but scoring rubrics are still necessary. Portfolio assessment, for example, suggests that a sampling of student materials will be collected over time; but how should we evaluate those materials once we have collected them? Portfolio assessment is a useful technique, but not a complete answer.

One of the most carefully conceived and promising recent projects in arts education, Arts PROPEL, focused on assessment. Arts PROPEL involved the development and field-testing of teaching and assessment materials in the arts by the Educational Testing Service and Harvard Project Zero, in cooperation with teachers and supervisors in the Pittsburgh Public Schools from 1986 to 1991 (Winner 1991). The project sought to observe and influence how students learn music, visual arts, and imaginative writing at the middle school and high school levels and to devise appropriate assessment strategies that would advance that learning. Arts PROPEL offers valuable insight and suggestions concerning the use of portfolios and long-term, process-oriented projects called *domain* projects.

Assessment standards in the arts are another essential prerequisite to satisfactory assessment. Assessment standards, based on the national content standards, will answer the question "How good is good enough?" Assessment standards are typically called *performance* standards in the other disciplines, but in the arts a different term is needed because of the specialized meaning of "performance." Assessment standards in the arts are difficult to write because it is not always possible to describe in words the characteristics of an adequate student response. Assessment standards will likely include audiotapes or videotapes of sample student responses to the evaluation tasks for performance standards or sample written responses to the evaluation tasks for nonperformance standards. The standards-development process is not completed until assessment standards are available. Efforts to develop assessment standards in the arts have begun.

One of the effects of the standards should be to reduce the mismatch between the rationales arts teachers offer for their programs and the public's perception of what actually happens in the arts classroom. This mismatch is particularly destructive when it exists in the minds of school administrators. Decisions concerning the support of arts programs are made on the basis of perceived reality, rather than on the lofty claims and abstract rhetoric of arts educators and advocates. When school curriculums, teachers' rationales, and the public's expectations for arts education are adjusted so that they are consistent with the outcomes specified in the standards, they will also be consistent with each other.

* * *

What should be taught in the arts has always seemed somehow more mysterious than what should be taught in math or biology. Part of the mystery has arisen from the traditional reluctance of arts educators to provide clear, straightforward answers to questions concerning their instructional goals. This reluctance, once tolerated as mere eccentricity, is no longer acceptable. Perhaps the most important function of the arts standards has been to strip away that mystery.

The arts have historically occupied a weak position in the competition for time in the curriculum. One reason is that they have been viewed as simply entertainment—a respite from the rigors of more serious study. The standards are based on a sound rationale for arts education. They can provide a gyrocompass by means of which arts programs, for the first time, can focus on important outcomes that truly reflect a national consensus.

The national standards for arts education are not perfect, but they represent a reasonable and appropriate reflection of the nation's aspirations based on the collective views of the diverse constituencies involved in the consensus-building process. School arts programs have been squeezed and starved for more than a decade of budget cuts and rampant narrow-mindedness. The standards movement in general, and the arts standards in particular, offer the best opportunity to rebuild and strengthen arts programs that many of us are likely to see in our professional lifetimes.

The arts are specified in the Goals 2000: Educate America Act among the education goals. They are included among the disciplines in which every student should demonstrate competence. The stage is set for a renaissance of arts education in the United States. The standards can provide the key. But first they must be implemented.

References

Consortium of National Arts Education Associations (CNAEA). (1994). *National Standards for Arts Education*. Reston, Va.: Author.

Goodlad, J. (1984). *A Place Called School*. New York: McGraw-Hill.

Lehman, P.R. (1988). "What Students Should Learn in the Arts." In *Content of the Curriculum,* edited by R.S. Brandt. 1988 ASCD Yearbook (pp. 109–131). Alexandria, Va.: ASCD.

Music Educators National Conference (MENC). (1994). *Opportunity-to-Learn Standards for Music Instruction*. Reston, Va.: Author.

National Assessment of Educational Progress (NAEP). (1994). *Arts Education Assessment Framework*. Washington, D.C.: National Assessment Governing Board.

National Education Commission on Time and Learning. (1994). *Prisoners of Time: The Report of the National Education Commission on Time and Learning*. Washington, D.C.: U.S. Government Printing Office.

National Endowment for the Arts (NEA). (1988). *Toward Civilization: A Report on Arts Education*. Washington, D.C.: Author.

Winner, E. (Ed.). (1991). *Arts PROPEL: An Introductory Handbook*. N.p.: Educational Testing Service and Harvard Project Zero.

Resources

The following organizations are members of the Consortium of National Arts Education Associations:

American Alliance for Theatre and Education (AATE)
Department of Theatre
Arizona State University
Tempe, AZ 85287-3411

Music Educators National Conference (MENC)
1806 Robert Fulton Drive
Reston, VA 22091

National Art Education Association (NAEA)
1916 Association Drive
Reston, VA 22091

National Dance Association (NDA)
1900 Association Drive
Reston, VA 22091-1502

2

Public-Professional Tensions in the Standards Debate

Miles Myers

The National Council of Teachers of English (NCTE) and the International Reading Association (IRA), in cooperation with the Council of Chief State School Officers (CCSSO), are now developing English content standards. Drafts of the standards themselves, which will continue to circulate throughout most of 1995 and which will be completed before November 1995, have elicited many interesting responses from public forums. It appears that the standards movement in general and the English standards movement in particular have, as probably almost anyone could have predicted, become sites of contention over the alleged failures, probable purposes, teaching methods, and curriculum content of K–12 schools. In other words, many tensions surround discussions of contemporary literacy.

What is "contemporary literacy"? Bereiter has given us the helpful reminder (Bereiter 1994, pp. 22–23) that all literacy practices cut across what Popper (1977) calls the three worlds: the patterns of the material objects and visible behaviors of World-1, the internal consciousness and cognitive processes of World-2, and the structure of immaterial ideas and concepts in World-3. Let's look at these worlds a little further:

- In English, we find the visible patterns of World-1 theaters (backdrops, exits), books (margins, covers), essays (titles, authors), computers (screens, keyboards), and social-organization (interaction in apprenticeships); and in other subjects, we find the World-1 patterns of bodies (biology and physiology), chemicals (chemistry), food (home economics), and so forth.
- In all subjects, we find the World-2 cognitive structures of internal mental images (senses), schemas (outlines), strategies (predicting), processes (chunking), and social interactions (scaffolding).
- In English, we find the World-3 conceptual structures of ideas (justice), theories (evolution), processes (synthesis), genre (novel and poem), and language (morphology, syntax).

Each world is generally, although not always, a translation of the other two. Therefore, the ideas in World-3 can be translated into physical objects, performances, or events in World-1 and into internal cognitive strategies in World-2. For example, ideas like the equality of men and women (or lack thereof) from World-3 can be recoded as the distribution of male and female labor in the workplace in World-1 and as the schemas and processes associated with gender in academic settings in World-2.

An adequate set of information and experience from each world is called *literacy*. Literate people have an adequate set; illiterate people do not. In schools, students typically learn about all three types of cultural capital, but inevitably, particular forms of literacy stress one type over another. Thus, the forms of literacy adopted by a nation change over time (Myers 1995), as follows:

- In the United States, from 1916 to 1983, *decoding/analytic literacy* was the primary form of literacy. In this form of literacy, teachers and textbooks delivered knowledge to students, who then studied the information and gave it back to the teacher on tests. In decoding/analytic literacy, classrooms were small lecture halls, most learning was individual, concepts were generic, and the self or learner was a passive receiver of information (Myers 1995, pp. 143–181).
- Current definitions of literacy emphasize *translation/critical literacy,* in which learning is both individual and collaborative (computers, collaborative groups); concepts are situated and embedded in a specific context or domain; and the self or learner is actively constructing information within a particular learning community or discipline, taking in a story and standing back from it, participating and observing, alternating between believing and doubting (Elbow 1986), confirming and disconfirming, and comprehending and criticizing (Langer 1989).

In this chapter, I use the terms "old" and "new" literacy to refer to *decoding/analytic* and *translation/critical* literacies, respectively. Keep in mind, however, that both are alive and well in schools today, and many controversies surround their definitions and applications.

The curriculum content standards of NCTE/IRA are an attempt to specify some of the details of the new literacy. The standards describe what students should be able to do in public performances (World-1); what they should know and use as internal, cognitive processes (World-2); and what they should understand and use as conceptual structures (World-3). These content standards are based on descriptions of the domain structure of language, literature, composition, and nonliterary documents, particularly the structure of documents of information and public discourse. Performance standards are test specifications for the content standards. Recent drafts of the content standards (NCTE and IRA 1994) suggest that students should know and be able to do, among other things, the following (from a draft, in no particular order):

1. Understand the central ideas in the literature of the United States and the traditions that are contributing and have contributed to it.

2. Write, speak, and respond thoughtfully and critically in a variety of genres for varied purposes and audiences.

3. Apply critical thinking and interpretive skills in comprehension of language and literature.

4. Understand and use the formal conventions of standard English.

5. Use multiple sources and forms of knowledge, including everyday experiences and disciplinary knowledge, to define, synthesize, hypothesize, draw conclusions, and evaluate information.

6. Use a range of technological forms of communication and understand and critically evaluate the conventions, demands, opportunities, and responsibilities of technologically based discourse.

7. Develop multiple strategies to understand, appreciate, interpret, and critique both literature and public discourse, both print and nonprint texts, both one's own work, and the work of others.

8. Understand and respond to literature and its aesthetic dimension.

9. Understand the ways in which readers, writers, speakers, listeners, and viewers are influenced by personal, social, cultural, and historical contexts.

10. Understand a variety of modes and explore ideas and feelings imaginatively through a variety of modes.

11. Become aware of, monitor, reflect on, and communicate about one's own processes and strategies in reading, writing, listening, speaking, and viewing.

12. Understand the varieties of language within and across individuals, cultural communities, and social situations.

Now a list like this, whether from a draft or not, begins to convey the shift in literacy, which underlies many standards statements, and it is this shift in the definition of literacy that underlies the public-professional contentions that have arisen in the English standards effort. Educators, policymakers, and the public continually debate issues such as the alleged failures of schools, the purposes of education, the place of attitudes and feelings in English curriculums, and the phonics/whole language controversy—just to name a few. Let's examine the details of some of these disputes.

Contention 1. The Alleged Failures of Schools

The first point of contention is whether or not schools are failing. Some critics claim that the quality of education in the United States is far worse now than it has ever been. Other people claim that the problem is that we are attempting to define a new "higher" standard of minimum literacy for everyone. An example of the first criticism is *A Nation at Risk* (National Commission on Excellence in Education 1983), which initiated the standards discussion by claiming that "the educational foundations of our society are presently being eroded by a rising tide of mediocrity" (p. 5). An example of the second claim is a series of reports from the National Assessment of Educational Progress (NAEP). In these reports, NAEP says that our primary curriculum problems in schools are not basic skills, but higher-order thinking at the intermediate and advanced levels. These distinctions have required NAEP to differentiate reading into different types of reading at different levels—basic, intermediate, advanced, and so forth (Mullis, Campbell, and Farstrup 1993).

Most of the available evidence suggests that the present standards movement is not a response to school failure to teach traditional skills but is a response to *new literacy needs*. (The review that follows comes from Myers 1994 and 1995). In 1993, the National Adult Literacy Survey (NALS) reported that over 80 percent of young adults in the United States, 18 to 26 years of age, could perform basic literacy tasks (Kirsch, Jungeblut, Jenkins, and Kolstad 1993); and NAEP reported that the "basics" of the old literacy had been taught by 1993 to 59 percent of 4th graders, 69 percent of 8th graders, and 75 percent of 12th graders (Mullis et al. 1993, pp. 7–8). Further, between 1977 and 1984, scores of 3rd and 8th graders rose dramatically on basic skills tests (ITBS); and between 1973 and 1982, reading scores rose 10 percentile points on the Stanford Achievement Test (SAT) (Kaestle, Damon-Moore, Stedman, Tinsley, and Trollinger 1991, p. 129) and were equal or higher on the Metropolitan Achievement Test (MAT) in 1970 than in 1958 (Kaestle et al. 1991, p. 131). There is substantial evidence of an increase in competence in basic skills throughout the population between 1916 and the 1980s. By the 1980s, most states were reporting above-average results on norm-referenced tests of basic skills in reading and writing (Cannell 1987); in fact, average reading levels went up 14 points in the United States between the early 1900s and the late 1980s (Linn, Graue, and Sanders 1990).

Thus, the present standards movement in English language arts is not the result of the failure of the schools, but the result of changing literacy needs in society. Furthermore, the current standards movement is not the first such movement in the United States. (The following review comes from Myers 1995.)

• The decision in the early 1800s to require recruits in the merchant marines to sign their name was a recognition that the country was leaving many of its oral customs behind and entering a new period of *signature literacy.*

• Signature literacy was followed by a period of *recitation literacy,* in which students memorized passages and then recited those passages aloud.

• In 1916, recitation literacy was replaced by *decoding/analytic literacy* (which we are calling the "old" literacy here), in which students silently and individually analyzed the parts of sounds, words, sentences, paragraphs, and different genres (Myers 1995).[1]

• In the 1980s and 1990s (as discussed earlier), we have seen a movement toward a new literacy, the current standards effort being one of the forums for defining this "new" literacy.

The old decoding/analytic literacy presented itself as universal, but the new literacy presents itself as contingent. English language arts professionals have not yet been able to explain to the general public this new conception of literacy as a contingent "construct" for solving contemporary problems. Thus, much of the public often concludes that

---

[1]Outside the United States, shifts in the definition of literacy include such events as the collapse of the religious "monopoly of writing" and the simultaneous emergence in the 11th and 12th centuries in England of vernacular writing.

we must be failing to do what we should have been doing all along. The fact is that the U.S. teacher is being asked to do what very few teachers across the world have even attempted, to teach *all* students "higher-order thinking skills." The essential point is that the public schools have *not* failed to do what they were asked to do. The standards project is an effort to define new curriculum goals for schools.

Contention 2. The Purpose of Education

A second area of contention between some members of the public and the profession is the purpose of public education. In general, most people agree that the purpose of schooling is to give young people the information and experiences they need to get along in the world, and "getting along" tends to mean that students get in school the necessary information and experiences to produce or to reproduce the kind of culture the public wants. At various times, however, schools have tended to emphasize one of four purposes:

- Identity or personal growth education
- Liberal or citizenship education
- Vocational or workplace education
- Academic or university education

Educators emphasizing personal growth education were often vigorously attacked for ignoring citizenship, academics, and workplace issues; those emphasizing a liberal or general education were often attacked for ignoring education for personal growth, for academic disciplines, and for getting a job; those emphasizing vocational education were often criticized for ignoring personal growth, academics, and citizenship; and those emphasizing academics were often criticized for ignoring personal growth and citizenship.

All four purposes—vocationalism, academics, citizenship, and personal growth—are a key part of the new literacy.

Let's look first at vocational or workplace education. In the old literacy, students prepared for a job either in a factory, an office, or a place with an academic ladder requiring degrees in higher education. In the new literacy, educators are realizing that many of the higher-order thinking skills formerly thought necessary only for the academic ladder are also necessary for students preparing for today's commercial workplaces. And people on the academic ladder are beginning to discover they need the technological skills of the modern office. Thus, vocationalism and academics are sharing more and more common ground.

Similarly, educators favoring a liberal education are now realizing that as the demands of citizenship in a contemporary democracy keep increasing, higher-order thinking skills become increasingly important for *all* students, not just the elite few.

In addition, people increasingly recognize that the marketplace and vocationalism depend on nonmarket values to survive. Trust and concern about others, for example—the essentials of personal growth education—are an essential foundation for markets and the workplace (West 1994). Moreover, many educators are recognizing that personal growth education—particularly sensitivity to other perspectives on life—is increasingly important to citizenship and to the new patterns of collaborative work in industry and academic workplaces.

Most parents expect K–12 schools to give the highest priority to workplace, academic, and citizenship needs. Parents agree that good schools are necessary to "keep and improve the slim competitive edge we still retain in world markets" and to enable all students "to participate fully in our national life" (National Commission on Excellence in Education 1983, p. 7). They know that good schools are necessary to improve the quality of democratic forums because "We need concerned people who are participants in inquiry, who know how to ask the right questions, and who understand the process by which policy is shaped" (Boyer 1987, p. 28). Most parents also expect schools to teach communal values of respect for democratic institutions, fairness to others, and honesty—all central issues in personal growth.

But the emphasis on personal growth seems to some parents not only to ignore content and skills, the primary responsibility of the public schools, but to intrude into an area reserved for the family and sometimes for the church. In many areas, Catholic Americans, Christian Americans, Japanese Americans, and Jewish Americans have set up weekend schools to teach their children the education of personal growth and various sectarian commitments. For these parents, Music TV (MTV) and the values of commercialism, sex, and exploitation have taken over the schools (and the media), and neither the schools nor the media can be trusted to teach a personal growth curriculum. Another group of parents, however, wants to ensure that the values of religious spirituality will be at the center of schooling. To accomplish this goal, these parents want a carefully monitored daily prayer or moment of silence to begin each school day. These two groups, though differing in their approaches, share a common belief that schools, as they are now constituted, are not equipped to teach personal growth education. "Of the People" is one national advocacy group pushing for a parental rights amendment to state constitutions, an amendment that says "the rights of parents to direct the upbringing and education of their children shall not be infringed" upon (Deily 1995, pp. 1–2).

For English teachers, the challenge is to find among these arguments about purpose a core curriculum that provides both clear content and values, both a common foundation and a student choice, and a concern both for personal growth and workplace skills. Furthermore, for all parents and teachers there is a need for clarity about student and teacher behavior toward others in schools. Many parents complain, for instance, that schools are no longer safe for their children. We must acknowledge that schools must have a moral vision, a vision shaping the way people are treated in a school committed to democratic values. Values are not the monopoly of religious institutions, despite our insistence that public schools are secular institutions.

Contention 3. Tension Between Skills and Meaning, Between Participation and Observation

A third criticism of English standards by some parents is that in contemporary English/English language arts, instruction in reading and writing does not focus adequately on a traditional World-1 list of generic, basic skills or World-2 cognitive processes, but instead focuses too much on World-3 ideas and meaning. These parents (and some members of the profession) oppose recent efforts to redefine classroom reading and writing as *literacy* activities in which students learn embedded skills and processes while focused on understanding what they read and write. These parents (and professionals) fear that attention to meaning and ideas in stories and essays has left some students without an adequate understanding of processes, phonics, spelling, and various parts essential for basic skills in reading and writing. The key question in literacy events, as Sylvia Scribner stressed, is always "What is leading?" (DiBello 1992, p. 114). It is ideas and conceptual purpose that are leading the activities of contemporary literacy events in schools teaching the new literacy. Skills and processes are situated or embedded within idea-driven literacy activities.

In the new literacy, the explicit study of language parts (sound-letter relationships, spelling, and punctuation) and the explicit recognition and practice of processes come during actual reading and writing activities focused on understanding and producing the ideas of reports, stories, studies, plays, and so forth. Students are expected to be able to participate in the development of ideas and, at the same time, to stand back and monitor or edit their efforts. Sometimes standing back means setting aside time for practicing particular skills.

The following descriptions of what students are expected to do in the idea-based programs of the new literacy reflect this emphasis on participation in literacy events in which time and attention is also set aside for skill practice:

- Take in the text and stand back from the text (Langer 1989)
- Participate in the belief of the text and analyze the disbelief of the text (Elbow 1986)
- Participate in and criticize the text (Frye 1965)
- Imitate as a participant and observe as a spectator (Harding 1937)
- Be seduced by the text and resist the text (Rosenblatt 1968)
- Compose meaning and edit parts as a recursive process (Sommers 1980)

In the words of apprentice theorists, idea-based or literature-based ways of learning to read must have two essential features—*invisibility* and *visibility*: "Invisibility in the form of unproblematic interpretation and integration into the activity, and visibility in the form of extended access to information" (Lave and Wenger 1991, p. 103).

Visibility takes the form of explicit observation of language, conscious practice of metacognition and other skills, drills now and then, and the development of both an interpretive and a critical, stand-back attitude. Invisibility takes the form of purposeful participation, involvement, and intentional engagement in an activity.

The point is that the old literacy and its emphasis on explicit observation and imitation does not work in an age demanding a new literacy of problem solving and interpretation. Most apprentice programs in and out of school are struggling with this change:

> Apprenticeships are supposed to acquire the "specifics" of practice through "observation and imitation." But this view is in all probability wrong in every particular. . . . To begin with newcomers' *legitimate peripherality* provides them with more than an "observational" lookout post: It crucially involves participation as a way of learning—of both absorbing and being absorbed in—the culture of practice (Lave and Wenger 1991, p. 95).

Students in most professions, as well as apprentices in trades, know that a balance between explicit instruction/observation and involvement/participation is the key to learning. For example, apprentice butchers complain that they need both time at the front counter cutting meat for customers and time in the back room studying how to improve the particular cuts they have made (Lave and Wenger 1991). This balance between observing parts and engaged participation is the key in the disputes over how to teach reading—for example, whether to study and observe explicit phonemic patterns or to participate in the actual reading of stories where phonemic awareness is an embedded skill. Should we assign specific goals, such as "learn short *e* sounds," which decoding/analytic literacy taught us can be easily drilled, observed, and measured; or should we assign broad goals, such as "Digging for the Dinosaur Story," which invite participation in literacy events? In the new literacy, the key is to learn to shift between participation in the broad goals and the explicit study of parts, always keeping the conceptual goals driven by purpose and intention at the center.

Some parents argue that some children, particularly those from the homes of the college educated, get explicit instruction at home in the observation of parts and in the skills of language use. The claim is that college-educated parents tell their children how to observe the spelling of words in letters to grandma and how to pronounce printed words like those on the cereal box. Therefore, these children come to school ready to develop their skills through participation in literacy events at school. The claim is that other students who receive little or no home instruction must begin with substantial, explicit instructions, concentrating on the observation and practice of particular skills and parts of language if they are to learn through participation. Most parents agree that language is learned through a mixture of observation and participation, and most agree that the proper mix of, first, language use through participation and, second, language study through observation and practice, will vary from one student to another.

Skillful teachers of the new literacy must weave these participation and study practices together, but learning how to weave together study and participation is not easy for teachers accustomed to teaching other forms of literacy in which the leading focus was memorizing the code from World-1 or practicing decoding processes from World-2. World-3 purposes, ideas, and intentions were either secondary or ignored altogether in the classrooms of general and remedial students. But are skills and processes being ignored now?

What Happened to Skill and Drill?

In fact, many parents and professionals oppose the teaching of literature-based or idea-based language arts on the grounds that in these approaches the study of phonics and of other skills is neglected. Some of these parents are certainly correct. In some reading programs, some states and districts shifted from a decoding/analytic approach to a literature-based or idea-based reading program by adopting a textbook and by *not* providing any staff development for teachers on how to weave together participation in the construction of meaning and the explicit study and observation of language. Yes, these parents were certainly correct that necessary skills instruction was sometimes missing in this shift. Says Bill Honig, former California State Superintendent, commenting on the current "reading crisis" in that state, "We made our mistakes because we weren't clear enough about this being a balanced approach" (Diegmueller 1995, p. 12). To attain this balance, any new program requires more than a new book. Without staff development, no new program can work; and idea-based or literature-based reading programs have often been implemented with little or no staff development.

Where would districts turn to find ways of weaving together participation and observation, use and explicit study? Kenneth Goodman (1986, p. 31) has suggested ways that academic tasks in the language arts can be organized around topics or themes of interest to students, and Ann Brown (1994) has suggested how various processes and skills can be embedded in an idea-driven model she calls Reciprocal Reading:

> Reciprocal teaching began as a method of conducting "reading group," once an established ritual of the grade school class. . . . Six or so participants form a group with each member taking a turn leading a discussion about an article. . . . The leader begins the discussion by *asking questions* and ends by *summarizing* the gist of the argument to date. Attempts to clarify any problems of understanding take place when needed, and a leader can ask for *predictions* about future content if it seems appropriate. These four activities [questioning, summarizing, clarifying, and predicting] were chosen because they are excellent comprehension devices. . . . Because thinking is externalized in the form of discussion, beginners can learn from the contributions of those more expert than they. So, unlike decontextualized skills approaches to reading, skills are practiced in the context of actually reading. . . . The integrity of the task, reading for meaning, is maintained throughout (Brown 1994, p. 7).

This description of an idea-based, or literature-based, approach to learning to read in English captures the important swing between observation (practicing skills) and participation (legitimate, peripheral participation) and between metacognition (questioning, summarizing, clarifying, predicting) and actual participation in a literacy event. At all times, the primary focus, driving purpose and intention, is the set of ideas in the reading. There is excellent evidence that the more time spent actually reading stories, the better the reading achievement (Fisher and Berliner 1985), that writing stories is an excellent way to learn letter-sound correspondences (Clarke 1988), and that reading things more than once helps improve reading skills (Dahl 1979).

Even so, some parents flatly oppose any mixture or balance of participation and observation and want to return to an exclusive focus on direct instruction in phonics, grammar, and isolated skills. Almost 20 years ago, Rosenshine (1979) outlined the instructional features of this "old" model of literacy, what he called *direct instruction*: large-group instruction, decision making by the teacher, limited choice of materials, orderliness, factual questions, limited exploration of ideas, frequent drill, and high percentages of correct answers (Rosenshine 1979, p. 47; Peterson 1979, p. 66). Yetta Goodman has commented that in this model and others like it, "instructional activities have been planned as if elementary students are learning literacy in a vacuum" (Y. Goodman 1987, p. xiv). Peterson, along with many others, argued that for contemporary students, "direct instruction" was "grim" and "undimensionable" (Peterson 1979, p. 67). But some parents prefer the direct instruction model because they believe it teaches not only specific skills but discipline and recognition of authority. These parents are not concerned about teaching "higher-order thinking skills." These parents want students taught discipline, recognition of authority, and specific basic skills, including phonics. The fear is that other approaches will not do that.

The Importance of Balance

These fears are generated, in part, by the tendencies of the public press and the courts to emphasize extremes. In a recent *Atlantic Monthly* (December 1994), Art Levine charged that many schools using idea-based or literature-based programs were no longer teaching necessary reading skills. It turns out that Levine also knows balance is necessary, but he withholds this point until the very end of his article:

> [The whole-language] stress on reading enjoyable children's literature rather than dull primers is surely worthwhile. . . . The emphasis on early writing wins broad support. . . . A majority of classrooms still devote too much of their reading-instruction time to simplistic workbooks and mind-numbing drills. Learning phonics this way is dull and time consuming (Levine 1994, p. 44).

Sometimes this public-professional tension over reading instruction finds its way into the courts. One reading program that followed closely the direct instruction model of the old literacy sued the California State Board for not teaching reading in its literature-based program. The California Curriculum Commission countercharged that the rejected program had an exclusive focus on observation and direct instruction, leaving out ideas and the use of language in discussions, in writing, and in reading quality literature. The Commission noted:

> This series sequences rote memorization, recitation, and workbook drills in a lock-step manner. Literature is lacking in quality, with controlled vocabulary appearing to be the determining factor in choice of selections. Few attempts are made to teach the language arts as interactive processes. Prior knowledge is not activated before students read. For example, in grade four teacher's edition, page 2, facts are given about Australia, but students are not asked what they may already know about that country. There is no evidence of writing being taught as a process. . . . Students are not guided through a range of higher-order thinking processes. . . . The discussion of issues and concepts is avoided (Engelmann 1989, p. 11).

The court ruled in favor of the California Curriculum Commission, but not before more than one witness testified that the adopted materials aimed for a balance of participation and observation, use and deliberate study, and ideas and skills. But court decisions tend to stress the extremes in a debate, and the effort to communicate the necessity of balance continues to be threatened by those who have successfully made money and political points out of the extremes. For teachers of English/ English language arts, the challenge is to communicate to the public and to fellow professionals why extremes will not teach the new literacy and why the new literacy requires a weaving together of ideas and skills in reading and writing instruction. The pedagogical solution is not a simple process of adding literature to direct instruction programs. The new literacy requires its own style of pedagogical balance (Honig 1995; Mills, O'Keefe, and Stephens 1992) or centering (Pearson 1995). Examples of efforts to design this balance in the teaching of reading are book club programs (Raphael and McMahon 1994), literature discussion groups (Applebee 1994, Daniels 1994), questioning-the-author strategies (Beck, McKeown, Worthy, Sandora, and Kuean 1993), and various other projects (see Honig 1995)—each of which weaves together phonemic, syntactic, and print awareness with participation and a focus on ideas and authentic purposes.

Contention 4. Tension Between Processes in Social Construction and Ideas

A fourth area of contention between the public and English teaching professionals is the emphasis of the new literacy on evidence, feelings, and collaborative learning in the social construction of knowledge.

How Do We Find Meaning in Texts?

In the old literacy, teachers often assumed that a book list *is* an English program. All meaning was in the text. This was so because the World-1 *objects* of English—the list of books, the phonics rules, the syntactic rules, the vocabulary list—were part of an understood, unified world. In the old literacy, teachers delivered the stable, consistent World-3 ideas of texts to students through a consistent set of World-2 processes, usually through a question-answer catechism or through lectures requiring extensive memorization.

But in the new literacy, designed for a fast-changing world with new information arriving every moment and with contextual variations, teachers assume that a book list is not a self-evident program. Books require interpretation—and reinterpretation—standing as they do as representations of the meaning in readers and in authors. In the English classes of the new literacy, readers help construct the ideas of texts in negotiations with texts, with the facts of the world, and with other readers and sometimes with authors; and writers shape information in negotiations with readers, with the facts of the world, and with other texts. A key part of the new literacy is learning the internal metacognitive strategies of these negotiations:

> [Academic learning is] active, strategic, self-conscious, self-motivated, and purposeful. . . . Effective learners generate best when they have insight into their own strengths and weaknesses and access to their own repertoires of strategies for learning. For the past twenty years or so this type of knowledge and control over thinking has been termed *metacognition* (Brown 1994).

Many parents fear that in the social constructivism of the new literacy, there is no *evidence* for ideas, only talk and practice of meta-cognitive skills in interactions with others. Rhetoric has always played an important role in methods of proof, because logical evidence alone cannot resolve all differences among different points of view. Learning to take the point of view of the other, shifting from one's "I" to another's "I," and shifting from "I" to a "third person" are all rhetorical practices that help recruit support for an idea; and community support is one of the types of evidence one can use to establish a proof (Gilbert and Mulkay 1984). But parents are worried about the possible relativism of answers, about the fact that rhetoric and style may have completely replaced "objective," rational methods as the way to arrive at (or construct) "answers." In traditional logic, shifting from "I" to "we" is not, strictly speaking, a method of proof.

Parental fears are increased when disciplinary spokespersons like Feyerabend (1988) claim that there is no rational method underlying so-called rational arguments and that all is talk and rhetoric in which one manipulates oneself and others into believing something is rational. Feyerabend has argued, for instance, that Galileo convinced physicists to adopt Galileo's physics and drop Aristotle's "not by meeting the standards required by some relevant type of rational argument but by deceptive rhetorical manipulation" (MacIntyre 1990, pp. 118–120; Feyerabend 1988, pp. 118–119). For some parents (and some English educators), *social construction* has a negative connotation; many people believe that teachers embracing the new literacy emphasize *talk alone* as the path to knowledge, as if one's personal experience were the source of all knowledge.

What are the common norms of logical proof that should govern social constructions in English classes? This question hit the pages of the public press in California in 1994 when Richard Paul, professor of philosophy at Sonoma State College, held a press conference in Sacramento. At this conference, Paul criticized the questions in the English language arts assessment of the California State Department of Education. He charged that English professionals had no common norms of logical proof for many of their questions:

> Do the assessors really know how to "impartially" assess whether or not a student reader is being "sensitive to a psychological nuance" . . . or can they impartially determine whether or not a student reader is entertaining a "challenging" idea . . . or whether a student perception is "acute" or not? (Paul 1994, p. 15).

He concluded: "Shame on the California Learning Assessment System, which has again failed to see the difference between a proper and an improper use of rhetoric and reason" (Paul 1994, p. 28).

In a reply to Paul, Sheridan Blau (1994) noted that Paul seemed unfamiliar with debates in English over how meaning is constructed and what proof means. For example, Blau suggested that Paul seemed quite unacquainted with the debates in English over how one uses author intention as evidence for textual meaning. Nevertheless, as Blau acknow-ledges, Paul's challenge makes a valuable point.

From one point of view, Paul's point is that we, as English teaching professionals, have not done a good job of explaining to the public (and, alas, to philosophers) what our common norms of logical proof are. First, we need to explain how learning to summarize a rival position does indeed help one understand the common assumptions of different positions. MacIntyre says, "The adherents of every standpoint in recog-nizing the existence of rival standpoints recognize also, implicitly if not explicitly, that those standpoints are formulated within and in terms of common norms of intelligibility and evaluation" (MacIntyre 1990, p. 5).

Second, we need to outline more clearly our methods of inquiry into the text. We need to be clear in our distinctions between an aesthetic reading in which we "fictionalize" a scene or object, approaching it as a spectator, and a nonaesthetic transactional reading in which we use the scene or object as a commodity in work or in citizenship. We also need to be clear in our distinctions between facts, which are comprehended, and versions, which are interpreted. That we can read a scene or object as either aesthetic or nonaesthetic does not mean there is not yet another, different distinction between the "facts" of texts, which we comprehend, and the versions or stories of texts, which we interpret. The facts of the text are there to be evaluated by traditional, logical means—the names of characters and their family relationships, the names of places and distances between them, when and where books were written. Students need to know what facts are and how to evaluate them. They also need to know what versions are and how to evaluate them—particularly how to evaluate the rhetorical patterns shaping versions.

What Is the Place of "Feelings" Questions in English Lessons?

Another related concern of many parents who are uneasy about social construction is the teaching practice of asking questions about feelings ("How did this scene make you feel?"). The pedagogical assumption is that students often need to begin with their feelings about something so they can connect the issues of the text to their own experience (see Lipman 1991, p. 49). In Los Angeles County Superior Court in 1994, one group of parents sued the Los Angeles Unified School District and the California State Board of Education on the grounds that "feelings" questions in state assessments violated a state law prohibiting schools from "invading" the privacy of students. The parents lost the case, but the State Board replaced "feelings" with "thinking" in the assessment questions (such as, "What do you feel about . . . ?" to "What do you think about . . . ?"). The judge ruled that feelings questions did not violate privacy because "the parables, stories, poems, etc., that go into the test all represent life situations that any objective observer would see, hear about, or otherwise experience" outside of school (O'Brien 1994, p. 4).

One of the ironies of this situation is that the law that the parents used to sue the California State Board of Education was originally introduced in the 1950s by, among others, left-wing parents who feared that teachers in the public schools would inquire into the left-wing feelings of their children and hold these feelings up for disparagement in the class. Today, right-wing fundamentalists have similar views; that is, they fear that their children's feelings about God and personal revelation will be held up for disparagement in class. The issue for these parents is to protect sectarian interests from being invaded or criticized by the public institutions. However, the American Civil Liberties Union (ACLU), which typically attempts to protect sectarian interests from mainstream domination, argued in this case that "asking students to express their 'feelings' about the story . . . makes students think," suggesting in a quotation from Justice Jackson that feelings are the source of ideas: "We must be ever vigilant not to 'strangle the free mind at its source'" (Ehrlich 1994).

In other words, the ACLU wants to protect the rights of people to speak out about their feelings, sectarian or not, because responses to feelings ultimately encourage the free expression of ideas. But parents who oppose the ACLU find feelings questions an intrusion into privacy. In one sense, these parents who oppose feelings questions are like some parents who oppose school prayers. Feelings questions, like school prayers, may be an intrusion into the religious life of the student. Other parents feel that feelings questions are simply another invitation to exercise Rhetorical Power and to ignore Logical Power and reason. Both groups of parents applauded the decision of the California State Board to change all "I feel" responses to "I think." The fact is, however, that the expressive response—feelings questions being one of those—is a very effective pedagogical device for getting response going; and once a response is on the table we can analyze and define it. The key point here is one that James Britton made many years ago about talking about personal experience in school—that is, students learn knowledge not by memorizing information from books but by learning to shape their own experiences and feelings at the point of utterance (Britton 1970), thereby translating personal intuitions about experience into language.

The danger, say some parents and many professionals, is that many teachers of English/English language arts do not go beyond talking about personal experience and feelings, as if individual reactions were the only source of meaning. These parents and professionals want teachers of English/English language arts to get students to look at intertextual evidence, for example—to study the evidence in other texts—and to look at *facts* in the world, and to write in the expository mode about knowledge and generalizations from subject matter disciplines. Personal experience and feelings alone, they say, are not enough. And most English teachers quite agree, but English teachers do not wish to ignore feelings and experience.

How Much Should Students Learn and Work Collaboratively?

Another related problem for many parents in social construction is collaborative learning. In decoding/analytic literacy, thinking took place in the heads of individual students who were required to work alone, silently, and without assistance from others or machines. In the new literacy in English, many kinds of problem solving are distributed to various collaborative systems: computers, spell-checkers, and other machines; networks of people with different kinds of expertise; and internalized voices for talking oneself through a problem. This shift from individualized to distributed intelligence requires classrooms that teach the social and cognitive skills of collaborative work and that are connected to the outside world through electronic networks and in-class publishing programs. For many parents and administrators, this kind of classroom seems too noisy, too full of cheating, too full of machines, and too preoccupied by interactions with agencies outside the school.

Have Processes Swamped Knowledge?

Many parents and other critics are also concerned that the new English standards will emphasize processes and activities and ignore ideas. English teachers generally recognize that both declarative and procedural knowledge, both processes and content, are essential in the curriculum—but some teachers have sometimes overemphasized (to parents) the processes that students use to learn and to interact in the world, and have often de-emphasized the structures, conventions, and content that students are learning. Some parents fear that a "cute" activity does not necessarily have any content. Many curriculum guides (as in the draft English standards) call for students to learn to write to different audiences, but these statements are often not translated into the declarative knowledge that is at stake—for example, the statements do not describe the structure of the different genres (autobiography, personal letter, editorial, research report). To ensure that the public understands the curriculum guides that are being written, teachers should recommend that a local task force review curriculum proposals (see the next chapter). Without such a review, public-professional misunderstanding seems certain.

Thus, parental concerns about social constructivism and processes focus on four related questions: (1) Why do English classes use so much talk and cultural conversations to find meanings, rather than using the factual and logical "evidence" available in books and in empirical tests of the world? (2) Why must teachers of social constructivism ask about experience and private "feelings" and thereby intrude into the personal life of students? (3) Why must students collaborate (and "cheat") in English classes? And (4) why have activities and processes swamped knowledge? In summary, Contentions 3 and 4 represent a tension over what is emphasized in the teaching of English/English language arts. Should the leading focus of English teaching be World-1 artifacts like published materials and observable systems like syntax and phonemes; or should the focus be World-2 schemas and processes like predicting, chunking, and personal memories; or should the focus be World-3 ideas and concepts like honor and justice?

What is emphasized as the focus or goal of an activity becomes, ultimately, the organizer of cognitive development and the determiner of particular forms of literacy (see DiBello 1992, commenting on the work of Sylvia Scribner). In Contention 3, parents are worried that a focus on ideas will lead to an absence of attention to the codes—grammar, punctuation, letter-sound relationships. In Contention 4, parents are worried that a focus on the cognitive processes of collaboration and internal feelings will lead to an absence of attention to the facts in World-1 and the structure of World-3 ideas and concepts. Carl Bereiter, commenting on these tensions among the three Worlds, says, "But in the most promising of approaches, the focus of activity is on World-3." He also adds, "Schools cannot abandon their fundamental concern with World-2," and "Constructivist and social approaches are both of value, but neither one quite provides the tool to do the job" (Bereiter 1994, pp. 22–23). Again, the key problem is finding the right balance and the public language to explain it.

Contention 5. New Conceptions of Literature

A fifth area of contention between parents and English teaching professionals is the way the teaching of literature has been reconceptualized. In the old literacy, books in English were divided into the works of literature and nonliterature. Literature was defined as works of fiction, poetry, biography, and some essays; and nonliterature was the public discourse of newspapers and magazines and the specialized discourse of history, science, and literary criticism.[2]

Ways of Reading

In the English of the new literacy, however, the boundaries between the literary and the nonliterary are often contested, tending to produce many books that are considered a combination of literary and nonliterary forms (see review of stance in Myers 1995). As a result, the study of literature has become the study of ways of reading texts, some texts typically inviting a literary or aesthetic reading and some typically inviting nonliterary, commodity reading. This means that some texts invite both a literary and a commodity reading, and other texts tend to invite either a literary/poetic reading or a use/commodity reading. The following are some ways of reading in the new literacy:

• In a nonliterary, commodity reading, one reads to use the text for some practical purpose—to compare descriptions of a place as information for a trip, to enjoy the plot of a well-known story, to pass an author-identification test, and to write an argument supporting a book's premise about gender differences.

• In a literary/poetic reading, one reads to enter an imaginative world as a spectator of individual lives—to enter the "private" feelings of individual characters at a crisis point in the story, to connect descriptions of characters to their settings and to other characters from other novels, and to evaluate the decisions of characters, comparing those decisions to comparable decisions in other texts and in one's own life.

• In a literary/poetic reading, one reads as a spectator, attempting to interpret events in the story from the point of view of different characters

---

[2]Decoding/analytic literacy's definition of literature as something artists created as aesthetic form was preceded by a history in which "literature" first meant something people had ("book learning"), then something people created as a form of verbal imagination, and then something people created as significant moral touchstones and aesthetic objects. In the new translation/critical literacy, literature is both a way of reading texts and a way of dividing books.

in the story or another story, or attempting to comprehend and enjoy the basic sequence of events.

• In a nonliterary/commodity reading, one reads as a participant, attempting to interpret the story to make political claims, or to correct the historical record, or to find one's way around town in a strange city.

These two ways of reading are what Barbara Hernstein Smith (1988) calls the *double discourse of value* in texts—the first being the values of beauty, contemplation, and spectator events like theater, paintings, and dramatic films, and the second being the values of use, means, and participatory commodities like flour, fuel, and faster freight trains. These two values have a long, overlapping history, including mixtures of these two values in an everyday event like buying a car or placing food on a plate. In addition, in these two ways of reading, readers, according to Scholes (1985), read for comprehension, appreciation, analysis, and criticism, examining the *text-in-text* (What is the plot?), the *text-with-another-text or set of events* (How do those texts or events help explain this text?), and the *text-against-text* (How does one text argue against another text?).

In the new literacy, most texts can be read either as literature or nonliterature. One could, for example, read a classified ad as a short story about a character's situation in life or as the public discourse about job and personnel information. The question then, of "What is literature?" has been changed to "When is literature?"—thereby shifting the emphasis of English from a taxonomy of works to a *stance* toward texts.[3] This does not mean we do not have lists of works that exemplify the kind of works that typically invite a literary reading.

For many parents and many professionals, this notion of ways of reading is troubling because for them a nonliterary reading of a piece of fiction turns the reading of short stories into cultural studies, not into a literary experience.[4] In a "cultural studies" reading of a text, the story could become an instance of gender history, class tensions, or racism, leading the reader to history and sociology but not necessarily to literature. The boundary between history and literature classes today is not

---

[3]Marshall, Smagorinsky, and Smith (1995), however, suggest that teacher delivery of meaning is still the usual practice in secondary literature classes, even among teachers who want to shift to constructivism.

[4]The Editorial Board of *PMLA*, the journal of the Modern Language Association, decided in 1994 not to add "culture" to *PMLA*'s area of interest, as defined in the journal's editorial policy: "Welcomes essays of interest to those concerned with the study of language and literature" [proposed "language, literature, and culture"] (Stanton 1994, pp. 359–365). One reason given was that members of the Editorial Board thought "culture" could be considered a way of reading literature or language.

always clear. In addition, many readers warn that cultural studies of reading can become as canned-and-delivered as any universal message in the old literacy. These readers want a literary reading to be an exploration of individual responses contending with World-3 ideas in specific circumstances, not a production of canned responses. Said one reader, objecting to one cultural studies approach to Alice Walker's "Everyday Use":

> I have been reading these stories all semester. Everytime black people show up it's the same thing. They're either poor or ignorant. . . . We haven't read one story with a positive black character. In fact, we haven't read one with a positive woman character. . . . We didn't read it right or missed something. Well, I can read'm right—most of the time anyway. I just do not like what I am reading. I am not staying home and making quilts with Mama. I want a different life (Trimmer 1990, pp. 161–162).

Fictionalized Nonfiction

For many parents and professionals, this notion of ways of reading is troubling for another reason: A literary reading of nonfiction can end up fictionalizing actual people. For example, for many parents and professionals, the very idea of reading a news report as "fiction" seems out of place in a responsible English class. In fact, in the view of many parents, the fictionalization of actual events—from Tom Wolfe's *The Right Stuff* to TV docudramas—has begun to play fast and loose with the real world of social rules governing intrusion into private lives.

For many parents, a strict division between literature and nonliterature is a necessary prohibition against reader speculation about the personal feelings and private lives of actual people. A clear literary code (or category of literature, such as "poetry," "novel," "short story," versus nonliterary "news article," "editorial," or "feature article") legitimizes voyeurism, as Chaim Potok (1994) put it recently. A literary reading of a newspaper report on a fire, for example, encourages one to speculate about the personal feelings of firefighters fighting a fire. If the story is fiction, then one is not directly intruding into the personal life of an actual person. If the story is a newspaper report of an actual event, then one is, according to some, intruding into someone's private life. Journalism may be reaching a crisis on this issue. The new journalism encourages a kind of mixture of literary and nonliterary production and consumption, and this mixture has helped produce an enormous increase in pop culture, grocery-counter newspapers, and TV docudramas presenting fictionalized accounts as journalism reports of actual events.

One troubling instance of this mixing of the literary and the nonliterary was Anthony Petrosky's presentation at an NCTE meeting of the tensions between his laboratory at the University of Pittsburgh and the headquarters staff of the National Board for Professional Teaching Standards (Petrosky 1994). Petrosky's paper moved back and forth between a series of poems about a husband and wife whose relationship was coming apart and nonliterary scenes showing the tense disagreements between NBPTS and Petrosky's staff. Why was this mixture uncomfortable for me? For one thing, this mixing of the literary and the nonliterary began to make the poems sound like fictionalized "real life." I did not want to know the people in the poem as actual people because I could not then enter the world of the poem and intrude on their private lives. As Chaim Potok might put it, voyeurism would then become illegitimate.

Literary fictionalization creates a screen that helps me engage with private lives of people by suspending disbelief of them as "real" people. It legitimizes voyeurism. I become, as a result of literary codes, conventionalized as a spectator into private lives; and as a spectator, my criticisms and judgments are at a distance, not a part of actual participation. The literary fictionalization in Petrosky's poems also held me back from any criticism of Petrosky's scenes of the tension between the lab staff and the NBPTS staff. If I had become a critical participant of the NBPTS scenes, then the literary screen might have dropped from the poems, and then I would have ceased to be a poetic spectator and would have become little better than a nonliterary peeping Tom.

In other words, my feelings about what I read were mixed because the "literary" nature of the work was mixed. Was it legitimate to identify fully with the characters in their poetry, to feel that it was proper to witness their private lives, because it was "only" poetry? (See Ferguson 1964 and Bakhtin 1981 for further discussion of how we use language codes to help us sort out the functions of different kinds of spoken and written discourse.)

When the functions of the different codes become uncertain, then the public becomes uncertain and uncomfortable about the values being communicated by radio, TV, texts, museums, and schools. If English teachers are the caretakers of these codes, then we need to be very careful about poetic-nonpoetic and participant-spectator distinctions. We, as English teachers, need to recognize that mixing stances too casually may blur important value distinctions that help us and our students live our lives.

Contention 6. Diversity Issues

A sixth area of contention between the public and English teaching professionals is diversity or pluralism—the practice of selecting texts and organizing discussions so as to contextualize World-3 knowledge in diverse settings. The reading program Distar—which represents the old literacy in its direct instruction approach—avoids all diversity problems because there is no need for World-3 content that involves students in discussions of different points of view. There is only a need for World-2 decoding processes and the observable artifacts or behaviors of World-1. In the new literacy in English, teachers attempt to situate meaning within the diverse perspectives of gender, history, ethnicity, geography, age, group, and class, as well as within the shared concepts that cut across all these boundaries. The result is a range of different points of view toward such themes as justice, responsibilities to others, the identification of strangers, tolerance of ambiguity, choice, and freedom. But many parents fear that the concepts of diversity and pluralism cannot be the goal of instruction because they are an invitation to relativism, an abandonment of what is shared in the culture. Many parents charge that multicultural education affirms every attitude, undemocratic attitudes included.

Who Should Choose Books?

In the old literacy, universal moral touchstones guided discussions of meaning in literature; in the new literacy, conflicting perspectives often guide the development of meaning in literature. But the purpose of the diversity in contemporary literature classes is not political representation, letting each ethnic group have its own books to read or letting every view be affirmed or celebrated. The purpose of this diversity is to introduce all students to the many traditions that have shaped and are shaping the literature of the United States, a literature embedded in a set of democratic commitments.

The purpose of this diversity is also methodological. Says Scholes (1985), "First, we locate the binary oppositions which organize the flow of value and power in our institutions; then we proceed to criticize or undo the invidious structure of those oppositions." In other words, the identification of difference helps us identify the concepts shaping the scene before us. Placing a female in an all-male setting (or vice versa) reveals suddenly the conceptual structure of gender in a given situation.

Stanley Fish (1980) gives the example from a Bob Newhart sketch of placing a disbeliever at the other end of a telephone conversation with Sir Walter Raleigh (paraphrase of both Fish and Newhart): "Walter, did I hear you right? Did you say you are growing leaves, rolling them up, sticking them in your mouth, and smoking them?" This story introduces *difference* into the Sir Walter Raleigh legend and thereby reveals something about smoking that otherwise might be invisible.

Scholes acknowledges that much in structuralism and deconstruction has been "misleading or unfruitful" but says that "the laying bare of basic oppositions" and the "critique of those oppositions seem to me immensely rich in its critical potential" and "likely to endure the excesses of its current vogue" (Scholes 1985, p. 4).

Concerns about diversity and difference in English classes led a group of parents to demand in 1994 that passages from stories by Alice Walker and Annie Dillard be removed from California's assessment of English. The State Board dropped Alice Walker's "Roselily" after a local newspaper compromised test security by printing sections of the story and eliciting public complaints about it. Parents complained that this story, which examined the emotional turmoil of a Christian woman who is about to marry a Muslim, created in the classroom tensions over religious differences, raising questions about religious values. Another passage from Alice Walker's "Am I Blue?" was deleted by the State School Board because the story "advocated" vegetarianism, another life-style difference—or, in the words of members of the State Board, the story was a "discussion of a particular dietary practice in political, dogmatic terms" (McDowell 1994). And another passage from Annie Dillard's "An American Childhood" was deleted on the grounds that it described a snowball fight that might have been viewed as "the depiction of violence" between two people of different races (McDowell 1994).

Many parents assume that if they remove books about diversity and difference, they can remove troubling diversity disputes from society. Of course, they cannot, as MacIntyre and others noted. The great interpretive disputes are not to be wished away. Says MacIntyre, "Texts have to be read against one another if we are not to misread them" (MacIntyre 1990, p. 229), and one of the purposes of schooling is to show students how, within democratic traditions, "to enter into controversy with other rival standpoints" (MacIntyre 1990, p. 231).

But why shouldn't parents be allowed to select the differences they want their children to consider and thus to select the books their children read, just as they might select the films or TV shows their children watch? What gives K–12 teachers a privileged position in the purchasing of books? What allows K–12 teachers to claim they are *selecting* books and that parents are *censoring* books? After all, selecting books in an English department or in a grade-level meeting is like going to an art auction. Since K–12 teachers have only so much money to spend on books, they vote for the books they like, often based on the readings they have found especially productive. In the end, the majority wins. These decisions about books, as Stanley Fish has said, "are a collective decision as to what counts as literature, a decision which will be in force only so long as a community of readers and believers continues to abide by it" (Fish 1980, p. 11). But if the book-selection process is little more than a contingent balloting process, then why shouldn't any group of parents be able to claim legitimately that they should participate in the voting? Or do the voting?

Again, why give teachers a privileged position in selection? There must be some extra, added value in teacher selections—otherwise, why allow it? But what extra value does the teacher bring to book selection? The first value is that teachers know the works that have survived over time as expressions of U.S. traditions. Contrary to the claims of some observers, teachers who are teaching the new literacy are not abandoning traditional works (see "Report from the Literature Center" in ASCD's *Curriculum Update*, June 1994). Instead, teachers are *adding* to the list of traditional literature such different voices as Toni Morrison, Maxine Hong Kingston, Amy Tan, and August Wilson. These are voices that have helped shape the values of U.S. literature, voices that we have sometimes rediscovered after a period of silence. Teachers are also adding different readings of traditional works, which, of course, have always had within them the potential for and a history of different readings (MacIntyre 1990, Graff 1987).

The second value is that teachers of English, because texts are their business, know how to bridge one place and another, how to revisit and contextualize the past, how to bridge the past and present, and how to pair different voices with traditional texts. To bridge the past and present, to bridge one place and another, to bridge what is shared in different times and places, English teachers in the new literacy are expected to initiate students into the situated meaning of different points of view in time (history) and space (culture, geography). One essential point to make in these pairings is that U.S. literature has had many influences and that culture conceals through its habits and, thereby, "blinds the educated to what needs to be seen" (MacIntyre 1990, p. 169). It is no longer possible to deny that global relationships shape our everyday lives. Even Western literature is a result of intercultural mixing from areas throughout the world.

Finally, English teachers are expected to develop an "eye" for greatness in books. What is "greatness"? In one answer to this question, Barbara Hernstein Smith argues that works that are selected again and again in different periods with different problems, all because they have contingent usefulness for helping people understand the age in which they live, may have the emerging extrinsic value of evolutionary adaptability (Smith 1988). The recognition of this extrinsic value may be another value that the public hopes English teachers will bring to book selection. Thus, the book selections of teachers are more than only a vote on what they like, although they are that, too. They are also estimates of a book's adaptability to different readings at different times, allowing K–12 readers to find in the text both bridges between old and new voices and a continuing adaptability that will help today's young readers connect to tomorrow's young readers.

Some teachers and other educators feel that the values teachers bring to book selection are undermined when parents ask that their children be given a teacher-selected option, other than the assigned book. In this time and place, however, there should be discussions between parents and teachers over the exercise of the parent option, and teachers should provide another teacher-selected option when the parents have strong objections to a book on religious or philosophical grounds. (See Bogdan 1992, p. 15, for further discussion.)[5]

What Is Proper Grammar?

This public-professional debate over the role of diversity in English classes is not limited to debates over what books to read and how to read them. The issue also turns up in grammar lessons. One commentator recently complained that she had read a draft of English standards in which standard English was called a "privileged dialect." The teachers, of course, were only trying to suggest that there are differences among dialects and that what gets privileged changes. The commentator charged, however, that this language of the "privileged dialect" undermined standards. English teachers, who had already dropped the criticized language from the next draft of the standards, were puzzled by the commentator's hysteria, unable to understand why language history and difference was of so little interest to a serious public commentator. In this instance, the effort of English teachers to explain how writing

---

[5]A request for an option is not the same as a parent request that no one read a particular book. This latter request should be handled under the *Right-to-Read Policy* of the National Council of Teachers of English.

conventions change over time was used by a commentator to raise fears that English teachers were not teaching contemporary standards.

In another example of grammar tension, a father called NCTE to complain that an Ohio teacher had unfairly graded his son in a parts-of-speech exercise. It seems that the son, who was born in India and educated in elementary schools in that country, was asked by his 7th grade teacher to classify the word "cow" as a person, place, or thing. The student hesitated, answered "person," and got a poor grade from the teacher. The problem of course, was that the student, given his perspective from his years in India, could not think of a "cow" as a thing (the right answer!) or as a place. To many people in India, cows have spiritual, living significance. NCTE asked Dennis Barron at the University of Illinois-Urbana to write an explanation to the father of what had happened; and the school principal, discovering that even parts of speech are embedded in cultural differences, decided to have a staff development program on the matter. For English teachers, these diversity tensions have been another reminder that professional language does not always have a clear public meaning.

Multiculturalism or Indoctrination? Where Is the Common Heritage?

Many parents recognize the importance of difference as a theme in today's shrinking world. But some parents ask, "Where is our common heritage? Does English take responsibility for what we share?"

Many parents are concerned that an emphasis on pluralism and diversity in English classes may lead to students' learning a different view of our traditions and our common heritage. Many parents support teaching students to understand and appreciate the ethnic contributions to the U.S. heritage, but they fear that the common heritage that *they* learned may get lost if new groups are added to the tradition. In *Multiculturalism and the Battle for America's Future*, Sandra Stotsky, a parent in Brookline, Massachusetts, is quoted as asking local parents, "How can you make sure your schools are offering an academically rigorous multicultural curriculum, not political indoctrination into one-sided and simplistic anti-Western and antidemocratic modes of thinking?" (Bernstein 1994, pp. 262–263). Stotsky (1995), in a recent *Phi Delta Kappan* article, charges that an experimental, elective American literature course at Brookline High School is, in fact, an "effort to dilute American literature and American national identity" (p. 609). Her concern is that "three of the twelve major authors suggested for study are

Canadian or South American" and argues, "Although students in American high schools should read Canadian or South American literature somewhere in their studies (particularly in a world literature course), what is at issue is whether they should be doing so in a course labeled 'American Literature'" (Stotsky 1995, p. 609).

Of course, the Brookline English Department may have had sensible reasons for its actions in this experimental, elective course. Or does literature from North America or South America help us understand what is special about our American literature? Stotsky charges that "one major problem in contemporary secondary school anthologies is the paucity of works about the experiences of European ethnic groups in this country" (Stotsky 1995, p. 608). The key question is, How are these issues to be reviewed in a local book list and a decision made? National trends do not always help us solve local questions. We have good evidence, for example, that traditional texts are not being abandoned in K–12 schools nationwide (see Applebee 1989, p. 2; Stotsky 1995, pp. 606–607). After reviewing the entire list of books used in secondary schools, Applebee concludes: "With only a few exceptions, the hundreds of selections on the list as a whole remained white (98 percent), male (81 percent), and Eurocentric (99 percent), firmly in the tradition established before the turn of the century" (Applebee 1995, p. 38). What is needed is obviously some kind of local task force that considers both the proposals and rationale of the teachers in the Brookline English Department and the proposals and rationale of parents like Stotsky and others (see Glatthorn chapter that follows). As things stand now, an attack is made on an English teacher or English Department, but there is no established procedure at the local level for letting English teachers present their views of their own program or for parents and teachers to exchange views. The public press, as noted earlier, stresses extremes, not understanding. We need a process for examining Stotsky's charges at the local level, a process very similar to NCTE's *Right-to-Read Policy* (NCTE 1982). If Stotsky is right, we should know it and correct the situation. European influences are not to be ignored. If she is wrong, we should know that, too.

Contention 7. Language for Discovery

A seventh concern of many parents about English classes of the new literacy is the use of language for discovery and thinking as well as for communication. In the old literacy, the primary emphasis of composition programs was the academic research report or the expository essay, both written in the third person (*it, he, she*). The exclusive concern was communication. Today, English professionals recognize that most third-person, academic research reports, arguments, and expository essays published for communication are developed first through writing for discovery—personal memos, rough draft letters, first-person narratives. This discovery process has been extensively documented in science laboratories (Gilbert and Mulkay 1984).

In the new literacy, English teachers assume that one of the primary purposes of writing—in addition to memory retention, persuasion, and communication—is exploring, refining, and thinking about an idea by writing about it. Teachers collect this discovery or "thinking" material to monitor how students are developing in their use of writing to learn and to solve problems. Parents who still assume that the only purpose of school writing is communication complain that teachers are allowing students to put memos and draft material into portfolios of student work without editing the errors and thereby encouraging error. Why, they ask, don't teachers have students throw that material away? Or if teachers are going to keep those memos, why don't teachers mark the errors in red? For many parents, the failure to correct this material is evidence of a tendency to ignore student errors and mistakes throughout society. We, as English teaching professionals, need to do a better job of explaining to parents the importance of using written language to discover ideas and clarify thoughts.

Contention 8. Noise and Movies

An eighth area of parental concern about the English of the new literacy is the increase in a wide range of sign systems in English classes. In the old literacy, there was almost an exclusive attention to the silent, printed page, both as something to consume by a reader and as something to produce by a writer. In the history of NCTE, this emphasis on the silent page led to the separation of the Speech Communication Association from NCTE; the separation of speech departments from English; the decline of public speaking, forensics, and debate as a vital part of secondary English departments; and the decline of oral language activities in elementary language arts. The result was the silent classroom of the old literacy.

In the English classes of the new literacy, however, we find more noise being produced by oral activities and by projects in multimedia communication, in which students learn to use print, graphics, film, and video. The noise produced by oral discussion groups and these new visual forms—film, television, live drama, charts, and graphics—is troublesome to many parents who peek into these classrooms and ask, "Why are they making so much noise? Why are they watching movies? That's what they do at home." Many parents, fearing the loss of books and silence in classrooms that house TV and audio units, are concerned that many English classes may not be investing the necessary time in silent reading of printed materials. Many parents fear that students may not be developing the reflective habits of mind required by print reading, in which the mind controls the pace of images and actions. Again, we should aim for balance, and we should explain to parents how a way of watching TV is a way of "reading" TV.

Summary

Each of these eight areas of parental concern relate to the following versions of the content standards being developed in English/English language arts:

1. Version of Content Standards: English/English language arts is taught as a historically contingent form of literacy.

Parental Concern: School failure is a failure to do what schools should have been doing all along.

2. Version of Content Standards: The purpose of English/English language arts is to prepare students for contemporary workplaces, academics, citizenship, and personal growth.

Parental Concern: Personal growth and identity is family business, and jobs and academics must come first, even ahead of citizenship.

3. Version of Content Standards: Reading in English/English language arts is taught as a contextualized activity, with participation in authentic events based on "real" purposes and with observation and study of metacognitive strategies and language.

Parental Concern: A wide range of activities and events, balancing participation and observation, detracts from exclusive attention to explicit, direct, and sequential attention to basic skills in reading.

4. Version of Content Standards: In English/English language arts, meaning is socially constructed.

Parental Concern: English teachers are getting students engaged in talk, as if that alone could lead to knowledge and evidence; are inquiring into students' feelings about events in texts, thereby invading the student's privacy; are getting students to collaborate in the construction of meaning, thereby encouraging cheating and indifference to individual responsibility; and are engaging students in one activity after another, each without any language content.

5. Version of Content Standards: Literature in English/English language arts is taught as a shifting stance between the literary and the nonliterary.

Parental Concern: Mixing one stance with another threatens to confuse the codes and values of different functions of language, leading to invasions of personal privacy by museums, books, the public press, and more and more public readers.

6. Version of Content Standards: Writing and reading in English/English language arts is embedded in the different perspectives of gender, class, ethnicity, history, geography, and so forth. In English/English language arts, students learn about common democratic commitments through the reading of literature and through participation in language activities.

Parental Concern: An understanding of these diverse perspectives, which English teachers find essential for citizenship and work, has begun to undermine the cohesion of our culture. Traditional literature and our common heritage are not being taught.

7. Version of Content Standards: In English/English language arts, students use language for discovery and thinking.

Parental Concern: Teachers are not correcting draft material, thereby encouraging student indifference to error.

8. Version of Content Standards: In English/English language arts, students are learning to compose and to interpret stories and messages in many different media.

Parental Concern: Students are making too much noise talking and wasting too much time watching movies, both of which take essential time away from the silent reading of print texts and the development of the reflective mind.

What steps should teachers and administrators take to deal with these parent concerns? First, the balance of participation and observation, between use and explicit study, needs to be carefully monitored to fit the needs of individual students. I recommend that each school conduct a portfolio assessment and that teachers review the data in these portfolios to determine the balance of work given to individual students.

Second, each school site should have a parent-teacher-student-administration committee that uses NCTE's *Right-to-Read Policy* (NCTE

1982, 1993) to handle all types of parent complaints about curriculum—from book censorship issues, to complaints about tests and instruction. This process gives parents a procedure for interacting with parents and for making their curriculum concerns known and gives professionals a reflective procedure for preparing a response for parents.

Third, each school site should have a standards document, either a course syllabus or a subject-matter framework, outlining the curriculum students experience in the school. In another age, with more unity, public institutions could assume that the public knew the goals of the institution. But in our time, mission statements and other kinds of standards documents are essential for establishing a compact with the public. The school site standards document should probably make clear that the faculty intends to pair new work with old in an effort to give all students access to diversity, that the faculty intends to use more multi-media projects and more oral language activities to expand the ways of knowing in the curriculum, and so forth. The existence of such a document, available for parent review at all times, enables parents and individual teachers to have some sense that classroom goals and practices have some public, institutional, and professional support.

One of the central problems in the tensions outlined here is a confusion of ends and means. For example, teachers often follow the reasonable cognitive principle of connecting old information to new in order to learn the new. Thus, in classrooms, teachers might use the patterns in local dialects (a means) to help students learn the patterns in standard English (the goal). Some parents, focusing on the means, not the goal, then ask, "Should local dialects be taught?" The answer, of course, is that students should study the patterns in various forms of language that give them power. Knowing that the local dialect of one's neighbors has a pattern often helps students understand the patterns of mainstream, standard English. Similarly, finding that the lines of a poem have a pattern that makes some kind of sense often leads students to examine the patterns in other texts that at first may seem difficult. The primary purpose of K–12 schooling is to give all students access to what they need to function effectively in mainstream society. Knowledge of patterns in English is obviously essential.

In summary, the English standards movement is a difficult project for English teachers, first because the new literacy calls for a kind of English not readily understood by many parents and second because English is, as always, one of the sites for debating society's larger goals and directions. Many of the same issues continually emerge in the public press—for example, in a debate over history standards ("Where is

Thomas Edison?" asks Lynn Cheney), in a debate over Smithsonian exhibits ("How is the Enola Gay going to be exhibited?" asks VFW leader), and in a letter to the editor congratulating the U.S. Department of Education for insisting that English teachers should teach Horatio Alger stories (the so-called canon of children's literature). Despite the difficulties of defining English standards that parents understand, the effort seems worth it. The payoff is schools that renew the tax-paying public's commitment to the K–12 public schools.

References

Applebee, A. (1989). *A Study of Book Length Works Taught in High School English.* Report Series 1.2. Albany: Center for the Learning and Teaching of Literature, State University of New York.

Applebee, A. (1994). *Toward Thoughtful Curriculum: Fostering Discipline-Based Conversation in the English Classroom.* Albany, N.Y.: National Research Center on Literature Teaching and Learning.

Applebee, A. (1995). "Transforming Tradition: Toward a Curriculum of Knowledge in Action." Unpublished manuscript. State University of New York, Albany, New York (to be copublished by NCTE and another publisher).

Bakhtin, M. (1981). *The Dialogic Imagination,* edited by M. Holquist, translated by C. Emerson and M. Holquist. Austin: University of Texas Press.

Beck, I., M. McKeown, J. Worthy, C. Sandora, and L. Kuean. (November 1993). *Questioning the Author: A Year-Long Classroom Implementation to Engage Students with Text.* Pittsburgh, Pa.: University of Pittsburgh, LRDC.

Bereiter, C. (October 1994). "Constructivism, Socioculturalism, and Popper's World-3." *Educational Researcher* 23, 7: 21–23.

Bernstein, R. (1994). *Dictatorship of Virtue: Multiculturalism and the Battle for America's Future.* New York: Alfred Knopf.

Blau, S. (1993). *Building Bridges Between Literary Theory and the Teaching of Literature.* Albany: National Research Center on Literature Teaching and Learning, State University of New York.

Blau, S. (1994). "Response to Richard Paul's Public Critique," Letter to Dale Carlson, Director of Assessment, California Department of Education, February 22, 1990.

Bogdan, D. (Fall 1992). "Reading as Seduction: The Censorship Problem and the Educational Value of Literature." *ADE (Association of Departments of English) Bulletin* 102: 11–16.

Boyer, E. (1987). *College: The Undergraduate Experience in America.* New York: Harper and Row.

Britton, J. (1970). *Language and Education.* London: Allen Lane; Penguin.

Brown, A.L. (November 1994). "The Advancement of Learning." *Educational Researcher* 23, 8: 4–12.

Cannell, J. (November 28, 1987). *Nationally Normed Elementary Achievement Testing in America's Public Schools: How All Fifty States Are Above Average.* Daniels, W. Va.: Friends for Education.

Clarke, L.S. (1988). "Invented Versus Traditional Spelling in First Graders' Writings: Effects on Learning to Spell and Read." *Research in the Teaching of English* 22: 281–309.

Dahl, P.R. (1979). "An Experimental Program for Teaching High Speed Word Recognition and Comprehension Skills." In *Communications Research in Learning Disabilities and Mental Retardation,* edited by J.E. Button, T. Lovitt, and N.T. Rowland. Baltimore: University Park Press, pp. 33–65.

Daniels, H. (1994). *Literature Circles.* New York: Stenhouse Maine.

Deily, M.-E. (June 7, 1995). "Parental Rights Movement Raises Support Questions," *Education Daily,* pp. 1–2.

DiBello, L. (October 1992). "Looking for 'What's Leading': A Legacy from Sylvia Scribner." *The Quarterly Newsletter of the Laboratory of Comparative Human Cognition* 14, 4: 114–116. (San Diego: University of California, Center for Human Information Processing).

Diegmueller, K. (June 14, 1995). "California Plotting New Tack on Language Arts," *Education Week,* pp. 1–12.

Ehrlich, D. (1994). "Censorship of Alice Walker Story," Letter to William D. Dawson, Acting Superintendent, California Department of Education, February 23, 1994, in archives of the American Civil Liberties Union Foundation of Northern California, San Francisco.

Elbow, P. (1986). *Embracing Contraries: Explorations in Learning and Teaching.* New York: Oxford University Press.

Engelmann, Siegfried, vs. State Board of Education, et al. (1989). Petition for Writ of Mandate (July 21, 1989), Memorandum of Points and Authorities in Opposition to Petition for Writ (October 6, 1989). Sacramento Superior Court, Sacramento, California.

Ferguson, C. (1964). "Diglossia." In *Language in Culture and Society,* edited by D. Hymes. New York: Harper and Row.

Feyerabend, P.K. (1988). *Against Method.* London: Routledge, Chapman, and Hall.

Fish, S. (1980). *Is There a Text in This Class?* Cambridge: Harvard University Press.

Fisher, C.W., and D.C. Berliner, eds. (1985). *Perspectives on Instructional Time.* New York: Longman.

Fishman, J. (1972). *The Sociology of Language.* Rowley, Mass.: Newbury House Publishers.

Frye, N. (1965). *A Natural Perspective: The Development of Shakespeare Comedy and Romance.* New York: Harcourt.

Gilbert, G.N., and M. Mulkay. (1984). *Opening Pandora's Box.* Cambridge: Cambridge University Press, pp. 58–59.

Goodman, K. (1986). *What's Whole in Whole Language?* Portsmouth, N.H.: Heinemann.

Goodman, Y. (1987). "Foreword." In *Supporting Literacy*, edited by C.E. Loughlin and M.D. Martin. New York: Teachers College Press, pp. xiii–xiv.

Graff, G. (1987). *Professing Literature.* Chicago: University of Chicago Press.

Harding, D.W. (1937). "The Role on the Onlooker." *Scrutiny* 6: 247–258.

Honig, B. (1995). *How Should We Teach Our Children to Read: A Balanced Approach.* Unpublished paper distributed by Bill Honig, May 1, 1995.

Kaestle, C.F., H. Damon-Moore, L. Stedman, K. Tinsley, and W.V. Trollinger. (1991). *Literacy in the United States: Readers and Reading Since 1800.* New Haven: Yale University Press.

Kirsch, I.S., A. Jungeblut, L. Jenkins, and A. Kolstad. (1993). *Adult Literacy in America.* Washington, D.C.: National Center for Education Statistics.

Langer, J. (1989). *The Process of Understanding Literature.* Report Series 2.1. Albany: National Research Center for the Learning and Teaching of Literature, State University of New York.

Lave, J., and E. Wenger. (1991). *Situated Learning: Legitimate Peripheral Participation.* Cambridge: Cambridge University Press.

Levine, A. (December 1994). "The Grand Debate Revisited." *The Atlantic Monthly,* pp. 38–44.

Linn, R.L., M.E. Graue, and N.M. Sanders. (1990). "Comparing State and District Test Results to National Norms: The Validity of Claims That 'Everyone Is Above Average.'" *Educational Measurement: Issues and Practice* 10: 5–14.

Lipman, M. (1991). *Thinking in Education.* Cambridge: Cambridge University Press.

MacIntyre, A. (1990). *Three Rival Versions of Moral Inquiry.* Notre Dame, Ind.: University of Notre Dame.

Marshall, J.D., P. Smagorinsky, and M.W. Smith. (1995). *The Language of Interpretation.* Urbana, Ill.: National Council of Teachers of English.

McDowell, M. (Chair of the California State Board of Education). (February 25, 1994). "Use of Alice Walker's 'Roselily' in the California Learning Assessment System." Press release, California State Department of Education, Sacramento, California.

Mills, H., T. O'Keefe, and D. Stephens. (1992). *Looking Closely: Exploring the Role of Phonics in One Whole Language Classroom.* Urbana, Ill.: National Council of Teachers of English.

Mullis, I.V.S., J. Campbell, and A.E. Farstrup. (September 1993). *NAEP 1992 Reading Report Card for the Nation and the States.* Washington, D.C.: U.S. Department of Education, Office of Educational Research and Improvement, National Assessment of Educational Progress.

Myers, M. (June 1994). "Work Worth Doing." *Council Chronicle.* Urbana, Ill.: National Council of Teachers of English, p. 24.

Myers, M. (1995). *Changing Our Minds: Negotiating English and Literacy.* Urbana, Ill.: National Council of Teachers of English.

Narayan, U. (1988). "Working Together Across Differences: Some Considerations on Emotions and Political Practice." *Hypatia* 3, 2: 113–132.

National Commission on Excellence in Education. (1983). *A Nation at Risk: Report of the National Commission on Excellence in Education.* Washington, D.C.: U.S. Government Printing Office.

National Council of Teachers of English. (1982). *The Students' Right to Know.* Urbana, Ill.: Author.

National Council of Teachers of English. (1993). *Guidelines for Dealing with Censorship of Non-Print Materials.* Urbana, Ill.: Author.

National Council of Teachers of English and International Reading Association. (October 1994). *Draft Standards for English/English Language Arts.* Urbana, Ill.: National Council of Teachers of English.

O'Brien, R. (Judge of the Los Angeles Superior Court). (1994). Tentative decision in: Greenfield and Thomason vs. the Los Angeles Unified School District and the State Board of Education, May 10, 1994. Case No. BS 028 375.

Paul, R. (1994). "Pseudo Critical Thinking in the Educational Establishment: A Case Study in Educational Malpractice." Sonoma, Calif.; Sonoma State University, Center for Critical Thinking and Moral Critique, Released to Press Sacramento, California, July 14, 1993.

Pearson, P.D. (May 15, 1995). "Reclaiming the Center." Unpublished manuscript, Department of Education, University of Illinois, Urbana.

Peterson, P.L. (1979). "Direct Instruction Reconsidered." In *Research on Teaching: Concepts, Findings, and Implications,* edited by P. Peterson and H. Walberg. Berkeley, Calif.: McCutchan Publishing Corporation, pp. 57–69.

Petrosky, A. (November 1994). "Schizophrenia, the National Board for Professional Teaching Standards, and Me." *English Journal* 83, 7: 33–42.

Popper, K. (1977). "Part I." In *The Self and Its Brain,* coauthored by K.R. Popper and J.C. Eccles. New York: Springer International.

Potok, C. (November 20, 1994). "Rebellion and Authority: The Writer and the Community." Presentation at the National Council of Teachers of English Annual Convention, Orlando, Florida.

Raphael, T., and S. McMahon. (October 1994). "Book Club: An Alternative Framework for Reading Instruction." *The Reading Teacher* 48, 2: 102–116.

"Report from the Literature Center." (June 1994). *Curriculum Update,* p. 5.

Richards, I.A. (1948). "Science and Poetry." In *Criticism: The Foundations of Literary Judgment,* edited by M. Schorer, J. Miles, and G. McKenzie. New York: Harcourt Brace.

Rosenblatt, L. (1968). *Literature as Exploration.* New York: Noble and Noble.

Rosenshine, B.V. (1979). "Content, Time, and Direct Instruction." In *Research on Teaching: Concepts, Finding, and Implications,* edited by P. Peterson and H. Walberg. Berkeley, Calif.: McCutchan Publishing Corporation, pp. 28–56.

Scholes, R. (1985). *Textual Power: Literary Theory and the Teaching of English.* New Haven: Yale University Press.

Smith, B.H. (1988). *Contingencies of Value: Alternative Perspectives for Critical Theory.* Cambridge: Harvard University Press.

Sommers, N. (December 1980). "Revision Strategies of Student Writers and Experienced Adult Writers." *College Composition and Communication* 31: 378–388.

Stanton, D.C. (May 1994). "What Is Literature—1994?" *PMLA* 109: 359–365.

Stotsky, S. (April 1995). "Changes in America's Secondary School Literature Programs." *Phi Delta Kappan* 76, 8: 605–613.

Trimmer, J.F. (October 1990). "Telling Stories About Stores." *Teaching English in the Two Year College* 17, 3: 117–121.

West, C. (1994). *Race Matters*. New York: Vintage Books.

Resources

Baron, D. (1994). *Guide to Home Language Repair*. Urbana, Ill.: NCTE.

Dunning, S., and W. Stafford. (1992). *Getting the Knack: 20 Poetry Writing Exercises*. Urbana, Ill.: NCTE.

IRA/NCTE Task Force on Assessment. (1994). *Standards for the Assessment of Reading and Writing*. Urbana, Ill.: NCTE.

McClure, A.A., and J.V. Kristo, eds. (1994). *Inviting Children's Responses to Literature*. Urbana, Ill.: NCTE.

Marshall, J., P. Smagorinsky, and M. Smith, eds. (1994). *The Language of Interpretation*. Urbana, Ill.: NCTE.

Nagy, W. (1988). *Teaching Vocabulary to Improve Reading Comprehension*. Urbana, Ill.: NCTE and IRA.

Purves, A., ed. (1994). *Encyclopedia of English Studies and Language Arts*. A Project of the National Council of Teachers of English. New York: Scholastic.

Standards for English/English Language Arts, copublished by NCTE and IRA. Contact:
National Council of Teachers of English
1111 West Kenyon Road
Urbana, IL 61801
Phone: (217) 328-3870

International Reading Association
800 Barksdale Road
P.O. Box 8139
Newark, DE 19714
Phone: (302) 731-1600

Strong, W. (1986). *Creative Approaches to Sentence Combining*. Urbana, Ill.: NCTE.

Tchudi, S.N., and M.C. Huerta. (1983). *Teaching Writing in the Content Areas*. Urbana, Ill.: NCTE.

Willis, M.S. (1993). *Deep Revision: A Guide for Teachers, Students, and Other Writers*. Urbana, Ill.: NCTE.

3

A Mastery Curriculum for English Language Arts

Allan A. Glatthorn

The preceding chapter by Miles Myers does an excellent job of delineating the current developments in English language arts and identifying the controversial issues that divide both the profession and the public. I would like to supplement Myers' chapter by offering some very specific recommendations for curriculum leaders and classroom teachers. In a sense, these recommendations are intended to advance Myers' insightful suggestion that each school site should have a syllabus outlining the curriculum that students experience in the school; the major difference articulated here is a belief that the curriculum should be a district concern to ensure effective coordination from kindergarten to grade 12 and afford equity across schools; individual schools should build upon the district curriculum, not develop their own.

The Central Issue

Standards projects have identified a range of issues in each curricular area. In English, the balance between process and content—or procedural and declarative—knowledge is central. The best way of resolving the issue and other related issues is the one implied earlier: A district task force should be appointed, composed of central office staff, school administrators, and classroom teachers. That task force should use their version of the procedures explained below in determining their own resolution of the appropriate balance between process and knowledge. The task force should solicit input from the parent/student/educator committee that Myers recommends.

Distinguish Between the Several Types of Curriculum

The task force should begin by deciding if they will use the "mastery" model of curriculum development that I have recommended elsewhere (e.g., Glatthorn 1994). In several of my published works, I have recommended that curriculum leaders make a distinction between four types of curriculum, based upon their degree of structure and their importance for all students:

• The *mastery* curriculum is high in structure and importance. It meets two criteria: It is the curriculum considered essential for all students; and it is best learned with a high degree of structure. It requires careful planning and explicit teaching. "Define *metaphor*" is an example of a mastery objective. The mastery curriculum, in this model, is seen as the province of the school district.

• As important as the mastery curriculum is the *organic* curriculum, the curriculum that is nurtured rather than taught. The organic curriculum does not have a high degree of structure; it is emphasized whenever appropriate, on a continuing basis, and is not assigned to a specific grade. "Enjoy poetry" is an example of an organic objective. The organic curriculum is fostered chiefly through staff development, not explicated in detail in curriculum materials.

• The *team-planned enrichment* curriculum is high in structure and low in importance. It is the enrichment planned by teachers and provided to all students, not just to the gifted. An objective that I would consider team-planned enrichment is "Explain how the structure of the Elizabethan theater affected Shakespearean drama." The team-planned component is the province of teachers.

• The *student-determined enrichment* is the piece of the curriculum that the students own—the current issues they would like to explore and the language-related questions for which they want answers. It is characterized by low importance and low structure.

Since neither the team-planned nor the student-determined enrichment curriculum requires districtwide planning, my comments from here on focus on the organic and mastery curriculums.

Develop the Knowledge Base

The next step in the curriculum project is to develop and synthesize the knowledge base. By reviewing the current literature, the curriculum task force should identify

1. Standards recommended by professional organizations.
2. The requirements of state frameworks and state tests.
3. Reviews of research in teaching the English language arts.
4. The recommendations of experts and the content of exemplary programs.
5. The nature of students' cognitive development.

Several excellent sources can be useful in accomplishing this task: the Flood, Jensen, Lapp, and Squire (1991) handbook; the *ASCD Curriculum Handbook* (1995); Langer and Allington's (1992) chapter on curriculum research in writing and reading; Applebee and Purves' (1992) chapter on curriculum in literature; and the analysis of standards by Kendall and Marzano (1995).

The results of that synthesis should be summarized in a form that can be used by the task force and in the staff development sessions explained below; the synthesis of the knowledge base should also be included in the curriculum guide.

Identify the Strands of the Mastery Curriculum

The task force's next charge is to identify the strands that will be used in planning the mastery curriculum. The strands are the recurring components of the curriculum; on the scope-and-sequence chart, they appear as the vertical dimension, delineating the major planning components of the curriculum. Curriculum workers and teachers should remember that identifying the separate strands is simply a planning device; teachers should be encouraged to integrate the strands as appropriate.

Some curriculum teams use what is often called the *tripod* of the strands: language, literature, and writing. The review of the knowledge base will suggest other conceptualizations. Kendall and Marzano identify the following general standards, which can be used as strands:

- Gathers information effectively through reading, listening, and viewing.
- Reads and responds to literature.
- Gathers information from technical documents, graphs, charts, and tables.
- Communicates ideas and information in writing.
- Understands and applies basic principles of language use.

In my own work, I have found that a different formulation of the strands seems to be effective in the planning process. The general strands and their specific elements that seem to have worked well in those curriculum projects follow:

- Reading and literature: Concepts; required literary works.
- Writing: Special types to be emphasized at each grade.
- Language study: Concepts; language history; language varieties, including dialects.
- Speaking and listening: Special speaking and listening skills required for more formal occasions.
- Mass media and information processing: Special skills involved in using the mass media effectively as both an entertainment medium and a source of information.

The way the strands are conceptualized obviously affects the structure of the curriculum; the curriculum task force, therefore, should give the matter serious consideration, critically reviewing the different recommended strands and deciding which will work best for the teachers in that district.

Identify and Emphasize the Organic Curriculum

The organic curriculum is in many ways the most important of the four in English language arts. The next major step for the committee, therefore, is to identify the major elements of the organic curriculum. Keep in mind that these are the important skills, knowledge, and attitudes that should be nurtured on every appropriate occasion, not specified for one particular grade. The task force should consider the following list, arranged according to the strands identified above:

1. Enjoy reading; value the literary experience; respond to literature in a variety of ways.

2. Value writing as a way of knowing and communicating; use the composing process flexibly.

3. Value language; appreciate the vitality of language; respect your own language and the languages of others.

4. Use oral language with sensitivity to audience, purpose, and occasion; listen courteously and attentively.

5. Use the mass media selectively and critically; locate, retrieve, evaluate, and apply information in the solution of language-related problems.

Those five sets of outcomes are essential for all students. They should be emphasized in every grade, in an approach and at a depth that is developmentally appropriate. They should be identified in the curriculum guide as recurring skills that serve as the core of the program—and they should be the focus of staff development programs for all English language arts teachers.

Secure the Recommendations of Informed Teachers

With the strands and the organic elements identified, the task force should then arrange for a series of staff development sessions for all those teaching English language arts. The purpose of these sessions is three-fold. The first is to orient the teachers to the curriculum project, explaining the rationale for the mastery approach, if the task force has decided to use that model. The second is to inform the teachers about the knowledge base and give them an opportunity to discuss it. The third purpose is to provide structured opportunities for teachers to exchange their experiential knowledge about a quality English language arts curriculum. In accomplishing this last purpose, they should review and modify the list of organic outcomes previously identified. The general intent is to develop an informed group of teachers who can then make sound recommendations.

When these sessions have been completed, the teachers should then be surveyed to determine what they would like to teach in the mastery curriculum for their grade level. The results of the survey should then be used in developing the first draft of a scope-and-sequence chart, which should then be critically analyzed and revised as necessary.

For task forces looking for specific recommendations, I offer the following advice (which represents only my own experience in developing English language arts curriculum; no consensus exists among experts and no research is available):

Reading and Literature. Identify a small number of literary terms and concepts that seem essential in understanding and communicating about literature. Assign three or four concepts to each grade, keeping in mind the difficulty of the concept and the developmental level of students. A specific list to consider follows: simile, metaphor, image, symbol, theme, rhythm, rhyme, character, plot, setting, comedy, tragedy, poem, novel, short story, drama, fiction, nonfiction, biography, and autobiography.

Also, identify for each grade one or two longer literary works that all students will read. The intent here is to develop a locally produced "canon" of literature, the great works of the past and the present, which all students should experience in some way—and whose study will not occasion excessive controversy in the community. Study of this canon will then be complemented with extensive individualized reading, which need not be specified in the curriculum guide. Advice from the "parent complaint committee" Myers recommended would be especially useful.

Writing. The task here is to identify the types of writing that will be emphasized in each grade, not specific writing skills. Several typologies are available. This one has worked successfully with several school systems: exposition; persuasion; writing about literature; academic writing (reports, summaries, and essay answers); practical and applied writing (the writing needed as a worker, consumer, and citizen); and personal and creative writing (letters, journals, stories, plays, and poems). Students should master a variety of forms, writing for real purposes and real audiences. Specific writing skills should be taught in context as needed.

Language Study. Provide a structured curriculum for learning grammar; the term *grammar* is used here to mean the structure of the language. Teach the structure of the English sentence in grade 8: subject, predicate, direct object, indirect object, predicate nominative, predicate adjective, and sentence patterns. Teach the parts of speech in grade 9: noun, verb, pronoun, adjective, adverb, preposition, and conjunction. Although the research is conclusive that such knowledge will not improve reading, writing, or speaking, it should be acquired as a tool in understanding the structure of English and other languages. (See Hillocks 1986 for a review of this research.)

Include two other aspects of language study. First, provide for study of the history of language (world language families, English language, and American language). Also include in selected grades the study of dialects and other varieties of language.

Speaking and Listening. If the English language arts classroom is a place where oral language is the basis of learning, then the mastery curriculum need only specify the special skills required for more formal communication. I recommend emphasizing classroom reports, debates and panel discussions, group discussions, job interviews, and college interviews.

Mass Media and Information Processing. Since the mass media have become so influential in modern life, the curriculum should make specific provisions for students to analyze the media in depth—the media's special nature, the tools they use, the way they shape values and reflect the culture, and how they can be used in information processing. Students should make systematic and recurring use of this basic information processing model: identify the need for information, retrieve information needed, evaluate information retrieved, and apply useful and reliable information in the solution of problems. The special skills needed in using different information modes should be taught in mastery units, assigning the close study of one or two of the media to each of the intermediate and secondary grades, with special attention to television and the computer. A sample sequence follows:

Grade 4: Newspapers and books
Grade 5: The computer
Grade 6: Television
Grade 7: Newspapers and magazines
Grade 8: The computer
Grade 9: Radio and television
Grade 10: Film
Grade 11: The computer
Grade 12: Television and emerging media

Concluding Note

Curriculum workers like to exchange this joke about English teachers: "Ask 10 English teachers what should be taught and you'll get 20 opinions." My experience has been otherwise: Informed teachers can, through open dialog, reach a consensus about what is essential in the

English language arts curriculum. The hope is that the Myers chapter, this addendum, and the IRA/NCTE standards released in the fall of 1995 can be useful in that process.

References

Applebee, A.N. (1991). "Environments for Language Teaching and Learning: Contemporary Issues and Future Directions." In *Handbook of Research on Teaching the English Language Arts,* edited by J. Flood, J.M. Jensen, D. Lapp, and J.R. Squire. New York: Macmillan, pp. 549–558.

Applebee, A.N., and A.C. Purves. (1992). "Literature and the English Language Arts." In *Handbook of Research on Curriculum,* edited by P.W. Jackson. New York: Macmillan, pp. 726–748.

Association for Supervision and Curriculum Development. (1995). *ASCD Curriculum Handbook.* Alexandria, Va.: Author.

Flood, J., J.M. Jensen, D. Lapp, and J.R. Squire, eds. (1991). *Handbook of Research on Teaching the English Language Arts.* New York: Macmillan.

Glatthorn, A.A. (1994). *Developing the Quality Curriculum.* Alexandria, Va.: Association for Supervision and Curriculum Development.

Hillocks, G., Jr. (1986). *Research on Written Composition: New Directions for Teaching.* Urbana, Ill.: ERIC Clearinghouse on Reading and Communication Skills.

Kendall, J.S., and R.J. Marzano. (1995). *The Systematic Identification and Articulation of Content Standards and Benchmarks: Update.* Aurora, Colo.: Mid-continent Regional Educational Laboratory.

Langer, J.A., and R.I. Allington. (1992). "Curriculum Research in Writing and Reading." In *Handbook of Research on Curriculum,* edited by P.W. Jackson. New York: Macmillan, pp. 687–725.

4

Foreign Language Curriculum in an Era of Educational Reform

Myriam Met

For foreign language instruction, reform began in the early 1980s, and since that time, views of language teaching and learning have been evolving. Today's approaches to foreign language curriculum and instruction are remarkably consistent with evolving views of curriculum and instruction across disciplines. These approaches are also consistent with the belief that all students can and should be proficient in at least one language in addition to English. This chapter examines language learning in the last decade, the issues that affect scope and sequence, the relationship of foreign language curriculum and instruction with those of other disciplines, and the questions and issues that will shape new directions for foreign language curriculums in the years to come.

Proficiency—The New Paradigm

In the early 1980s, the American Council on the Teaching of Foreign Languages (ACTFL), in collaboration with the Educational Testing Service (ETS), embarked on an ambitious effort to develop a common yardstick to assess the language proficiency of learners. This yardstick was based on the U.S. government's Foreign Service Institute rating scales and calibrated against the norm of the educated native speaker. ACTFL also collaborated with ETS to develop more fully detailed descriptors for the lower end of the performance continuum, where most school learners would place. The resulting rating scales, the ACTFL/ETS Proficiency Guidelines, provide a performance-based measure of the range of tasks or functions that learners might perform, the contexts and topical areas in which they might perform, and the degree to which their performance is grammatically and socioculturally accurate. The rating scales were originally developed to describe the skills of listening, speaking, reading, writing, and culture, although most attention has been paid to the rating scales and their accompanying measure of oral proficiency, the ACTFL Oral Proficiency Interview (OPI).

The ACTFL Proficiency Guidelines have had—and continue to have—a dramatic and far-ranging impact on curriculum and instruction. First and foremost, the guidelines refocused attention on performance and on the integration of declarative and procedural types of knowledge. While acknowledging that knowledge of vocabulary, grammar, and cultural characteristics are essential components of language learning, the proficiency movement (as it has come to be called) now stresses putting such knowledge to use. Like initiatives in mathematics and science, the proficiency movement puts emphasis on learners' knowledge *in use,* on what they *do* with what they know. The professional issues that have framed the birth of and debates about proficiency-oriented curriculum and instruction closely parallel the issues and debates that have surrounded the whole language movement in reading/language arts. Questions about the role and place of "grammar" are similar to those about "phonics," and the professional explorations of instructional practices that are consonant with these viewpoints have also been parallel. Thus, since the mid-1980s, the language profession's performance-based orientation to learning and assessment has been much in keeping with that of other academic disciplines.

Several characteristics have come to be associated with proficiency-based instruction, many of which will be familiar to those knowledgeable about trends across disciplines. Because proficiency-based instruction is performance oriented, it follows that decisions about curriculum and instruction should be strongly linked to the ways in which the learner may be expected to perform in real-life situations. Thus, the content of the curriculum derives, in large part, from the *authentic* communicative needs of the learner. Many of these needs are fairly universal and predictable for U.S. students in grades K–12, for if the purpose of language learning is to interact with native speakers (whether in the United States or abroad), it follows that there are some kinds of interactions that may be identified and addressed in curriculum. This notion of authentic, real-life uses of language also finds its way into other aspects of instruction: the tasks students are asked to perform in class should be consistent with (or simulate) real-life language tasks; the language students are taught should be authentic (not "school talk"); and authentic materials, drawn directly from the culture, should be a primary medium through which students access new language and culture.

While the proficiency guidelines have had a clear and positive effect on language curriculum and instruction, they have also sometimes been misused in secondary schools. The guidelines and accompanying rating scales are global descriptions of what learners can and cannot do at progressive stages of development relative to the proficiency of an adult-educated native speaker. It was never intended that the proficiency guidelines drive curriculum.

> Because the *ACTFL Proficiency Guidelines* are evaluative in nature and identify in a global way some of the stages through which language learners typically pass, they have interesting implications for curricular design. However, the guidelines neither provide a curricular outline nor imply that a particular type of syllabus or sequence of instruction should be followed (Omaggio Hadley 1993, p.13).

However, some state and local curriculum objectives have been derived, in part, from the performance descriptors; and some curriculum frameworks have equated years or hours of instruction with specific levels of proficiency. This is as inappropriate as developing a secondary school English curriculum consistent with the content of the verbal section of the Scholastic Assessment Test (SAT), or suggesting that by the end of 10th grade, students will attain a score within a given range on the verbal section of the SAT.

Despite this inappropriate use, the proficiency guidelines and rating scales have had a strong and positive effect on conceptualizations of language teaching and learning in the last decade. Curriculum and related classroom practices increasingly reflect the constructs that undergird a proficiency-based orientation.

Curriculum Today:
Scope, Sequence, and Methodology

This section examines some of the key questions related to proficiency-based curriculum, such as scope (what should be taught?), sequence (when should it be taught?), and instruction (how should it be taught?). These questions are of particular interest as the language profession moves toward implementing national standards and toward a new plane in the proficiency movement.

The Scope of the Language Curriculum

The proficiency-based curriculum reflects a multifaceted view of the purposes of language learning. This view is quite distinct from that of the past, when language learning was primarily an intellectual endeavor designed to provide access to great works of literature. The content of past curriculums reflected this perspective by focusing on grammar and translation. Today, most foreign language educators would agree on a dual agenda: first, that language learning is inherently valuable both as a field of intellectual pursuit and as part of a well-rounded education; second, that language learning can prepare students to meet real-life needs for language use, whether in the United States or abroad. The focus on authentic language used for authentic purposes means that curriculum must be far broader than simply knowledge of grammar plus some vocabulary to flesh out that grammatical skeleton. Research from the various fields in linguistics has led to an understanding that language proficiency is far more complex than knowledge of grammar rules. Rather, it is an interaction of at least four competencies:

1. Grammatical competence—knowledge of vocabulary, pronunciation, morphology, and syntax;

2. Sociolinguistic competence—the ability to adjust one's communication to be appropriate to the situation and participants;

3. Discourse competence—the ability to combine utterances at the discourse level resulting in cohesion and coherence; and

4. Strategic competence—the ability to use paraphrase, circumlocution, or repair strategies to get one's message across (Canale 1983, Canale and Swain 1980).

In U.S. schools today, most students take only two to three years of a foreign language, just long enough to attain rudimentary, survival skills in that language. As a result, decisions about what to teach are relatively uncomplicated: students generally learn fundamental language that allows for basic communication and survival. A cursory review of state curriculum frameworks and of language textbooks—whether used at the secondary or postsecondary level—reveals remarkable consensus about the content of a core, proficiency-based language curriculum.

Proficiency-based language curriculums are designed around the three primary constructs of the ACTFL Proficiency Guidelines: (1) functions—the tasks to be performed with language (e.g., requesting or expressing preferences), (2) contexts and contents—situations and topics (e.g., ordering food in a restaurant), and (3) accuracy—grammatical correctness and sociocultural appropriateness. Curriculums for the early stages of language development are designed to enable students to communicate to fulfill certain basic functions related to familiar topics or survival situations. Such functions include greetings and leave-takings, expressing preferences, making requests, and obtaining or providing information. These functions are expressed through rather simple linguistic means, such as "I like/don't like," "Do you have," "My address is," and "Where is the." As learners advance through levels of proficiency, the functions may not change, but their linguistic expression will become more sophisticated and rely on more complex grammatical structures or elaborated forms. For example, although novice learners may express preferences with "I like/don't like," more proficient learners can access a range of expressions to reflect nuances of preference, such as "I detest" and "I am particularly fond of." Similarly, novice learners make simple (and often not very polite) requests beginning with "Do you have" or "I need a." Later in their language development, students can express these functions in a more acceptable and also more grammatically complex manner by starting with "Would you happen to have" and "I wonder if I might trouble you for a."

Contexts and contents typically found in first- and second-year curriculums include the self (personal and biographical information), family and friends, the house and its furnishings, school (subjects, schedules, and supplies), body and health, leisure activities, clothing, and weather. As learners become more proficient, the topics may expand to include current events, social issues, and the environment. In addition, the contexts in which the learner functions may also become more demanding: face-to-face interaction with native speakers (as opposed to face-to-face with peers or a sympathetic teacher), more challenging and diverse types of textbooks and other materials, and relatively decontextualized media, such as the telephone or radio broadcasts.

As learners become more proficient, their accuracy improves. They call upon their broadening repertoire to communicate with increased grammatical accuracy, lexical precision, and sociocultural appropriateness. Thus, the proficiency-based curriculum is recursive, spiraling functions, contexts, and contents so that students are continually refining their ability to function in the language. Their broadened repertoire of linguistic resources and cultural knowledge enables students to communicate with greater flexibility, precision, elaboration, and complexity.

Even though there is certainly a common core of language (functions, contexts, and contents) that all students will need to communicate, decisions about the content of the curriculum for advanced-level students may be as varied as are the needs of the learners. As noted earlier, decisions about the content of the curriculum derive from the communicative needs of learners. As the purposes of language use may vary considerably among learners, so too may the specific language skills that they will eventually need. However, since it is difficult to predict how most students will put their language skills to use, designing curriculums for advanced students presents a serious challenge. Currently, because very few U.S. students reach this advanced level prior to leaving secondary school, curriculum developers have yet to confront this challenge— a challenge that might become quite real as more students begin language learning earlier and continue for longer sequences than is currently the case.

Culture and the Curriculum

Perhaps no area of a foreign language curriculum is more subject to diversity than the area of culture. Although all foreign language educators agree that culture is an integral and essential part of a language curriculum, reaching consensus on the content is less easily achieved. Academia does not appear to have a commonly shared definition of "culture," in part because the definition within academia reflects the perspectives of a number of disciplines: anthropology, sociology, the arts, and humanities. Second, there is the question of balance: whether to emphasize the system of cultural attitudes and values through which cultural information can best be understood or to emphasize the information itself (the *why* in balance with the *what*). Finally, for French and Spanish—the most commonly taught languages in U.S. schools—there is no single culture of speakers of those languages, but rather diverse cultures spanning the globe. Foreign language professionals struggle with the challenge of determining whose culture and how much of each should be taught.

To add to the complexity of this issue, many teachers feel uncomfortable about teaching culture. Unlike their confidence in their proficiency in the target language—which most teachers have—many feel they have only limited cultural competence. It is difficult to be well-informed about the cultures of many diverse target language speakers. Some aspects of culture, such as daily lifestyles and socioculturally appropriate language use, are continually in flux. More important, while teaching about the cultural products and heritage of speakers of a language may seem relatively straightforward, helping U.S. students understand the underlying belief systems that shape the lives of target language speakers is fraught with dangers that range from stereotyping to trivialization. As a result of these many challenges, the content of the culture component of foreign language courses remains far more subject to individual or local variation than does the content of the language component.

The Sequence of the Foreign Language Curriculum

Like mathematics teachers, foreign language teachers have long thought of their curriculum as sequential and hierarchical. Stemming from the work of structural linguists, the language curriculum traditionally has been a grammatical sequence ordered from the simple to the more complex. Grammar is typically the organizing principle of curriculums, with grammatical and syntactic structures presented in their order of complexity. Although many curriculums today are organized around contexts and contents, such as getting around town or shopping for clothes, little has changed about the general sequence of grammar topics. These have remained unchanged for decades, despite evidence that this order of presentation bears little relationship to the order in which grammar structures are acquired (Richards 1985), and despite suggested alternative criteria for the selection of grammar teaching points for the early stages of language development. Galloway (1987) suggests that grammar topics should reflect learner needs, and that ease of acquisition be weighed in relation either to the structure's frequency in authentic speech or to the flexibility and versatility of its use in a variety of contexts.

These recommendations have met with some, although limited, success. For example, such grammar concepts as giving commands, the forms and placement of double object pronouns, and certain uses of the subjunctive used to receive a great deal of instructional emphasis; today, they receive less emphasis or are placed later in the syllabus. Others have been modified so that certain verbs or structures are introduced only when needed to communicate about a given topic. For example, in the past, when introducing Spanish stem-changing verbs, teachers taught students all the verbs in that category and held students accountable for conjugating them correctly. Today, when working with a unit that enables students to discuss leisure time activities, many Spanish teachers would teach, for instance, the stem-changing verb *jugar* ("to play," as in, to play baseball), but not the stem-changing verbs *dormir* and *morir* ("to sleep" and "to die"), because those verbs are not needed to talk about leisure time activities. Decisions about when to introduce these stem-changing verbs will reflect the communicative objectives of the curriculum rather than the traditional grammar sequence.

The sequence of culture objectives both reflects tradition and departs from it. Today's culture curriculum provides a greater role for culture in the anthropological sense—the daily life patterns and belief systems of target language speakers that provide the cultural context in which the language is rooted. Some culture topics are relatively self-evident in both their importance and placement. Culturally appropriate greetings and leave-takings occur early in the language curriculum. Differing definitions of times of day, such as when afternoon begins and ends, must still be taught early, in part because appropriate greetings depend on this understanding. Cultural notions of family, descriptions of homes, food habits, customs, holidays, and special events are still regularly included in beginning levels of the curriculum because students learn early to talk about the family, the house, food, and special occasions in the target language. In these instances, the language and culture curriculums are inextricably linked—one can hardly become an effective communicator in a language without an understanding of the cultural meanings that the language evokes. Determining the sequence of other aspects of the culture curriculum, such as the history or aesthetic contributions of the target culture, depend on individual teachers, local school decisions, and textbook content.

Instructional Practices: Putting Scope and Sequence into Action

As stated above, the proficiency movement has had a significant impact on how languages are taught. A growing research base in language learning and linguistics is consistent with constructivist theory. Many of today's instructional practices thus result from newly emerging understandings of what language is, how languages are used in authentic communication, and how learning in general—and language learning in particular—are facilitated.

Research has shown that comprehension plays an important role in language acquisition and development. Learners need extensive opportunities to hear language used in meaningful and comprehensible ways. Frequent opportunities for such *comprehensible input* (Krashen 1982) enable learners to match what they hear and read with what they experience, do, and see. The importance of comprehensible input has resulted in a renewed appreciation of the role of context in making meaning, and on the need to emphasize listening and reading comprehension tasks as part of the teaching/learning process. Intake occurs when learners notice and "take in" features in the comprehensible input. Thus, by attending to such language features in the input as vocabulary, syntax, and discourse markers, learners begin to construct an understanding of the language system and its component features.

This significant role of comprehensible input means that teachers need to use the target language in class as much as possible, for if language is acquired by understanding what is heard, then it follows that students need to hear the language used in meaningful, comprehensible ways to the fullest extent possible. New methodologies (Asher 1984, Krashen and Terrell 1983) that capitalize on the significant role of comprehension in language development had gained widespread acceptance by the mid-1980s; many of these methodologies continue to be in vogue today.

Although comprehensible input is a necessary condition for language acquisition, it is not the only condition. Learners need opportunities to produce language as well. Learners must be able to produce comprehensible output (Swain 1985) because communication involves negotiating meaning—working to make oneself understood and understand others. By "testing the waters" of their constructions in the give-and-take of human interaction, language learners discover the ways in which their constructions are accurate enough to be understood by others. The need to repair their messages requires learners to map meanings onto forms, so that meanings are conveyed with accuracy and precision. Through the processes of input and intake, learners construct an internalized representation of the language system and the complex interactions of its many components (Ellis 1993). Increasingly sophisticated and complex input, when coupled with the demands of output tasks, together provide feedback on the accuracy of these constructions, which results in further language development and growth.

Since the primary goal of language learning is effective language use in communication, it is clear that a significant portion of instructional time must be devoted to using language knowledge (as opposed to just acquiring knowledge of the components of language) and in ways that most closely approximate the authentic communications that take place outside the classroom. Language use always involves making meaning— whether interpreting the meanings of others, expressing one's own meanings, or engaging in the natural give-and-take that characterizes most human interactions (negotiating meaning) (Savignon 1991). Authentic communicative interactions are characterized by the following features:

• They are contextualized. Communicators have a shared agreement about the topic at hand; they usually share common background knowledge, scripts, and schemata related to the topic; and their interactions frequently incorporate features of the physical context into their communications (e.g., gestures and body language, objects or other features in the immediate environment).

• They have a purpose. In real life, people use language to get things done, whether their goal is to accomplish a task, transact a purchase, exchange information, express an opinion, or simply socialize.

• They involve an authentic, meaning-driven exchange of information. Authentic communication is usually characterized by an *information* or *opinion gap*. That is, parties in a conversation often exchange information or opinions unknown to one another. In contrast, inauthentic classroom talk communicates little *new* information because it is frequently characterized by display questions such as "What is this?" and "What's the weather today?"

In foreign language classrooms, the characteristics of authentic communicative interaction imply that students should be engaged in tasks that allow them to exchange real meanings of their own creation, for a real purpose, and for a real audience in a task that is as authentic as possible. Peer collaboration through pair and group work is an important feature of the language classroom. In addition to the well-documented benefits of collaborative learning in all disciplines, when small-group interactions are appropriately structured in language classrooms, they provide increased opportunities for language use in meaningful contexts. Small-group interactions also provide the critically important opportunity to negotiate meaning, allowing students opportunities to test the accuracy of their constructions of the language system and to refine these constructions when their communication is less than effective. Research suggests that such interaction is essential to language growth (Doughty and Pica 1986, Long and Porter 1985, Swain 1985).

The research base that informs today's foreign language curriculum and related instructional practices differs substantially from the former Skinnerian model of language learning. Today's view of second or foreign language development is well aligned with constructivist theory, a theory that also informs the whole language approach to first language reading/language arts. Constructivism is a theory of human learning that holds that

> people are not recorders of information but builders of knowledge structures. To know something is not just to have received information but also to have interpreted it and related it to other knowledge. . . . (T)he goal of all . . . instructional activities is to stimulate and nourish students' own mental elaborations of knowledge and to help them grow in their capacity to monitor and guide their own learning and thinking (Resnick 1989, pp. 5–6).

In both traditional reading and foreign language classrooms, instruction has been based on a bottom-up approach: Students learned each of the parts in analytical fashion and were expected to synthesize the parts into the whole. Today, language development is seen as a holistic process, in which the whole (meaning) is greater than the individual parts, and in which the parts must always be placed at the service of and in the context of the whole. In neither reading nor foreign language instruction today are the parts—phonics and grammar, respectively— abandoned. Rather, the parts are seen as integral to the overall meaning-making process, but not the primary point of departure. Foreign language classrooms today present students with meaningful interactive communicative tasks that stand in stark contrast to the days when class periods were devoted to having students parrot mindlessly after the teacher or performing excruciatingly boring, meaningless, rote grammar exercises.

Other parallels exist between reading/language arts and foreign language instruction. In both fields, language is viewed as an integrated complex of skills; listening, speaking, reading, and writing do not develop in isolation from one another. Traditionally, foreign language educators viewed the sequence of skills development as relatively fixed; students learned to listen, then to speak, then to read what they could understand and speak, and then to write what they could say. Culture was viewed as a fifth skill. In contrast, language is viewed today as growing from interactions among listening, speaking, reading, and writing, which may be reciprocal in their development and effects. For example, although listening comprehension is a primary vehicle for language development, reading also serves as a significant source of comprehensible input. Speaking is more than merely talking. The oral expression of meaning depends on knowledge of discourse rules and sociocultural rules of communication as much as it does on knowledge of words or grammar rules. By engaging in spoken interactions, learners can elicit comprehensible input from each other. Thus, speaking helps to maintain a cycle of communication that ultimately can improve language knowledge and performance. And, unlike past views of the writing skill, writing is no longer thought to depend on the ability to speak. Writing may actually precede oral production. Allowing students to outline or develop ideas in print can often contribute to increased fluency and clarity of their oral messages.

Another research-based practice foreign language education shares with reading is strategies-based instruction. Learners of foreign languages, like those learning to read in their first language, benefit from explicit instruction in learning strategies (Chamot and Kupper 1989, Oxford 1990). Metacognitive, cognitive, and affective strategies enable students to be self-directed and self-regulating learners. For example, early readers in a first or foreign language can call on background knowledge or use the titles and illustrations of text to predict what the text will be about. This strategy facilitates the construction of meaning, a process that has more to do with what resides in the learner's head than what is found on the printed page.

Integrating Language and Culture

As noted earlier, cultural knowledge and skills underlie effective communication because culture provides the anchoring context for language and determines what speakers really mean by what they say. Culture, then, cannot be relegated to a fifth skill or be taught only on Friday afternoons. Rather, culture must be integrated into all aspects of language teaching. This is particularly true for those aspects of culture that affect how the language encodes meaning. For example, Spanish speakers place great importance on interpersonal relationships, and therefore, on greetings. In Spanish-speaking cultures, it is considered rude to begin discussing a potential purchase with shopkeepers without at least greeting them first. And if the vendor and client are known to each other, inquiries about families are also in order. In several languages, it is inappropriate to respond to a compliment by saying "thank you." And, in Japanese, *how* you say "thank you" depends on a variety of factors, including the relationship between the speakers, their sex and age, and the cause that occasions the need to proffer thanks.

Thus, for the English speaker learning another language, simply knowing how to translate from English to another language without understanding the cultural meanings speakers assign to words can lead to miscommunication or even interpersonal dysfunctions. Because effective communication with native speakers depends on the kinds of cultural knowledge just described, culture must be integral to language skills—not a fifth skill.

Foreign language classrooms need to provide for linguistically and culturally authentic interactions, both face to face and through print. Authentic reading materials provide insight into culture and language as an integrated system. They are examples of the "culture communicating with its own" (Galloway 1992, p. 98), examples of native speakers/culture bearers communicating with each other through a shared language and culture. The role of culture in language use provides yet another compelling reason for classroom tasks that are authentic, meaningful, and purposeful.

Curriculum Across the Grades

Most foreign language instruction in the United States begins in high school, but programs at the elementary and middle school levels are expanding rapidly. This expansion reflects a growing recognition that waiting until high school allows insufficient time in a student's academic career to attain a usable level of language proficiency. And, if U.S. students are ever to achieve world-class academic standards (and the forthcoming U.S. national standards), they will need to start language learning earlier and stay with it longer.

At all levels, foreign language curriculum designers are swiftly translating the trends described above from the pages of the professional literature into the classroom. Despite philosophical similarities, differences in implementation are associated with different levels of schooling. Elementary school foreign language programs are probably more communicative in orientation than those at any other level, in large part because a communicative approach is the most developmentally appropriate. Indeed, it is hard to imagine teaching languages to young children in any way other than through a holistic, meaning-focused, authentic approach. Children develop language skills by participating in meaningful, engaging activities, such as stories, drama, games, role-plays, interesting tasks, and projects. Interdisciplinary instruction is becoming more widespread as teachers draw on content from across the curriculum for language practice and development (Curtain and Pesola 1994, Met 1991).

Big books and familiar stories are common. Vocabulary development in a food unit can be integrated with mathematics (using nonstandard units of measurement) when students weigh fruits and vegetables, or vocabulary can be integrated with science when students determine whether a food is a fruit or vegetable based on which part of the plant is eaten. Culture not only is a curriculum focus of most elementary school programs, it has a natural fit with the concepts of the social studies curriculum and with the multicultural outcomes frequently found among the goals of many schools or districts.

Middle school instructional practices widely reflect the tenets of communicative, proficiency-based instruction. It is not clear whether this is due to the learner-centered, constructivist focus that now permeates many middle schools or whether it is in response to the developmental characteristics of the students themselves. What is clear is that middle school language teachers increasingly tend to use collaborative task structures, focus on interesting tasks for language practice, and provide concrete supports for contextualization, such as visuals, hands-on manipulatives, and role-plays. In some middle schools, as in some high schools, however, more traditional forms of instruction persist.

At the high school level, language curriculum and instruction continue to reflect the shift from a grammar-based curriculum to a proficiency-based curriculum. In fact, many states have already developed curriculum frameworks that are proficiency based (see LaBouve 1993 for a detailed discussion). Professional associations and local inservice opportunities have helped teachers gain the knowledge and skills needed to make this transition. However, because many high school teachers (who also form the overwhelming majority of K–12 teachers) have limited access to subject-specific professional development, change occurs slowly. Further, most elementary and some middle school teachers find their students may have difficulty with abstract grammar concepts. Therefore, many students do not receive in-depth instruction in the structure of the target language until they reach high school. For high school students who advance beyond the first two years of foreign language study, reading and writing at higher levels of sophistication, including exposure to literature, take on a greater role than in the earlier grades.

Influences on the Curriculum

Among the most powerful influences on what gets taught, to whom, and how, is the organization and administration of schools.

Most foreign language instruction in the United States begins at the high school level. In 1990, the most recent year for which data are available, approximately 39 percent of public high school students were enrolled in a foreign language course (Draper 1991). (This figure does not represent students who may have completed one to three years of language study previously.) The data show an across-the-board growth in foreign language enrollments, with increasing interest in Spanish and in less commonly taught languages such as Japanese, Chinese, and Russian, and stable enrollments in German and Latin. Most students, however, still take only two years of a high school foreign language, although there are small increases in third year (and above) enrollments from previous years. Length of sequence is of serious concern to foreign language educators because the goals of proficiency (and those of national standards) cannot be attained in only two or three years of language learning. In fact, many foreign language educators believe that this short sequence does little more than prepare students to be polite tourists. If our need for a language-competent nation is ever to be attained, or if U.S. students are to attain world-class standards in challenging academic coursework, the length of foreign language sequences must be extended to include an earlier start and sustained study. In a handful of states, eligibility for more prestigious high school diplomas includes a foreign language requirement, but at present, New York is the only state that requires foreign language study for graduation.[1]

High school students are often more interested in meeting college entrance or diploma eligibility requirements than in gaining a usable level of language skill. Their lack of universal or extended foreign language study partly shapes the content of the curriculum. Unlike other nations where language study is taken for granted as an integral part of schooling, the U.S. viewpoint has been that foreign languages are peripheral to the core curriculum. In fact, most Americans do not appear to believe that proficiency in any language other than English is a necessary skill for full participation as a productive member of society or the economy. In contrast to many countries where students study languages long enough to gain a usable proficiency in it, and where they also have

---

[1]All students must take a foreign language to graduate. On request, special-needs students may have the requirement waived or reduced.

a reasonable expectation of using their language skills, U.S. students acquire very minimal skills. As a result, the stated goals of proficiency-based curriculums can only be partially attained. In a somewhat discouraging feedback cycle, students' inability to use their skills, even within their own multilingual communities, further erodes public belief in the efficacy and utility of language learning, resulting in further minimal investment in such instruction and learning.

While foreign languages are almost universally available in U.S. high schools, the same cannot be said for middle schools. Data on middle school course offerings and enrollments are discouraging. Epstein and MacIver (1990, 1992) report that only about one-third of public schools that include 7th and 8th grades offer a year-long foreign language course. Of these, only 14 percent report enrolling half or more of students in these grades. In contrast, the picture is somewhat better in private schools that include grades 7 and 8. Approximately two-thirds of these schools offer a year-long course, and 58 percent report enrolling half or more of their students. Similarly, Draper (1991) reported that only 12.44 percent of U.S. public school students in grades 7 and 8 were enrolled in a foreign language course in 1990. Students will find it difficult to attain challenging academic standards if the opportunity to learn is not available.

The shift from junior-and-senior-high-school to middle-and-high-school configurations has also dramatically affected foreign language course offerings and enrollments. In particular, the middle school emphasis on exploratory experiences has resulted in a proliferation of short-term exploratory foreign language courses. In some districts, long-standing sequential programs have been replaced by exploratory courses, because some middle school administrators have interpreted the professional literature to mean that only exploratory courses should be offered in the middle grades (see Met 1994 for a fuller discussion). Exploratory courses tend to have minimal language outcomes, emphasizing instead simply the development of positive attitudes toward learning other languages and cultures. Although there is no doubt about the value of exploratory courses, they often require that students delay the development of language proficiency until later grades.

Within the foreign language teaching profession itself there is serious debate over the relative merits of exploratory and sequential programs (Kennedy and DeLorenzo 1994; Knop and Sandrock 1994a, 1994b; Met 1994). Most foreign language educators believe that the goals of exploratory courses are worthwhile, but some feel that these goals can be achieved as effectively through a well-designed sequential program in the middle school. Others suggest that exploratory courses be limited in duration (e.g., six weeks to a semester), so that students do not spend two to three years in such courses at the expense of developing some usable level of proficiency.

The middle school movement has had a serious impact on the organization and administration of language programs. Because foreign language teachers rarely form part of the "core" interdisciplinary team, they are frequently marginalized and excluded from the academic life of the school. Decisions about interdisciplinary themes or units are often made by the core team. For foreign language teachers to participate in interdisciplinary units, however, they need to be part of the decision-making process, because students' limited ability to use language (whether orally or through print) places constraints on the ways in which foreign language can contribute to achieving the units' outcomes. Foreign language teachers can usually contribute to the team or school's interdisciplinary unit through connections with the target culture, but they often find themselves forced to teach in English to do so. And while such participation may legitimately further the cultural objectives of the language curriculum, teaching in English impedes language growth.

Just as the middle school foreign language curriculum is determined by program model or course offerings, so too is that of the elementary school. A growing number of elementary schools offer foreign languages, and some states (e.g., Arizona, Louisiana, North Carolina, and Oklahoma) now require it. Some school systems have initiated programs not only in recognition of the importance of foreign languages in a global society, but also in light of the growing body of research on the cognitive and academic benefits of early language learning. In a 1987 survey, Rhodes and Oxford (1988) found that approximately one in five elementary schools offered foreign language instruction. (Although no new data have been published, this number has increased significantly since the 1987 survey because at least three states have subsequently implemented mandated elementary school language programs.)

Elementary programs fall on a continuum of time, intensity, and intended outcomes. At one end are Foreign Language Exploratory (FLEX) programs. FLEX programs are typically short in duration (one to two years), and classes typically meet a few times a week for 30 minutes or less. FLEX programs emphasize exposure to new cultures and some language objectives. Foreign Language in the Elementary School (FLES) programs, by contrast, have more clearly focused language outcomes, also stress cultural learning, and are part of an extended sequence of language learning. Students in FLES programs have language instruction no fewer than 75 minutes per week in no fewer than three sessions; some even have 70 minutes of language instruction daily. Clearly, a wide range of organizational formats falls within this program model. Many FLES programs are content based; they draw upon the content of the school curriculum for content and language tasks.

The most intensive and extensive program model is immersion. In this model, students study the regular school curriculum through the medium of a foreign language for no less than half a day.

Program models have an obvious effect on the curriculum. FLEX curriculums have limited language content and focus on culture. FLES curriculums are hierarchical and sequential—that is, concepts, skills, and knowledge acquired at one level are reinforced, enriched, and expanded at the next, resulting in growth in language proficiency. In immersion programs, the curriculum is the school's curriculum in the subjects taught through the foreign language (e.g., math and science). Language growth is the outcome of instruction in these subjects. Many immersion programs have acknowledged the need for a language scope and sequence in the immersion language and have begun to develop and pilot test such curriculums.

Articulation from grade to grade and from elementary to middle to high school is a key factor, and unless carefully planned, curriculums at each of these school levels may repeat what was taught previously.

Teachers and the Curriculum

An old Spanish proverb says *El papel aguanta todo* (You can put anything on paper). The curriculum is only a paper document. The real curriculum is in the hands of teachers. Teachers filter curriculum through their belief and knowledge systems. Curriculum reform is facilitated when teachers have state-of-the-art knowledge of theory and related instructional practices. Therefore, preservice education and the professional development of practicing teachers are vitally important.

The proficiency-oriented curriculum requires that teachers be competent speakers of the language and that classes be conducted primarily in the target language. Because the development of students' oral proficiency rests heavily on their comprehension skills, guidelines and standards developed by a number of professional associations have all called for Advanced or Advanced Plus performance on the ACTFL oral rating scales (Lafayette 1993). ACTFL and the American Association of Teachers of Spanish specify an Advanced Plus rating. The American Association of Teachers of German state in their professional standards (1992), "Teachers of German have a command of the language that allows them to conduct their classes in German with ease and confidence" (p. 9). Similarly, standards for French teachers, offered by the American Association of Teachers of French (AATF), describe the importance of language proficiency:

> The ability to speak, understand, read, and write French well encourages teachers to use French in class, providing expansive and accurate models for their students. . . . It also allows them to maintain contact with French-speaking cultures, giving them current information to share with their students (AATF 1989, p. 11).

In addition to language proficiency, the cultural competence of teachers also influences curriculum and its delivery. The extent to which a teacher has competence in the area of culture determines the place of culture in that teacher's curriculum—that is, *if* it is taught, *what* is taught, and *how* it is taught. Skills in cross-cultural communication are essential for both preservice and inservice practitioners. And, teachers need an understanding of the basic cultural framework of attitudes and values and of how these have been expressed through aesthetic expressions and in a culture's daily life patterns. They also need knowledge of the culture's history and geography. All the major professional associations that have issued guidelines or standards for teacher preparation have included a strong focus on cultural competence.

Instructional Materials and Resources

Curriculum is also influenced by available resources such as instructional materials and technology. Like many other disciplines, foreign language instruction was more textbook driven in the past. Nonetheless, textbooks (as well as nonprint materials) play a role in shaping today's curriculum, particularly when state or local curriculum documents are lacking. In 1992, 17 states had no curriculum frameworks; another 10 did not require that schools adhere to the state's frameworks (Phelps 1993). Current reform initiatives in almost all states are likely to affect these data. In the interim, however, decisions about curriculum thus rest with local school districts, schools, and teachers. Here an interesting interplay takes place: once the curriculum is written, texts are then selected to support it. Teachers are, however, familiar with the content of existing or new text materials as they are developing curriculum. By their very contents, these commercial materials help mold what teachers think the curriculum content ought to be. The quantity of space devoted to certain topics—even to the exclusion of others—together with the placement and prominence of such topics in the text sends powerful messages about appropriate curriculum content. Yet at the same time, publishers produce what they think teachers will buy, particularly since textbook production is a multimillion dollar risk. In this interplay, then, it is easy to see how the process of curriculum development and reform can be affected by published materials. Although textbooks neither determine curriculum nor impede reform, they are part of an interrelated, interlocking system.

Technological resources have the potential to significantly influence curriculum design and delivery. These resources, however, are not common in the typical foreign language classroom, although this picture is likely to change as technology becomes more accessible and widespread. Distance learning already brings opportunities for language study to areas where resources (human or financial) are scarce—areas where enrollments in languages such as Japanese or Russian are low, or where there is a shortage of qualified teachers. Little research is available at this time to document the ways in which distance learning shapes the content of curriculum or to attest to its efficacy. In some schools, students communicate across the globe via electronic telecommunication. Global e-mail provides meaningful and authentic opportunities for students to communicate through writing, particularly in geographic areas where students might not otherwise have direct access to native speakers of the language. The Internet can provide access to foreign language resources, references, and data that far exceed those currently available in the typical school or community library. Although technology has the potential to transform foreign language education, this potential is still only in the exploratory stage.

Foreign Language Curriculum in the Coming Decades

Proficiency: The Next Generation

As the proficiency movement has matured, notions of communicative language use have become more sophisticated. For the last decade, to allow for authentic meaningful and purposeful communication, students have been presented with tasks in which the information exchanged is personalized: They describe their personal experiences, their opinions on a variety of relevant topics, or their preferences. There is now a growing recognition that even though personalized activities are engaging and provide opportunities for authentic exchanges of information, students must also be able to communicate about ideas. As a result, there has been significant interest in extending and expanding content-based foreign language instruction so that students use language as a tool for learning new information. In this approach, content drawn from other disciplines is taught through the new language. This content may be the primary source of course objectives, with language outcomes as important secondary objectives. Or, the primary course objectives may be the language outcomes, with content serving as a vehicle for language use. In reality, content-based instruction represents a range of approaches to integrating content and language learning, all of which offer an expanded view of language: moving beyond interpersonal communication to the use of language as a tool for accessing and processing new information.

Setting Standards in Foreign Languages

Several standard-setting initiatives have emerged in the last few years. Because of the extensive work related to the ACTFL Proficiency Guidelines and related endeavors, a high degree of consensus already existed in the early '90s within the foreign language community about appropriate goals, processes, and approaches to assessment. This consensus facilitated rapid progress in standards-setting projects. Perhaps the best known is the National Standards in Foreign Languages project funded by the U.S. Department of Education as part of the Goals 2000: Educate America Act initiative. Content standards in foreign languages are under development through a joint effort of ACTFL, the American Association of Teachers of French, the American Association of Teachers of German, and the American Association of Teachers of Spanish and Portuguese.[2] Although these voluntary national standards will not be completed until late 1995, they have already been disseminated in draft form. The standards and related benchmarks will be developed in five broad goal areas, describing how students will do the following:

- Communicate in a language other than English.
- Gain knowledge and understanding of other cultures.
- Connect with other disciplines and acquire new information.
- Gain insight into own language and culture.
- Participate in multilingual communities and global societies.

---

[2]For further information about the National Standards in Foreign Language Education, contact Jamie Draper, ACTFL, 6 Executive Plaza, Yonkers, NY 10701.

Another standard-setting project is *Pacesetter,* a project of the College Board. *Pacesetter* is an initiative being undertaken in five disciplines, including Spanish, to develop challenging standards, course materials, and related assessments to be attained by all students, not simply the college bound. *Pacesetter* is remarkably consistent not only with the proficiency movement, but also with the draft goal statements of the national foreign language standards. The three major goals of *Pacesetter Spanish* are

• Students will use language to acquire additional knowledge in any area appropriate.

• Students will gain a better understanding of their own and other cultures by (1) developing knowledge of the *facts* of target cultures, (2) observing the *acts* of target cultures, and (3) discovering the *meanings* important to cultures so that greater sensitivity and awareness may develop.

• Students will use and understand oral and written Spanish in a culturally acceptable manner to participate effectively in everyday situations at home and abroad.

In addition to national standards and *Pacesetter,* many states have undertaken standards development as well.

Standards, Articulation, and Assessment

Recognizing that high standards cannot be achieved unless students are able to move from one level of instruction to the next or from one setting to the next, several projects are under way to provide clear expectations for student performance and to ensure appropriate articulation as students progress through levels of performance from middle school to high school to postsecondary education. The Articulation and Achievement Project is a collaborative endeavor of the New England Network of Academic Alliances in Foreign Languages, the College Board, and ACTFL. This project has worked "to develop articulated standards and student achievement levels for foreign language education in grades 7–14" (*Provisional Learning Outcomes Framework* 1994).[3] The New England collaborative's framework describes five stages of language development and provides descriptors of functions, contexts, content,

---

[3]For further information, contact Claire Jackson, Assistant Superintendent for Curriculum and Instruction, K–12, the Public Schools of Brookline, Massachusetts; Donald Reutershan, Foreign Language Consultant, Maine Department of Education; or Robert Orrill, Executive Director of the Office of Academic Affairs, The College Board.

text type, accuracy levels, and assessment strategies for each stage. Like other standards initiatives in foreign languages, the framework is strongly consonant with the tenets of proficiency-based outcomes, instruction, and assessments.

Similar projects are under way in Ohio[4] and Colorado.[5] In Ohio, the Collaborative Articulation and Assessment Project also addresses issues of curriculum and articulation. Its two main objectives are "the establishment of a clear articulation plan and the development of valid foreign language early assessment measures" (*The Collaborative Articulation and Assessment Project,* n.d.). As part of the development of articulation plans and assessment measures, faculty from high schools, a community college, and a four-year institution in the Columbus area have worked to identify a common core of learning upon which proficiency-oriented tests will be based. In Colorado, Project Span (Standards- and Performance-Based Academic Networking) is a three-year, K–16 project in five disciplines (including Spanish) to develop performance standards and indicators, to identify benchmark performance tasks to assess student progress relative to established performance standards, and to design scoring criteria for these tasks. Project Span anticipates that development of standards, indicators, and assessments will lead to reassessment (and redesign) of curriculum and instruction at both the precollegiate and postsecondary levels.

In other states, standards and assessments are also linked. In Oregon, Pennsylvania, and Texas, students will need to perform at a specified level on the ACTFL proficiency rating scale to meet state standards. In the case of Oregon and Pennsylvania, high school graduation will be tied to proficiency in future years. Seven states—Alaska, Colorado, Nebraska, Oregon, South Dakota, Texas, and Wisconsin—are developing foreign language content standards or curriculum frameworks (along with standards for other disciplines), with the support of the Secretary's Fund for Innovation in Education. Two of these states—Nebraska and Texas—are using these federal funds solely for foreign languages.

---

[4]For further information, contact Diane Birckbichler, Project Director, Ohio State University, National Foreign Resource Center.

[5]For further information, contact Francis A. Griffith, Assistant Vice Provost for Assessment, University of Northern Colorado.

The Shape of Things to Come

National, state, and other standards will be a shaping force in foreign language curriculum and instruction for decades to come. It is likely that the national standards will be set at a challenge level that can best be met by students who begin foreign language learning and continue with the learning over a long sequence of time.

Setting high standards in foreign languages has been a source of thoughtful discussion among professionals. On the one hand, there is the serious concern that U.S. students currently study languages for too short a time to peg any kind of challenging academic standard to today's enrollment patterns. But to set standards that truly reflect challenging world-class levels means that schools will have to design and implement far more extensive programs than exist at present. Extending programs both to the lower grades and to continued study into the junior and senior years of high school will require additional human and financial resources, some of which are in very short supply in today's economic climate. If standards are set high, will schools simply choose to ignore voluntary standards in foreign languages? On the other hand, if standards are set at a level accessible to most schools, will the mandate to set challenging, world-class standards have been met?

Attaining high standards in foreign languages will need to be accomplished through programs that begin in elementary or middle school and that continue through high school. Extended sequences will mean that schools will need to develop new curriculums for those levels and that existing curriculums be revised to reflect an earlier start. Advanced levels of instruction currently constitute a very small percentage of secondary school foreign language course enrollments. But as sequences are extended, the number of students with higher levels of proficiency will increase, requiring more attention to appropriate curriculum content and materials. Further, as discussed earlier, the purposes to which learners put their language skills increasingly influence curriculum content as learners advance. These purposes will need thoughtful consideration as curriculums are developed or revised to accommodate more proficient high school students. Higher levels of student proficiency will have implications for classroom practices, so that instructional practices appropriate to the development of advanced level skills will need to be a more salient feature of professional development. Because so few high school students develop advanced levels of proficiency at present, most professional development for teachers until now has focused on the initial stages of language acquisition.

If teachers influence the curriculum based on their knowledge of subject content and their pedagogical skills, then initiating and sustaining curriculum reform clearly rests heavily on teachers' access to ongoing professional development. Indeed, new standards will require increased in-depth opportunities for teachers to become skilled and knowledgeable in enabling students to meet those standards. The foreign language curriculum of the 1990s and beyond relies on teachers for its effective implementation, as is the case for all curriculum areas. Indeed, the close relationship between professional development and educational reform has been noted in much of the discussion of forthcoming national standards and is one of the goals listed in the Goals 2000: Educate America Act. The need for professional development, however, may be greater among foreign language teachers than for other professionals, because fewer resources have been available in recent years to address their professional growth than have been available for teachers of mathematics and science, for example.

National standards will affect both veteran and preservice teachers. Beyond the demands of today's curriculum, teachers will need to know

• Effective means of developing communicative competence in students of all ages, abilities, and achievement levels, and in differing program models.

• The culture(s) of target language speakers and how to best convey their own knowledge to students.

• How language and culture are related and how and what aspects of this information should be taught to students at different ages and levels of language proficiency.

• How to make connections between foreign language and other disciplines.

• Foreign language resources for students to acquire new knowledge through the language.

• How to make authentic print and nonprint materials accessible to students who may have limited proficiency in the foreign language.

• Resources in the community and the world beyond and how to access them.

• How to reach a broader and more diverse student population.

• How to make learning accessible to students at different ages and stages of cognitive development.

• Classroom-based strategies for performance assessment.

• How to use technology to promote language growth and cultural insights.

The effective implementation of national standards in foreign language will require extensive teacher professional development, presenting challenges to university-based teacher educators, school-based administrators, and professional associations. At the postsecondary level, it has been suggested that only a very small percentage of methods professors are trained in foreign language methodology or applied linguistics (Van Patten 1993). Indeed, a significant number of methods courses are not subject-specific, but cover all disciplines taught at the secondary level.

Whether novices entering the profession or veterans of some years, all teachers should have access to continued professional growth. The literature on teacher professional growth is unequivocal on the importance of sustained opportunities for teachers to acquire new theoretical perspectives and their incorporation into classroom practices (Joyce and Showers 1982). Teachers need opportunities for consistent guided practice to transfer skills acquired in training workshops to the classroom. For example, the peer coaching model, as described by Joyce and Showers (1982), includes (1) studying the theory of a new teaching approach, (2) observing repeated expert demonstrations, (3) practicing the new approach under sheltered conditions (e.g., teaching peers in a workshop setting), and (4) practicing new skills in the classroom with peers providing feedback in a supportive, collegial fashion.

Opportunities to learn new theories and to apply them are constrained by a number of factors. Many schools and school districts do provide some inservice training days, but frequently these are focused on schoolwide concerns such as substance abuse prevention or mainstreaming initiatives. There are few inservice training opportunities provided by most schools or districts that are subject-matter specific. In a study of one state, Wolf and Riordan (1991) found that most foreign language teachers have limited access to subject-matter specific professional development. Many foreign language educators believe these findings are generalizable to a large number of states. To meet the demands that national standards will impose on curriculum and instruction, local schools and districts will need to plan and implement foreign language-specific professional development opportunities, whether alone or in collaboration with other agencies and institutions. Turnkey training models (train-the-trainers) will be a useful approach to increasing the number of qualified personnel. State departments of education and professional associations will need to engage extensively in outreach activities and focus on sustained change. Most important, teachers will need opportunities to be reflective practitioners and assume control of their own professional growth, with seminars and study groups that promote and provide time for reflection.

Conclusion

The foregoing discussion should make clear the extent to which foreign language curriculum and instruction have progressed in the last decade. As is true for educators in other disciplines, the foreign language profession is performance oriented, relies on a constructivist view of learning, and is engaged in promoting high levels of achievement for all students. Foreign language curriculum and instruction are not only influenced by theory, research, and standards, but are also shaped by the realities of schools, teachers, and available resources. In the coming decades, as national standards and the constructivist views of learning that underpin them gain prominence and acceptance, the interrelationship of curriculum, instruction, and assessment will be more tightly bound than ever. If schools will make available the opportunity for sustained foreign language study, and if they implement the curriculum and instructional practices that the profession advocates, U.S. students will be able to attain world-class standards of foreign language proficiency.

References

American Association of Teachers of French. (1989). "The Teaching of French: A Syllabus of Competence." *AATF National Bulletin* 15 (special issue).

American Association of Teachers of German. (1992). *Professional Standards for Teachers of German.* Cherry Hill, N.J.: Author.

Articulation and Achievement Project. (1994). *Provisional Learning Outcomes Framework.*

Asher, J. (1984). *Learning Another Language Through Actions: The Complete Teacher's Guidebook.* Los Gatos, Calif.: Sky Oaks Publications.

Canale, M. (1983). "From Communicative Competence to Communicative Language Pedagogy." In *Language and Communication,* edited by J.C. Richards and R.W. Schmidt. London: Longman.

Canale, M., and M. Swain. (1980). "Theoretical Bases of Communicative Approaches to Second Language Teaching and Testing." *Applied Linguistics* 1: 1–47.

Chamot, A.U., and L. Kupper. (1989). "Learning Strategies in Foreign Language Instruction." *Foreign Language Annals* 22: 13–28.

Collaborative Articulation and Assessment Project. (n.d.). Columbus, Ohio: National Foreign Language Resource Center.

Curtain, H., and C.A. Pesola. (1994). *Languages and Children: Making the Match.* New York: Longman.

Doughty, C., and T. Pica. (1986). " 'Information Gap' Tasks: Do They Facilitate Second Language Acquisition?" *TESOL Quarterly* 20, 3: 305–325.

Draper, J. (1991). *Foreign Language Enrollments in Public Secondary Schools, Fall 1989 and Fall 1990.* New York: American Council on the Teaching of Foreign Languages.

Ellis, R. (1993). "The Structural Syllabus and Second Language Acquisition." *TESOL Quarterly* 27, 1: 91–112.

Epstein, J., and D. MacIver. (1990). *Education in the Middle Grades: Overview of National Practices and Trends.* Columbus, Ohio: National Middle School Association.

Epstein, J., and D. MacIver. (1992). *Opportunities to Learn: Effects on Eighth Graders of Curriculum Offerings and Instructional Approaches.* Baltimore: Johns Hopkins University Center for Research on Effective Schooling for Disadvantaged Students.

Galloway, V. (1987). "From Defining to Developing Proficiency: A Look at the Decisions." In *Defining and Developing Proficiency: Guidelines, Implementations, and Concepts,* edited by H. Byrnes and M. Canale. Lincolnwood, Ill.: National Textbook Co.

Galloway, V. (1992). "Toward a Cultural Reading of Authentic Texts." In *Languages for a Multicultural World in Transition,* edited by H. Byrnes. Lincolnwood, Ill.: National Textbook Co.

Joyce, B., and B. Showers. (1982). "The Coaching of Teaching." *Educational Leadership* 40, 1: 4–10.

Kennedy, D., and W. DeLorenzo. (1994). "Point: The Case for Exploratory Programs in Middle/Junior High School." *Foreign Language Annals* 27: 69–73.

Knop, C., and P. Sandrock. (1994a). "Counterpoint to the Exploratory Approach." *Foreign Language Annals* 27: 74–76.

Knop, C., and P. Sandrock. (1994b). "Point: The Case for a Sequential Second Language Learning Experience at the Middle Level." *Foreign Language Annals* 27: 77–83.

Krashen, S. (1982). *Principles and Practice in Second Language Acquisition.* Oxford: Pergamon Press.

Krashen, S., and T.D. Terrell. (1983). *The Natural Approach: Language Acquisition in the Classroom.* New York: Pergamon Press.

LaBouve, R. (1993). "Proficiency as a Change Element in Curricula for World Languages in Elementary and Secondary Schools." In *Reflecting on Proficiency from the Classroom Perspective,* edited by J. Phillips. Lincolnwood, Ill.: National Textbook Co.

Lafayette, R.C. (1993). "Subject Matter Content: What Every Foreign Language Teacher Needs to Know." In *Developing Language Teachers for a Changing World,* edited by G. Gungermann. Lincolnwood, Ill.: National Textbook Co.

Long, M., and P. Porter. (1985). "Group Work, Interlanguage Talk, and Second Language Acquisition." *TESOL Quarterly* 19, 2: 207–228.

Met, M. (1991). "Learning Language Through Content: Learning Content Through Language." *Foreign Language Annals* 24: 281–295.

Met, M. (1994). "Current Foreign Language Practices in Middle Schools." *Foreign Language Annals* 27: 43–58.

Omaggio Hadley, A.C. (1993). "Proficiency: Origins, Perspectives, and Prospects." In *Reflecting on Proficiency from the Classroom Perspective*, edited by J. Phillips. Lincolnwood, Ill.: National Textbook Co.

Oxford, R. (1990). *Language Learning Strategies: What Every Teacher Should Know.* New York: Newbury House/Harper and Row.

Phelps, R. (May 19, 1993). "The Weak and Strong Arguments Against National Testing." *Education Week,* p. 30.

Resnick, L.B., ed. (1989). *Knowing, Learning, and Instruction: Essays in Honor of Robert Glaser.* Hillsdale, N.J.: Lawrence Erlbaum Associates.

Rhodes, N.C., and R.L. Oxford. (1988). "Foreign Languages in Elementary and Secondary Schools: Results of a National Survey." *Foreign Language Annals* 21, 1: 51–69.

Richards, J.C. (1985). *The Context of Language Teaching.* Cambridge: Cambridge University Press.

Savignon, S.J. (1991). "Communicative Language Teaching: State of the Art." *TESOL Quarterly* 25, 2: 261–277.

Swain, M. (1985). "Communicative Competence: Some Roles of Comprehensible Input and Comprehensible Output in its Development." In *Input in Second Language Acquisition*, edited by S. Gass and C. Madden. New York: Newbury House Publishers.

Van Patten, B. (1993). *Proficiency: Paradigm Shift or Flash in the Pan?* Paper presented at the annual meeting of the Northeast Conference on the Teaching of Foreign Languages, New York.

Wolf, W.C. Jr., and K.M. Riordan. (1991). "Foreign Language Teachers: Demographic Characteristics, Inservice Training Needs, and Attitudes Toward Teaching." *Foreign Language Annals* 24, 6: 471–478.

Further Reading

Adair-Hauck, B., R. Donato, and P. Cumo. (1994). "Using a Whole Language Approach to Teach Grammar." In *Teacher's Handbook: Contextualized Language Instruction*, edited by J. Shrum and E. Glisan. Boston: Heinle and Heinle Publishers.

Johnson, D.W., and R.T. Johnson. (1989). *Cooperation and Competition: Theory and Research.* Edina, Minn.: Interaction Book Company.

Kagan, S. (1992). *Cooperative Learning.* San Juan Capistrano, Calif.: Resource for Teachers Inc.

Littlewood, W. (1981). *Communicative Language Teaching.* New York: Cambridge University Press.

Met, M., and V. Galloway. (1991). "Research in Foreign Language Curriculum." In *Handbook of Research on Curriculum*, edited by P. Jackson. New York: Macmillan.

Nunan, D. (1989). *Designing Tasks for the Communicative Classroom*. Cambridge: Cambridge University Press.

Nunan, D. (1991). "Communicative Tasks and the Language Curriculum." *TESOL Quarterly* 25, 2: 279–295.

Omaggio Hadley, A.C. (1994). *Teaching Language in Context*. Boston, Mass.: Heinle and Heinle Publishers.

Slavin, R.E. (1983). *Cooperative Learning*. New York: Longman.

5

Health Education: A Foundation for Learning

Deborah Haber and Christine Blaber

> *In the great work of education . . . our physical condition, if not the first step in point of importance, is the first in order of time. On the broad and firm foundation of health alone, can the loftiest and most enduring structure of the intellect be reared.*
>
> —Horace Mann, Educator

The Urgent Need for New School Health Education

For the first time in U.S. history, young people are less healthy and less prepared to take their places in society than their parents were (National Commission on the Role of the School and the Community in Improving Adolescent Health 1990). One in five children lives in poverty, and one in four lives in a single-parent family (U.S. Department of Commerce, Bureau of the Census 1989, 1990). Four to six of every 25 elementary-age children live with a family member who abuses alcohol or other drugs (American Association of School Administrators 1990). Every year, 675,000 children are abused or neglected (Children's Defense Fund 1990, National School Boards Association 1991).

We have learned that although a number of factors affect the health and well-being of young people, many health risks they face are associated with the following types of risk behaviors (Kolbe 1990):

1. Behavior that results in intentional and unintentional injuries.
2. Drug and alcohol abuse.
3. Behavior that results in pregnancy and STDs, including HIV infection.
4. Tobacco use.
5. Excessive consumption of fat and calories.
6. Insufficient physical activity.

Even though today's children face the same developmental tasks young people have always faced, the obstacle course of life has become more difficult. Children and youth navigate through and around conflicting messages, risky behaviors, and mounting pressures without benefit of the support systems that were once in place. Families are often isolated and scattered from one another; working parents are stretched thin by demanding schedules; and neighborhoods do not provide the community safety net they once did—and often are not safe at all.

As a society, we acknowledge these risks, and we worry about how to help young people manage them. Educators and communities have looked to schools to address some of the health concerns because they realize that children who come to school in poor health or with personal problems will be less able to learn. Clearly, schools should not be responsible for meeting all the needs of all children. Nonetheless, when students' physical and social needs directly affect their ability to learn, the school must step in to help.

In 1990, the National Commission on the Role of the School and the Community in Improving Adolescent Health stated, "Unhealthy teenagers are . . . unlikely to attain the high levels of education achievement required for success in the 21st century. And thousands of these young people will experience school failure, which for many will be a precursor to an adult life of crime, unemployment, or welfare dependency." The commission recommended that schools become more personal; improve both the health and learning environments; provide a "new" kind of health education; and improve collaboration inside and outside of schools to assure that students receive the physical, social, and emotional help they need.

Exactly what is this new kind of school health education? It is part of a larger health initiative known as a comprehensive school health program. Such a program includes the development and integration of health instruction, health services, school environment, counseling and guidance services, physical education, food services, staff wellness, and integration of school and community efforts (Allensworth and Kolbe 1987) (see Figure 5.1).

FIGURE 5.1

Model for Comprehensive School Health Program

Source: Adapted from "The Comprehensive School Health Program: Exploring an Expanded Concept," by D.D. Allensworth and L.J. Kolbe, 1987. *Journal of School Health* 57, 10:409. Adapted with permission. Kent, Ohio: American School Health Association.

What Is School Health Education?

Quality school health education is comprehensive, interweaving a variety of health content areas and emphasizing the reduction of such risk behaviors as violence, tobacco, alcohol and other drug use, unintended pregnancy, and HIV/AIDS. Quality education goes beyond the learning of health information by helping students identify attitudes and develop skills that promote health and well-being. It is also developmentally appropriate and culturally sensitive and may be integrated across the curriculum. Ideally, health education is taught sequentially in kindergarten through grade 12 by trained teachers (Allensworth 1993, Seffrin 1990).

Healthy students generally choose healthy options, are able to realize their potential, avoid risky behaviors, and cope effectively in stressful environments. To help them, health education must provide opportunities to

- Obtain accurate, health-related information.
- Identify misconceptions.
- Recognize healthy behaviors and norms.
- Understand their susceptibility to specific health threats.
- Recognize pressures that put them at risk.
- Identify, practice, and carry out actions that will help them protect their health and well-being.

For health education to effectively support the health and well-being of students, it must become a significant part of a school curriculum. In a recent survey, state superintendents of education identified a lack of administrative support as the primary barrier to implementing comprehensive school health programs at the local level (Chambers Butler 1993). Because administrators decide the importance of health education in relation to other subject areas, they must make a commitment to health education for quality instruction to occur.

To embrace health education as part of the curriculum, administrators need to carry out the following activities:

- Provide adequate time for instruction. The American School Health Association (Allensworth 1993) recommends a minimum of 50 hours of instruction for each elementary and middle grade and 150 hours by a certified health educator at the high school level.
- Give teachers involved in developing and implementing a school health program adequate ongoing training and support and require that they be certified in health education.

• Provide resources to conceptualize and develop the health education program as a whole, reinforcing and integrating the essential core of health information, beliefs, skills, and themes. The health curriculum (whether it is prepackaged or locally developed) must be structured sequentially to assure adequate skill development. Such a plan differs from many health curriculums, which are developed using a categorical, piecemeal approach.

• Require the use of up-to-date materials and methods that focus on risk behaviors. Some traditional health areas may receive less emphasis.

• Make students' needs and involvement the heart of the health education program. Ensure that activities are student centered, hands on, and interactive. Encourage teachers to use a variety of teaching strategies, and allow adequate time to learn and practice critical skills (see Figure 5.2).

• Maintain a supportive school environment and encourage teachers to develop a classroom environment that also gives students a sense of security, belonging, respect, and personal and social competence (Fetro 1994).

• Do not isolate health education. Ideally, it is part of a comprehensive health program that considers all the health needs of a student. Offer opportunities to connect the health program with other disciplines, the community, and other related programs in the school.

• Ensure that opportunities for family support and involvement are built into the program; family involvement can have a positive influence on students' health behaviors (Allensworth 1994).

Structure and Content of a Health Education Curriculum

As in all subject areas, competing priorities about what should and can be taught at a particular grade level occur. A continual dilemma for health educators is choosing between time spent covering health facts and time needed for skill mastery or for activities that examine the attitudes and beliefs influencing health behaviors.

Educators tend to focus on health facts, forsaking the more complex tasks of skill development or attitude assessment. Often, this decision is based on a concern that students "need to know" a particular piece of health information. Sometimes, however, the decision is a result of a teacher's feeling more comfortable providing information than facilitating skill development.

FIGURE 5.2
Health Skills

Self-Assessment
The ability to look at one's own health beliefs, knowledge, skills, attitudes, and behaviors and clarify where one is in relation to where one would like to be.

Risk Assessment
The ability to analyze situations and actions and assess the degree of potential risk, hazard, or opportunity.

Communication
The ability to interact with others, read and listen with understanding, articulate health needs, and express caring concern for the health and well-being of oneself and others.

Decision Making
The ability to identify critical choices, consider alternatives, assess the health consequences of each alternative for oneself and others, choose a healthful course of action, act with conviction, and evaluate the real outcomes of the decision.

Goal Setting
The ability to develop plans for the future and to identify and take steps to reach one's goals.

Health Advocacy
The ability to act to enhance the health and well-being of people in one's family, school, workplace, community, state, nation, and world.

Healthy Self-Management
The ability to make situation and lifestyle behavior choices that result in attaining and maintaining one's physical, emotional, social, and environmental health.

Conflict Resolution
The ability to recognize conflict situations and to identify and use strategies that resolve the conflict effectively and safely.

Anger Management
The ability to recognize healthy and problematic patterns of expressing anger and to develop and practice anger management strategies that are effective and safe.

Refusal/Resistance
The ability to recognize, predict, and resist pressure situations involving peers by "saying no" effectively when one chooses to do so.

Source: Education Development Center, Inc. (1994), *Reach for Health Curriculum,* Newton, Mass.: Author.

Curriculum decision makers and teachers should consider whether imparting health information contributes to students' ability to carry out healthy behaviors (i.e., is the knowledge functional?) or whether the facts are pieces of information that students can learn to access when needed. Given the rapid pace at which new health-related information is generated, students will benefit more by learning how to locate health information and resources than they will by learning health facts. Curricular decisions must be based on what will help students maintain healthful behaviors and prevent involvement in risky ones.

A health education scope-and-sequence chart that is organized using the traditional method of health instruction shows how the 10 major health content areas are covered from kindergarten through grade 12. The content areas are injury and violence prevention; community health; environmental health; family life; nutrition; personal health; disease prevention and control; tobacco, alcohol, and other drug use; consumer health; and mental and emotional health. Many health education textbooks typify this approach.

A disadvantage with this method is that the curriculum becomes narrow and categorical, supporting a "topic-of-the-month" approach to health education and focusing primarily on conveying health information. Also, educators frequently do not make important connections among the health content areas for students. Because health education is rarely taught in every grade from kindergarten through grade 12, educators find that this approach leaves too much health content to squeeze into too few classroom hours.

A strong case can be made for developing health education curriculums that focus more on the six risk behaviors (listed earlier in the chapter) that the Centers for Disease Control and Prevention (CDC) has targeted and less on other topics (Kolbe 1990). These behaviors result in the most deaths and premature illnesses.

Fetro (1992) asserts that using personal and social skills, rather than health content areas, as the organizing principle for the health education curriculum is effective for the following reasons: students learn key skills in depth and examine the connections among the skills; students focus on their positive, health-related behaviors rather than on how to avoid negative behaviors; and skills tend to be less emotionally charged than health content areas. Fetro also reduces the 10 health skills shown in Figure 5.2 to four: decision making, communication, stress management, and goal setting.

Educating young people to master health skills involves five steps:

1. Introduce the skill.
2. Present the steps for developing the skill.
3. Model the skill.
4. Practice and rehearse the skill.
5. Provide feedback and reinforcement.

One might assume that health education teachers would be fairly comfortable using health-related skills in their personal lives and teaching them to students. But the skills-based approach to health education is relatively new and fairly complex; teachers need expanded preservice and inservice programs to help them learn about and teach the skills.

Health education curriculums do not need to focus exclusively on health knowledge, health risk behaviors, or health skills. The new national health education standards provide a useful model for integrating the traditional health content areas with the priority youth risk behaviors targeted by CDC and the standards. One can envision the health education scope-and-sequence chart of the future as a three-dimensional model incorporating health knowledge, health risk behaviors, and health skills.

Whether the health education curriculum is organized by content areas, risk behaviors, skills, or a combination, topics should be introduced at one grade level and reviewed and reinforced in later years. The ideal curriculum is sequenced so that students can build on prior knowledge and skills, applying what they have learned to new and more complex situations. In reality, because most districts do not have a comprehensive plan for K–12 health education, the content of the health curriculum and teaching methods used at one grade level may bear little resemblance to those at the next level.

Some combination of the following factors typically determines how the health education curriculum at various grade levels is sequenced: students' mental and physical development; their health needs and interests; key learning objectives in health knowledge, affect (e.g., beliefs, attitudes, values, and feelings), and behavior; state and local regulations on health education; and input from families and the community. The new national health education standards and performance indicators should prove to be a helpful addition in making decisions about sequencing.

The following example illustrates how a particular health theme, "people's image of their bodies affects feelings and behaviors," is played out at different grade levels in response to students' varying developmental needs (National [Sexuality Education] Guidelines Task Force, p. 14). In early elementary school, the report suggests that the class focus on issues such as "individual bodies are different sizes, shapes, and colors." In upper elementary school, the curriculum moves to a focus on themes such as "a person's appearance is determined by heredity, environment, and health habits." The middle school/junior high curriculum explores issues related to puberty, self-image, and feelings. And in high school, students examine such issues as "physical attractiveness should not be a major factor in choosing friends or dating partners."

Integrating health education across subject areas requires careful planning to ensure that critical health information, attitudes, skills, and behaviors are adequately addressed and that the connections among topics are explored. When health is integrated haphazardly, a certain amount of student learning may occur, but meaningful or lasting student outcomes is unlikely.

Health Education Standards

Because health education commonly receives little attention or time in most schools, national content standards have been needed to help place it on the national, state, and local policy agenda. National standards also offer needed objective guidelines for assessing health education curriculum and instruction.

The Joint Health Education Standards Committee (1994a)—composed of members from the American School Health Association; Association for the Advancement of Health Education; American Public Health Association; and Society of State Directors of Health, Physical Education, Recreation, and Dance—has developed seven national health education standards:

1. Students will comprehend health promotion and disease prevention concepts.

2. Students will demonstrate the ability to locate valid health information and appropriate health products and services.

3. Students will demonstrate the ability to practice health-enhancing behaviors and reduce health risks.

4. Students will analyze the impact of culture, media, technology, and other factors on health.

5. Students will demonstrate the ability to use effective interpersonal communication skills that enhance health.

6. Students will demonstrate the ability to use goal-setting and decision-making skills that enhance health.

7. Students will demonstrate the ability to advocate for personal, family, and community health.

Each standard has a rationale; grades 4, 8, and 11 have related student performance indicators. For example, for Standard 1, a performance indicator for grade 4 is students will describe the human body systems; for grade 8, students will describe how body systems are interrelated; and for grade 11, students will analyze the effect of personal health behaviors on body systems.

The committee defines the ultimate goal of the standards as improved education for students and improved health for all people in the United States. The members also anticipate that the standards will ensure a common purpose and consistency of concepts in health instruction, improve student learning, provide a basis for assessing student performance, provide a foundation for curriculum development and instruction, and serve as a guide for enhancing teacher preparation and continuing education.

The standards link health education to major education themes, including the importance of helping develop well-educated, literate people for the 21st century. Health-literate individuals are defined as able to function in the following roles:

• Critical thinkers and problem solvers who identify and creatively address health problems and issues at multiple levels, ranging from personal to international.

• Responsible, productive citizens who realize their obligation to assure that their community is kept healthy, safe, and secure so that all citizens can experience a high quality of life.

• Self-directed learners with a command of the changing health promotion and disease prevention knowledge base.

• Effective communicators who organize and convey beliefs, ideas, and information about health through oral, written, artistic, graphic, and technological means.

The health education standards and performance indicators provide a framework for a health education curriculum; state boards of education and local school districts should determine how to attain the standards and perhaps develop additional community-specific ones. School districts should select a curriculum and make instructional decisions based on the characteristics and needs of students, their families, and the community.

The most carefully crafted standards are meaningless unless resources are available in the school system to implement health education programs that will allow schools to work toward achieving the standards. To accompany the standards and performance indicators, the Joint Health Education Standards Committee (1994b) created a framework of system standards that target schools, families and community agencies; state departments of health and education; teacher preparation institutions in collaboration with state agencies; and national health and education agencies. The system standards are designed to address the infrastructure needed to support the achievement of student standards.

Influences and Trends

A number of trends are influencing health education today. Educators are focusing on teaching critical health skills, developing a health promotion model, and encouraging parent and community involvement. They have also found that theoretical approaches that can be applied in a wide variety of health areas provide a framework for health instruction that works. The diversity of students is creating a greater need for health education curriculums that meet the needs of all students. Such considerations are changing the direction of school health education programs.

The Changing Focus of Health Education

Health educators have learned much about what is needed to delay the onset or decrease the incidence of health-compromising behaviors. Thirty years ago, health education focused on conveying information about physical and emotional risks. In the 1970s, instruction began to incorporate affective strategies (e.g., values clarification, self-esteem work, and enhanced decision making). In recent years, because we have learned that information and affective exploration alone are not enough, health education has evolved to include psychosocial approaches that incorporate a focus on critical health skills. Specifically, health education programs that are based on skills training, peer involvement, social learning theory, and community involvement have been shown to have the greatest impact (Gold 1994).

In another development, we have shifted away from the health instruction model, which is teacher centered, fact based, hygiene focused, and textbook driven, and toward the health promotion model. This change has involved moving beyond just teaching health in the classroom to advocating for health throughout the school. As a result, many schools are addressing issues such as staff wellness, the safety of the school environment, parent involvement, and health as an attainable and desirable goal for all (Pine 1985).

Research indicates that an individual's health status and health risk result from a number of factors, including health knowledge, perceived risk, attitudes toward health care, social interactions, and perceived norms (Allensworth and Symons 1989; Benard 1988, 1991; Dryfoos 1990). Programs that focus on these factors and the highest-risk behaviors are most likely to be successful. Health education is becoming more finely tuned by targeting specific behaviors and risks and by focusing on the development of key skills that have implications for several risk areas.

At the same time, researchers and health educators acknowledge that even instruction based on sound theories and focused on skill development is not enough. Health education must be coupled with more broad-based, multifaceted efforts that connect schools with parents and other community members.

The process of change continues. Allensworth (1994) describes characteristics of a traditional health instruction program and contrasts them with those of a health education program in a health-promoting school (see Figure 5.3).

Trends in Behavioral Research

In recent years, trends in behavioral research have affected the focus and direction of school health education. Most notably, educators have used theoretical approaches that are effective in a variety of categorical health areas (e.g., tobacco, alcohol, and drug use prevention; and pregnancy prevention) as the basis for developing health education curriculums. The theoretical models usually include social learning theory, social inoculation theory, social influence model, health belief model, and cognitive behavior theory. These theoretical approaches can provide the framework for developing health instruction that works. For example, the social learning theory proposes that an individual is more likely to carry out an action when that person understands what has to be done, believes that he or she can do it, and believes that the action will be effective (Kirby, Barth, Leland, and Fetro 1991). Applying this theory to the health education curriculum means that if the aim is to enable students to refuse drug use, students need to understand what has to be done to "say no." They must learn the steps of "saying no" (direct teaching), observe someone saying no (teacher modeling and role playing), and practice saying no (role playing).

FIGURE 5.3

Comparison of a Traditional Health Instruction Program with a
Health Education Program in a Health-Promoting School

Traditional Health Program	Emergent Health Program
Emphasizes knowledge and attitude changes that would lead to behavior change.	Applies multiple theories and models to promote health-enhancing behaviors.
Organizes program around 10 content areas.	Focuses on 6 priority behaviors within 10 content areas.
Views school health program in terms of instruction, services, and environment.	Promotes expanded program: instruction, environment, food services, physical education, guidance and counseling, work site health promotion, and integration of school and community.
Makes health instruction the focal point.	Replaces health "instruction" model with health "promotion" model.
Pays little attention to coordination or comprehensiveness. Curriculums spotty; offerings uneven.	Identifies and develops comprehensive prekindergarten through grade 12 curriculum.
Considers health education in limited terms.	Coordinates health promotion activities throughout school and community, including infusion of health content areas across curriculum.
Promotes coordination through school health advisory council.	Promotes program coordination within school through interdisciplinary and interagency teams.
Uses didactic, teacher-led instruction and acquisition of facts.	Encourages active student participation, using methods that match teaching techniques with instructional goals.
Responds to crises one by one.	Recognizes commonality of skills needed to address various health issues and includes common skills in curriculum.
Considers adoption of health-promoting behaviors a result of instruction.	Takes wider view of school, including the relationship with community; effort to develop a caring school community with high expectations for all students.
Does not routinely involve parents in school health program.	Considers family involvement in the lessons and in the development of the total program as central to the health-promoting school.

Source: Adapted from "The Research Base for Innovative Practices in School Health Education at the Secondary Level," by D.D. Allensworth, 1994. Journal of School Health 64, 5: 181. Adapted with permission. Kent, Ohio: American School Health Association.

Researchers from the field of tobacco, alcohol, and drug use prevention have been studying children and young people who do not become involved in risky behaviors. In particular, they have focused on those young people who—seemingly against all odds—have been able to navigate successfully past the many risks factors in their lives, do well in school, and succeed in reaching their personal goals. These young people are said to be "resilient." The body of work that emerged has significance, not only in the field of risk prevention education, but for all health instruction.

The resilient youth is one who works, plays, loves, and expects well (Benard 1991). That person possesses problem-solving skills, social skills, autonomy, and a sense of purpose and future. Young people are thought to become resilient to risk factors through a complex interaction of protective factors within themselves, their peers, families, communities, and schools. Protective factors are the "positives" in children's and young people's lives. They are the positive conditions, such as prosocial behaviors, competent role models, and high expectations, that help keep youth safe.

Researchers have identified protective factors characterizing competency in the areas of self and peers, families, communities, and schools (see Figure 5.4). Comprehensive risk prevention programs work toward including and developing as many protective factors as possible.

School setting and health education contribute to the development of resilient young people by reducing risk factors and providing instructional and schoolwide activities aimed at enhancing protective factors. To be successful, risk prevention education must be a broad-based, communitywide effort that helps youth develop the attitudes, skills, and attributes necessary for healthy development.

Providing Health Education That Honors Diverse Students

The demand for inclusive, appropriate curriculums taught by trained staff touches every discipline and corner of the school program. Philosophical discussions about what the nature of such programs should be abound. Ultimately, the most critical question to address is whether school curriculums and materials are reaching the needs of all children and youth. This question is particularly important in health education.

To meet students' needs, the following elements should be present:

• Health education must be relevant. Educators must become aware of the cultural, social, economic, and political contexts of their students and understand how families, cultural values and beliefs, and communication styles affect health.

FIGURE 5.4

Protective Factors

Within the Community
Clear norms for families and schools
Clear rules and regulations
Intergenerational ties
Competent role models
External support systems

Within Youth and Peers
Ability to set goals
Good sense of humor
Autonomy
Ability to develop friendships
Strong sense of the future
Belief in oneself
Good health
Average intelligence

Within the Family
Religious Affiliation
Consistent rituals and traditions
Clear rules and regulations
Domestic responsibilities
Significant relationship with parent or
caregiver

Within the School
Clear rules and regulations
Competent role models
Great expectations for all children
Social competencies
Relationship with significant adult
Goal-directed behavior
School ethos (values)
Easy temperament

Source: From *Fostering Resiliency in Kids: Protective Factors in the Family, School, and Community,* by B. Benard, 1991. Portland, Oreg.: Western Center for Drug–Free Schools and Communities. Reprinted with permission.

- Health educators must understand the community and environment in which students live—What resources, strengths, and challenges are present (Sancho 1994)? What concerns and needs are expressed? Focus groups with students, parents, and other community members are useful tools in acquiring this information (Davis 1994).

- Health educators must view students as individuals with unique backgrounds, concerns, and needs, rather than stereotyping them according to particular groups. Health educators must hold high expectations for all students and provide learning opportunities that enable students to feel they can take actions to preserve and promote their health and well-being. Ongoing training and staff development are needed to help educators address these issues.

- Materials must be tailored to meet students' needs. The following questions may help teachers (Education Development Center 1991):

◊ Are my students—their ethnicity, sex, sexual orientation, age, physical abilities, economic condition, geographic setting—reflected in the role playing?

◊ Are health issues that are critical for my students emphasized appropriately?

◊ Is the language and reading level in the materials appropriate for my students?

◊ Are issues raised in the health education curriculum consistent with community norms and school policies?

◊ What can I add or change to make the materials more appropriate for the diverse needs of my students?

Schools working to develop a comprehensive approach to the health and well-being of students often convene a health advisory board composed of school staff, parents, community members, and students. This group is usually charged with helping guide philosophical, policy, and programmatic decisions related to student health issues. The group can also help form guidelines for instructional programs that meet the diverse needs of students and the community.

Challenges and Opportunities

Advocates of a comprehensive health education program face challenges and opportunities in many areas. They must work in the general education community to develop a closer relationship with mainstream education so that each group can understand and support the other; in the school community to help with restructuring, teacher training, integration of health education into other subject areas, and family participation; and in the neighborhood to develop support and deal with controversy.

Developing Better Linkages Between Health and Mainstream Educational Trends

In some ways, the school-based "subject" of health education is different from other school-based subjects. Health is not only a subject but also a state of being. It is a personal as well as a societal issue. Trends in health status, findings from health education research, and current critical health issues that affect society influence health education more than research from the educational mainstream. Traditionally, mainstream educators and health educators do not travel in the same circles. They often participate in different professional organizations, read different journals, and use different resources to obtain information relevant to their profession.

Interestingly, the very nature of health, and research on health behavior, are leading health educators unknowingly in the direction of major trends in mainstream education. In the *Journal of Health Education*, the Association for the Advancement of Health Education (1992) asserted that "the purposes of [school] health education do not stand apart from the purposes of education itself . . . Education is not concerned merely with knowledge acquisition . . . individuals [must] apply that knowledge . . . The ultimate goal of health education, therefore, is to liberate an individual's potential strengths, energies, and creative powers so that personal actions become deeply satisfying and humanly constructive" (pp. 4–5).

Mainstream educators have been concerned with such issues as the relevance of curriculum, applicability and transfer of learning outside the school setting, and authenticity of instruction. For more than a decade, health education has been moving toward providing more meaningful, student-centered, hands-on interactive activities, as well as helping students develop and practice life-related skills needed outside the classroom. In the best health classrooms, children and young people construct their own meanings and explore areas that they are interested in.

Despite these obvious connections, health educators frequently do not know about, let alone become involved in, significant trends in mainstream education until after the trends have influenced the school setting where they work. Even preservice training has been slow to incorporate such linkages. We need to find ways to link health educators with current educational thinking—and to link mainstream educators to health.

For example, health educators should be key players as schools plan and provide inservice opportunities for teaching and learning issues (e.g., authentic assessment, integration of technology, thematic and integrated learning, and theories of learning). Health education can contribute much to restructuring efforts aimed at addressing the needs of the whole learner.

Incorporating Health Education into School Restructuring

Health educators need to work in tandem with mainstream school reformers and with others who care about children's health and well-being to build a broad base of support for policies and programs supporting healthy students and health-enhancing schools.

—Sullivan and Bogden 1993

School restructuring, in its broadest definition, involves fundamental changes in every aspect of the current educational system. The ultimate goal of restructuring is to make schools more effective; the underlying belief is that schools must change the way they do business.

In applying this goal to health, educational leaders are now acknowledging the critical links between student health/well-being and student learning (National Commission on the Role of the School and the Community in Improving Adolescent Health 1990, Carnegie Council on Adolescent Development 1989, American Association of School Administrators 1990). Such a recognition creates an opportunity for health educators to bring a comprehensive view of health to the planning table.

It is reasonable to think that the kind of education that results in students who are healthy also results in students who learn. Many perspectives and goals embedded in school restructuring are also part of effective comprehensive school health education:

• Focusing on the whole child or student.

• Identifying clear goals and student outcomes (e.g., students will make healthful choices and avoid risk behaviors).

• Using relevant curriculums that aid the learning of health-enhancing information, skills, and attitudes.

• Implementing student-centered learning.

• Encouraging active, hands-on, and cooperative learning.

• Focusing on critical thinking/higher-order thinking for students.

• Training teachers to ensure effectiveness.

• Involving parents in learning activities.

• Considering school climate.

• Collaborating within a school and between a community and a school.

• Including all eight components of a comprehensive school health program.

School restructuring plans provide opportunities for health educators to work within the educational mainstream and to help integrate health-related goals into the plans. Mainstream educators can also benefit from the health education perspective.

According to Jones, Miller, and Tritsch (1994), restructuring is producing health education challenges:

• Because health education rarely enjoys a central position within schools, health educators may not be involved in helping develop outcomes and goals (state or local) that guide future plans.

• Changes in school governance and control may make adoption of controversial health education topics (e.g., sexuality and HIV) more difficult, particularly if health educators are not included in the decision-making process.

• Assessment of student outcomes is an important part of many restructuring efforts. Assessment of certain long-term health-related outcomes that involve the development and maintenance of health-enhancing behaviors may be problematic.

Failure to become actively involved in the decision-making process can result in a diminished role for health education in students' lives. Active and enthusiastic participation in the planning processes can lead to enhanced health education and services for children and youth.

Preparing Teachers

In health, as in other disciplines, a successful instructional program results from an effective curriculum taught by well-trained teachers. A solid health education curriculum in the hands of an untrained or unmotivated teacher is unlikely to produce positive outcomes. Unfortunately, this situation occurs often in health education.

At the elementary school level, classroom teachers teach health education. Most have had no preservice training in health education (Burks and Fox 1994). At the secondary school level, the myth that "anyone can teach health" frequently prevails. In many schools, specialists in other disciplines, with little or no formal training or interest in health education, are assigned to teach the subject, with predictably disappointing results (Lohrmann, Gold, and Jubb 1987).

Until preservice programs provide adequate preparation in health education for all elementary educators *and* until secondary schools hire only certified health educators to teach health, ongoing, targeted inservice programs will continue to be essential for teachers implementing health curriculums. This is a particularly significant issue as more schools integrate health topics into a variety of disciplines.

The cry for increased staff development opportunities in health education for *all* teachers is growing louder (American Cancer Society 1993, Varnes 1994). Nonhealth educators have important roles in protecting the health of young people. Such roles include being healthy role models, managing the classroom environment in a health-enhancing manner, advocating for a healthy school environment, identifying and helping troubled students, acting as a resource for accurate health information, and integrating health topics into the curriculum (Haber 1994).

Integrating Health Education into Other Subject Areas

A three-year study of middle-grade students found that health knowledge and positive behaviors increased as students had more health instruction. Fifty or more classroom hours yearly produced significant attitudinal changes (Connell, Turner, and Mason 1985). Since schools rarely devote this much time to annual health instruction, expanding opportunities for integrating health awareness into other content areas is critical and ensures that students receive an "effective dose" of health education at every grade level.

At the secondary school level, educators use four primary models of structuring health education: (1) all health instruction occurs in a designated health course (most traditional method); (2) in the absence of a core health course, health topics are "inserted" in other subject areas for a few days or weeks each year; (3) a designated health course is offered, and teachers in other disciplines (e.g., science, social studies, language arts, mathematics, physical education, home economics, and counseling) integrate health content and skills into their curriculums; and (4) no designated health course is given, but a health education specialist coordinates integrating health into other subject areas and acts as a resource person.

Anecdotal evidence suggests that when schools do not plan a comprehensive, coordinated approach to health education but simply insert health topics randomly into other subject areas, student gains in health knowledge and skills are diminished. This decrease is probably because teachers in other subject areas are more likely to teach the facts about a given health issue rather than address critical health attitudes and skills.

Models 3 and 4 are thought to be the most effective for organizing health instruction at the secondary school level (see Figure 5.5.) The restructured middle school also provides an ideal setting for integrating

FIGURE 5.5
Model for Integrating Health and Education into Other Subjects

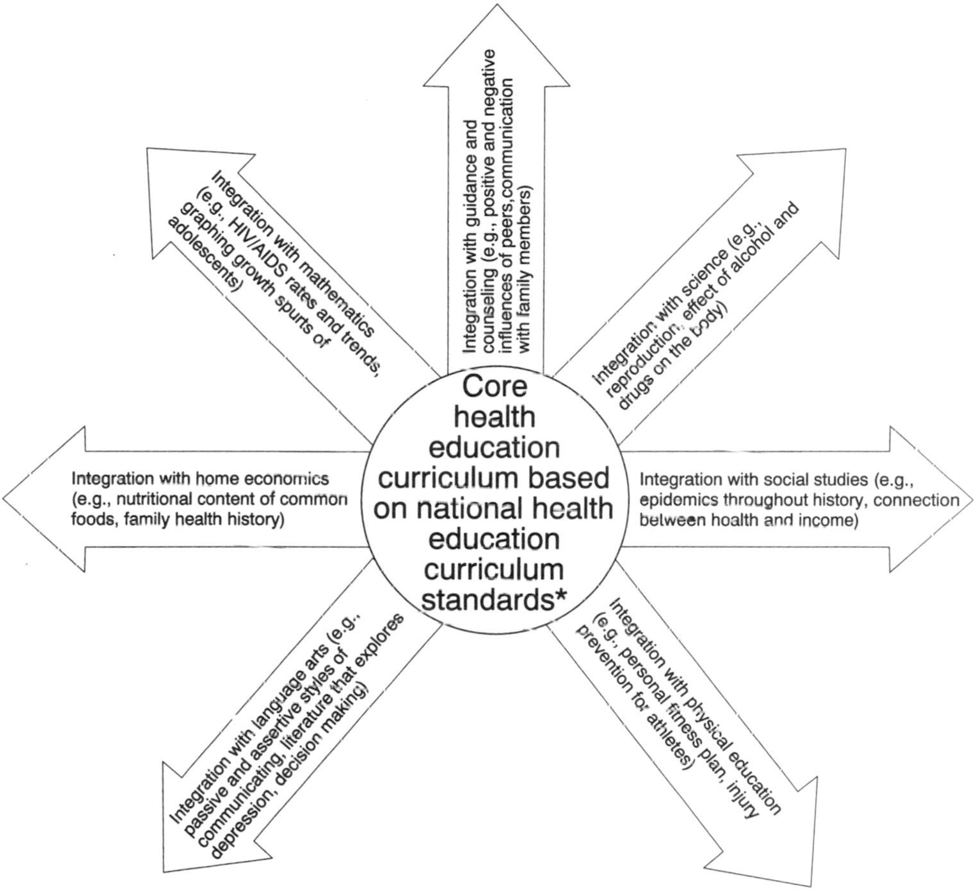

Integration with guidance and counseling (e.g., positive and negative influences of peers,communication with family members)

Integration with mathematics (e.g., HIV/AIDS rates and trends; graphing growth spurts of adolescents)

Integration with science (e.g., reproduction; effect of alcohol and drugs on the body))

Integration with home economics (e.g., nutritional content of common foods, family health history)

Core health education curriculum based on national health education curriculum standards*

Integration with social studies (e.g., epidemics throughout history, connection between health and income)

Integration with language arts (e.g., passive and assertive styles of communicating, literature that explores depression, decision making)

Integration with physical education (e.g., personal fitness plan, injury prevention for athletes)

*Students will
1. Comprehend health promotion and disease prevention concepts.
2. Demonstrate the ability to locate valid health information and appropriate health products and services.
3. Demonstrate the ability to practice health-enhancing behaviors and reduce health risks.
4. Analyze impact of culture, media, technology, and other factors on health.
5. Demonstrate ability to use effective interpersonal communication skills that enhance health.
6. Demonstrate ability to use goal setting and decision-making skills that enhance health.
7. Demonstrate ability to advocate for personal, family, and community health.

health education into other subject areas. Teachers of both health education and other subject areas can collaborate to develop and implement multidisciplinary units on a variety of health topics. The personal and societal significance of health topics (e.g., HIV/AIDS, substance abuse, and environmental issues) leads to exciting opportunities for multidisciplinary curriculum development. Teachers and administrators alike are frequently pleased to find that health education can be a powerful vehicle for addressing educational objectives across subject areas. The promise for interdisciplinary teaching of health is great, but it requires a high degree of commitment and coordination from teachers and administrators, ongoing teacher support, and opportunities for staff development in health education and multidisciplinary curriculum planning.

Involving Families

Children's health behaviors are heavily influenced by those of their parents and other family members. Involving families in school health education can lead to positive outcomes: family members have increased opportunities to enhance their health knowledge and skills; families have a clearer understanding of what is being taught in health education and can more actively support children's positive health behaviors; and family members can become vocal advocates for school health programs. And most important, a growing number of studies (Perry, Luepker, Murray, Kurth, Mullis, Crockett, and Jacobs 1988) have shown that parent-child interactions decrease the likelihood of children engaging in risky behaviors.

Learning activities that occur at home and involve students and their families (e.g., homework and special projects) are perhaps the most successful method for increasing family involvement in health education (Perry et al. 1988). These activities aim to enhance family dialogue about health issues by having students review and discuss with significant family members health education topics being explored in class. Students who do not have strong relationships with caring family members should be encouraged to carry out these activities with another reliable, trustworthy adult.

School health programs seeking to increase meaningful family involvement need to move beyond traditional programs in which parents are passive clients in their child's education. It is time for schools to reach out to family members so that they can become active participants and collaborators in their children's learning experiences (Fruchter, Galletta, and White 1992).

Dealing with Controversy

Because health education addresses such sensitive issues as sexuality, alcoholism and drug abuse, physical and sexual abuse, mental health, and family relationships, the curriculum can be highly controversial. Several national and state surveys have shown that most parents support health education programs in public schools. In recent years, however, several conservative groups (many representing the Religious Right) have waged attacks against school health education.

Criticism has come from individuals or groups that have a genuine desire to negotiate a process with school systems—a process that would create a more accurate or appropriate health education program for young people. Criticism has also come from extremely conservative groups that are fundamentally opposed to teaching health education in public schools on the grounds that it invades family privacy, teaches children to develop a sense of personal responsibility and decision-making capabilities (which these groups see as teaching children to challenge adult authority), and exposes young people to information on topics such as sex, violence, and alcohol and other drugs that they would be better off not knowing about (Van Patten 1994).

Some opposition groups hope to dismantle the system of public education in the United States—and they see health education programs as an easy initial target. The People for the American Way's annual report (1993) states that attacks on the freedom to learn identify health education programs (in particular, sex education, drug abuse prevention, and self-esteem units) as one of the most common targets of groups attempting to censor and challenge U.S. public education.

School boards must have the following systems in place to support their health education curriculum:

• A policy describing how the health education curriculum and instructional materials are selected. Many districts create a community advisory panel to help in curriculum selection. Materials should be available for public viewing at an accessible public place.

• A policy outlining how complaints or concerns about the curriculum will be addressed. Clear procedures on how challenges are to be brought forward are essential, and the board must adhere to the policy if challenges arise (Morris 1992, Newman and Farrell 1991).

In the early stages of developing a school health education program, educators should identify and build relationships with supportive community members. Citizens who participate in the curriculum selection process or who are on an ongoing health advisory board can be powerful allies if the curriculum is attacked. Teachers, administrators, and board members must understand and support the philosophy of comprehensive school health education, as well as the specific curriculum that is implemented.

Controversy surrounding school health education cannot be avoided. In fact, it is healthy. Constructive public dialogue can strengthen effective implementation of new programs. Teaching staff, administrators, and board members, however, need to ensure that the integrity of the curriculum is maintained.

Health Education Research and Evaluation

The preponderance of health education curriculums available today are categorical in nature—that is, they focus on one or two health topics rather than on the broad range of issues addressed in comprehensive health curriculums. Not surprisingly, then, most health education evaluations describe the effectiveness of such categorical programs. In addition, because students' health-related knowledge, beliefs, and attitudes are much easier and less controversial to assess than their health-related behavior, few evaluation studies have examined the effect of health instruction on students' behavior, health status, or educational performance (National Coordinating Committee on School Health 1993).

To date, the only comprehensive health education curriculums that have undergone large-scale, controlled outcome studies are Growing Healthy (kindergarten to grade 6), Know Your Body (kindergarten to grade 6), and Teenage Health Teaching Modules (grades 7 to 12).

In the landmark study documenting the effectiveness of school health education, an earlier version of the Growing Healthy curriculum (called the School Health Curriculum Project or SHCP) was evaluated in comparison with three other health education curriculums (Connell et al. 1985). Involving 30,000 students across 20 states, the study found that health education is an effective means of helping children improve their health-related knowledge and attitudes. Students who participated in SHCP showed the strongest gains in health knowledge, attitudes, and behavior. In addition, based on self-reports, almost three times as many students in a control group began smoking in the first half of 7th grade compared with students enrolled in a SHCP class.

The Know Your Body program has been evaluated among a variety of populations. In one study of 1,105 children in 15 schools in the New York City area, students who had participated in the Know Your Body program for six years had significantly lower rates of cigarette smoking onset, reduced saturated fat consumption, and increased carbohydrate consumption compared with control group students (Walter, Vaughan, and Wyndner 1989).

The Teenage Health Teaching Modules (THTM) is the first comprehensive school health curriculum at the secondary school level to have undergone a large-scale controlled evaluation. The study (Errecart, Walberg, Ross, Gold, Fiedler, and Kolbe 1991), which involved almost 5,000 students in seven states, indicated that THTM produced positive effects on the health-related knowledge and attitudes of middle and high school students. High school students reported positive changes in several health behaviors, including reduced use of tobacco, alcohol, and other drugs.

As research validates more health education curriculums, the next wave of research is beginning to focus on how effective programs are adopted, tailored, and maintained in new settings (Ross, Errecart, Lavin, Saavedra, and Gold 1989). As Seffrin (1990) points out, the ultimate effectiveness of health education programs is dependent on many factors beyond the curriculum itself, including teacher training, the extent and degree of program implementation, the amount of time allotted for instruction, involvement of parents and family, and community support.

In addition to research on the effectiveness of health instruction, school health education has benefited from findings in other disciplines. Gold's work (1994) reveals lessons that have a direct bearing on school health education:

• Integrated approaches that target a variety of risk factors have the greatest potential.

• Consistent, mutually supporting messages must be conveyed through the school's efforts in health education, health services, and health environment.

• One program cannot reach all audiences equally well. Literacy, gender, race, ethnicity, culture, and social groupings must be addressed when developing programs.

• Preventing relapse of unhealthful behaviors is as equally important as demonstrating the existence of healthful behaviors.

Comprehensive health education curriculums typically are multilayered programs addressing a variety of health content areas through activities designed to build students' health knowledge, attitudes, and skills. Although evaluation of comprehensive programs such as Growing Healthy, Know Your Body, and Teenage Health Teaching Modules demonstrates that these programs are effective, the comparative effectiveness of specific program subcomponents is unclear. In other words, we know *that* they work, but not necessarily *why*. This situation, coupled with the limited classroom time available for health education, has prompted one group of researchers (Resnikow, Cherry, and Cross 1993) to argue that research should be conducted to determine the "active ingredients" of health education programs. The hope is that schools could save time and money by using the findings of such studies to reduce their health education program to its most effective components.

References

Allensworth, D.D. (1993). "Health Education: State of the Art." *Journal of School Health* 63, 1: 14–23.

Allensworth, D.D. (1994). "The Research Base for Innovative Practices in School Health Education at the Secondary Level." *Journal of School Health* 64, 5: 180–187.

Allensworth, D.D., and C.W. Symons. (1989). "A Theoretical Approach to School-Based HIV Prevention." *Journal of School Health* 59, 2: 59–65.

Allensworth, D.D., and L.J. Kolbe. (1987). "The Comprehensive School Health Program: Exploring an Expanded Concept." *Journal of School Health* 57, 10: 409–412.

American Association of School Administrators. (1990). *Healthy Kids for the Year 2000: An Action Plan for Schools*. Arlington, Va.: Author.

American Cancer Society. (1993). *National Action Plan for Comprehensive School Health Education*. Atlanta, Ga.: Author.

Association for the Advancement of Health Education. (1992). "A Point of View for Health Education." *Journal of Health Education* 23, 1: 4–6.

Benard, B. (1988). *An Overview of Community-Based Prevention. OSAP Prevention Monograph 3: Prevention Research Findings*. Washington, D.C.: U.S. Department of Health and Human Services.

Benard, B. (1991). *Fostering Resiliency in Kids: Protective Factors in the Family, School, and Community*. Portland, Oreg.: Western Center for Drug-Free Schools and Communities.

Burks, A., and E. Fox. (1994). "Why Is Inservice Training Essential?" In *The Comprehensive School Health Challenge: Promoting Health Through Education*, edited by P. Cortese and K. Middleton. Vol. 2. Santa Cruz, Calif.: ETR Associates.

Carnegie Council on Adolescent Development. (1989). *Turning Points: Preparing American Youth for the 21st Century*. New York: Author.

Chambers Butler, S. (1993). "Chief State School Officers Rank Barriers to Implementing Comprehensive School Health Education." *Journal of School Health* 63, 8: 130–132.

Children's Defense Fund. (1990). *A Report Card, Briefing Book, and Action Primer.* Washington, D.C.: Author.

Connell, D.B., R.R. Turner, and E.F. Mason. (1985). "Summary of Findings of the School Health Education Evaluation: Health Promotion Effectiveness, Implementation, and Costs." *Journal of School Health* 55, 3: 316–321.

Davis, S.M. (1994). "General Guidelines for an Effective and Culturally Sensitive Approach to Health Education." In *The Multicultural Challenge in Health Education,* edited by A.C. Matiella. Santa Cruz, Calif.: ETR Associates.

Dryfoos, J.G. (1990). *Adolescents at Risk: Prevalence and Prevention.* New York: Oxford University Press.

Education Development Center, Inc. (1991). *Teenage Health Teaching Modules: Teachers' Guide for Grades 9 and 10.* Newton, Mass.: Author.

Education Development Center, Inc. (1994). *Reach for Health Curriculum.* Newton, Mass.: Author.

Errecart, M.T., H.J. Walberg, J.G. Ross, R.S. Gold, J.L. Fiedler, and L.J. Kolbe. (1991). "Effectiveness of Teenage Health Teaching Modules." *Journal of School Health* 61 (special insert),1: 26–30.

Fetro, J.V. (1992). *Personal and Social Skills: Understanding and Integrating Competencies Across Health Content.* Santa Cruz, Calif.: ETR Associates.

Fetro, J.V. (1994). "Personal and Social Skill Development Is Basic." In *The Comprehensive School Health Challenge: Promoting Health Through Education,* edited by P. Cortese and K. Middleton. Vol. 1. Santa Cruz, Calif.: ETR Associates.

Fruchter, N., A. Galletta, and J.L. White. (1992). *New Directions in Parent Involvement.* Washington, D.C.: Academy for Educational Development, Inc.

Gold, R.S. (1994). "The Science Base for Comprehensive Health Education." In *The Comprehensive School Health Challenge: Promoting Health Through Education,* edited by P. Cortese and K. Middleton. Vol. 2. Santa Cruz, Calif.: ETR Associates.

Haber, D. (1994). "Health Education: A Role for All." *ASCD Curriculum/Technology Quarterly* 3, 4: 1–3.

Joint Health Education Standards Committee. (1994a). *Draft National Health Education Standards and Performance Indicators.* Reston, Va.: Author.

Joint Health Education Standards Committee. (1994b). *Draft National Health Education System Standards.* Reston, Va.: Author.

Jones, E.H., N.S. Miller, and L. Tritsch. (1994). "School Restructuring: How Is the Health Program Affected?" In *The Comprehensive School Health Challenge: Promoting Health Through Education,* edited by P. Cortese and K. Middleton. Vol. 2. Santa Cruz, Calif.: ETR Associates.

Kirby, D., R.P. Barth, N. Leland, and J.V. Fetro. (1991). "Reducing the Risk: Impact of a New Curriculum on Sexual Risk-Taking." *Family Planning Perspectives* 23, 6: 253–263.

Kolbe, L.J. (1990). "An Epidemiological Surveillance System to Monitor the Prevalence of Youth Behaviors That Most Affect Health." *Health Education* 21, 6: 44–48.

Lohrmann D.K., R.S. Gold, and W.H. Jubb. (1987). "School Health Education: A Foundation for School Health Programs." *Journal of School Health* 57, 10: 420–425.

Morris, C. (1992). "Pressure Groups and the Politics of Education." *Updating School Board Policies* 23, 9: 1–5.

National Commission on the Role of the School and the Community in Improving Adolescent Health. (1990). *Code Blue: Uniting for Healthier Youth.* Alexandria, Va.: National Association of State Boards of Education.

National Coordinating Committee on School Health. (1993). *School Health: Findings from Evaluated Programs* (Publication No. 1993-357-637/90247). Washington, D.C.: U.S. Government Printing Office.

National Guidelines Task Force. (n.d.). *Guidelines for Comprehensive Sexuality Education Kindergarten–12th Grade.* New York: Sex Information and Education Council of the United States.

National School Boards Association. (1991). *School Health: Helping Children Learn.* Alexandria, Va.: Author.

Newman, I.M., and K.A. Farrell. (1991). *Thinking Ahead: Preparing for Controversy.* Lincoln, Nebr.: Nebraska Department of Education.

People for the American Way. (1993). *Attacks on the Freedom to Learn: 1992–1993 Report.* Washington, D.C.: Author.

Perry, C.L., R.V. Luepker, D.M. Murray, C. Kurth, R. Mullis, S. Crockett, and D.R. Jacobs. (1988). "Parent Involvement with Children's Heath Promotion: The Minnesota Home Team." *American Journal of Public Health* 78, 9: 1156–1160.

Pine, P. (1985). *AASA Critical Issues Report: Promoting Health Education in Schools—Problems and Solutions.* Arlington, Va.: American Association of School Administrators.

Resnikow, K., J. Cherry, and D. Cross. (1993). "Ten Unanswered Questions Regarding Comprehensive School Health Promotion." *Journal of School Health* 63, 4: 171–175.

Ross, J.G., M.T. Errecart, A.T. Lavin, P. Saavedra, and R.S. Gold. (1989). *Final Report: Teenage Health Teaching Modules Evaluation.* CDC Contract No. 200-86-3932. Silver Spring, Md.: Macro Systems, Inc.

Sancho, A.R. (1994). "A Multiethnic Perspective on Comprehensive Health Education." In *The Multicultural Challenge in Health Education,* edited by A.C. Matiella. Santa Cruz, Calif.: ETR Associates.

Seffrin, J. (1990). "The Comprehensive School Health Curriculum: Closing the Gap Between State-of-the-Art and State-of-the-Practice." *Journal of School Health* 60, 4: 151–156.

Sullivan, C., and J.F. Bogden. (1993). "Today's Education Policy Environment." *Journal of School Health* 63, 1: 28–32.

U.S. Department of Commerce, Bureau of the Census. (1989). "Money, Income, and Poverty Status in the United States." In *Current Population Reports Series P-20, 445.* Washington, D.C.: Author.

U.S. Department of Commerce, Bureau of the Census. (1990). "Table C—Marital Status and Living Arrangements." In *Current Population Reports Series P-20, 445.* Washington, D.C.: Author.

Van Patten, M.M. (1994). "Dealing with Controversy in the School Health Program." In *The Comprehensive School Health Challenge: Promoting Health Through Education,* edited by P. Cortese and K. Middleton. Vol. 2. Santa Cruz, Calif.: ETR Associates.

Varnes, J.W. (1994). "Preservice Education: Providing Health Knowledge for All Teachers." In *The Comprehensive School Health Challenge: Promoting Health Through Education,* edited by P. Cortese and K. Middleton. Vol. 2. Santa Cruz, Calif.: ETR Associates.

Walter, H.J., R.D. Vaughan, and E.L. Wyndner. (1989). "Primary Prevention of Cancer Among Children: Changes in Cigarette Smoking and Diet After Six Years of Intervention." *Journal of the National Cancer Institute* 81: 995–999.

Resources: National Organizations*

American Association of School Administrators (AASA)
1801 North Moore Street
Arlington, VA 22209

American School Health Association (ASHA)
7263 State Route 43
P.O. Box 708
Kent, OH 44240

ASCD Comprehensive School Health Education Network
Attn.: Deborah Haber/Jaki Ellis
c/o Education Development Center, Inc.
55 Chapel Street
Newton, MA 02158

Association for the Advancement of Health Education (AAHE)
1900 Association Drive
Reston, VA 22091

Centers for Disease Control and Prevention (CDC)
Division of Adolescent and School Health
4770 Buford Highway, N.E.
Atlanta, GA 30341

Children's Defense Fund
25 E Street, N.W.
Washington, DC 20001

Comprehensive Health Education Foundation (CHEF)
22323 Pacific Highway South
Seattle, WA 98198

Council of Chief State School Officers (CCSSO)
School Health
One Massachusetts Avenue, N.W., Suite 700
Washington, DC 20001

Education Development Center, Inc. (EDC)
Comprehensive School Health Education Training Network
55 Chapel Street
Newton, MA 02158

Education, Training, and Research Associates (ETR Associates)
P.O. Box 1830
Santa Cruz, CA 95061

National Association of School Health Education Coalitions (NASHEC)
1001 G Street, N.W., Suite 400 East
Washington, DC 20001

National Association of State Boards of Education (NASBE)
1012 Cameron Street
Alexandria, VA 22314

National Center for Health Education (NCHE)
72 Spring Street, Suite 208
New York, NY 10012

National Education Association (NEA)
Health Information Network
1201 16th Street, N.W.
Washington, DC 20036

National School Boards Association (NSBA)
Comprehensive School Health
1680 Duke Street
Alexandria, VA 22314

* You may also want to consult the local chapters of the American Cancer Society, American Heart Association, American Lung Association, and American Red Cross.

Resources: Publications

American Association of School Administrators. (1990). *Healthy Kids for the Year 2000: An Action Plan for Schools.* Arlington, Va.: Author.

American Cancer Society. (1993). *National Action Plan for Comprehensive School Health Education.* Atlanta, Ga.: Author.

Carnegie Council on Adolescent Development. (1989). *Turning Points: Preparing American Youth for the 21st Century.* New York: Author.

Cortese, P., and K. Middleton, eds. (1994). *The Comprehensive School Health Challenge: Promoting Health Through Education.* Vols. 1–2. Santa Cruz, Calif.: ETR Associates.

Council of Chief State School Officers. (1991). *Beyond the Health Room.* Washington, D.C.: Author.

Education Development Center, Inc. (1994). *Choosing the Tools: A Review of Selected K–12 Health Education Curricula.* Newton, Mass.: Author.

Education Development Center, Inc. (1995). *Educating for Health: A Guide to Implementing Comprehensive School Health Education.* Newton, Mass.: Author.

English, J., A. Sancho, D. Lloyd–Kolkin, and L. Hunter. (1990). *Criteria for Comprehensive Health Education Curricula.* Los Alamitos, Calif.: Southwest Regional Educational Laboratory.

Fetro, J.V. (1992). *Personal and Social Skills: Understanding and Integrating Competencies Across Health Content.* Santa Cruz, Calif.: ETR Associates.

Fruchter, N., A. Galletta, and J.L. White. (1992). *New Directions in Parent Involvement.* Washington, D.C.: Academy for Educational Development, Inc.

Healthy People 2000: National Health Promotion and Disease Prevention Objectives. (1990). Washington, D.C.: U.S. Department of Health and Human Services.

Joint Health Education Standards Committee. (1994). *Draft National Health Education Standards and Performance Indicators* and *Draft National Health Education System Standards.* Reston, Va.: Author.

Kane, W.M. (1993). *Step by Step to Comprehensive School Health: The Program Planning Guide.* Santa Cruz, Calif.: ETR Associates.

Matiella, A.C., ed. (1994). *The Multicultural Challenge in Health Education.* Santa Cruz, Calif.: ETR Associates.

National Commission on the Role of the School and the Community in Improving Adolescent Health. (1990). *Code Blue: Uniting for Healthier Youth.* Alexandria, Va.: National Association of State Boards of Education.

National Association of State Boards of Education.

National Coordinating Committee on School Health. (1993). *School Health: Findings from Evaluated Programs* (Publication No. 1993–357–637/90247). Washington, D.C.: U.S. Government Printing Office.

National Health/Education Consortium. (n.d.). *Bridging the Gap: A Health Care Primer for Education Professionals* and *Bridging the Gap: An Education Primer for Health Professionals.* Washington, D.C.: Author.

National School Boards Association. (1991). *School Health: Helping Children Learn.* Alexandria, Va.: Author.

6

The Family and Consumer Sciences Curriculum

Sharon S. Redick

In 1978 Marjorie Brown published *A Conceptual Scheme and Decision-Rules for the Selection and Organization of Home Economics Curriculum Content* and thus began a series of writings that would revolutionize thinking about curriculum in home economics. Brown's writings (1978, 1980, 1985, 1986) and those she coauthored with Beatrice Paolucci (1979) began a massive movement that generated dialogue and reflection about what home economics ought to be. Later, numerous writers (Meszaros 1981, Hultgren 1986, Hultgren and Wilkosz 1986, Wilsman 1986, Laster 1989) examined Brown's work, further expanding the dialogue and debate about the definition, mission, and focus of home economics.

Author's Note: In June 1994, at its 96th annual meeting, the American Home Economics Association voted to change the name of the professional association to the American Association of Family and Consumer Sciences. The Home Economics Division of the American Vocational Association changed its name to Family and Consumer Sciences in December 1994. Many state and local programs have also changed to this name. In this chapter, I use the terms *home economics* and *family and consumer sciences* interchangeably, with the term *family and consumer sciences* reflecting the current name.

Brown argued that the philosophical base underlying home economics should be reconsidered, its purpose reconstructed, and its curriculum orientation redirected. Steeped in Habermas's theory (Habermas 1992), Brown wrote extensively on why home economics is not a technical science (its traditional designation):

> A technical scientist uses concrete knowledge to manipulate objects in a certain way to produce a certain end. . . . Home economics has historically claimed to be concerned with humans who meet the concrete situations of everyday life and who are, among their other roles and activities, members of families. Home economics as a technical science would manipulate people. Certain specific goals are set by the professional which may or may not be in the interest of the individual or of the society in which the individual seeks or has attained a degree of mature status. . . . The technical procedure used by a professional is one which expects passive acceptance and with whom the professional does not engage in open communication: such professional action is not liberating (Brown 1986, pp. 49–50).

In contrast, she described home economics as a critical/practical science. The "practical" is derived from the German *praktisch*—pertaining to conscious thought processes that reach fulfillment in action. Brown continues her argument by noting that a practical scientist would

> conduct open and undistorted communicative action with those whom they serve and give attention in the content of that communication to the meanings and the logic for validating those beliefs, meanings, and norms significant to family life and development of the individual (Brown 1986, p. 51).

This new direction for the field produced both followers and foes. Responding to the negative reaction to their position, Brown and Paolucci contended that any scholarly discipline requires continuous examination and redefinition of its theoretical and operational bases over time. Despite the criticism, or perhaps because of it, Brown's followers grew, and they discussed and debated her ideas at professional meetings and gatherings across the country.

Changes in the concept of the family in the late 1970s and early 1980s prompted educators to look more closely at the family and consumer sciences curriculum. As the divorce rate increased, a variety of family structures emerged and with them, new problems that threatened the economic, social, and psychological well-being of the family and its individual members. Family functions—the roles of individuals and family members—also took on new meanings as the family turned away from a production orientation to become primarily a consumption unit.

In the face of such changes, educators could not help but ask, "Is the curriculum content relevant? Is family and consumer sciences addressing the critical, problematic areas of individual and family life?" Brown (1978, 1980), Brown and Paolucci (1979), and others answered these questions with a resounding *no* and proceeded to propose a reconceptualization of the field.

The Aim and Mission of Family and Consumer Sciences

The ultimate aim of family and consumer sciences is to improve the quality of home and family life. Although this aim is widely accepted, various views of the field have existed over the years. Thomas (1986, p. 169) describes six views of family and consumer sciences education:

1. *Education for women,* focusing on traditional roles and tasks of women as homemakers, wives, and mothers.

2. *Manual training,* focusing on products and processes of production.

3. *The application of science,* focusing on improving the environment.

4. *Household management,* focusing on improving the quality, influence, and effectiveness of households.

5. *Family development,* focusing on strengthening the family system and improving family practices.

6. *Intervention,* focusing on reducing or removing barriers or deficits that make certain groups disadvantaged.

Some of these views, such as home economics as education for women only or as manual training, are not held by those in the field today, but they are part of the general public's perception of home economics. Thomas (1986) notes that given such diversity of focus, it is not surprising that both the general public and educators are confused about what the nature of programs is or should be. The evolution that has taken place in this field is not immediately apparent.

Considering the values of the past and the needs of contemporary families, Brown and Paolucci (1979, pp. 46–47) proposed the following mission for the family and consumer sciences profession:

> To enable families, both as individual units and generally as a social institution, to build and maintain systems of action which lead to (1) maturing in self-formation and (2) enlightened, cooperative partici-

pation in the critique and formulation of social goals and means for accomplishing them.

In discussing this mission as it applies to family and consumer sciences education, Kister (1989, p. 1) stated the following:

> The family fosters physical, social, moral, aesthetic, and spiritual conditions of the home and family in order to nurture optimum development of each family member. Families to a great extent determine who a person is and what a person becomes—families can and should provide for the humanness of our society. Home economics education helps students be critically reflective of social forces influencing families and prepares them to be proactive in economic, social, political, and technological change. Home economics education prepares youth and adults for the work of the family as well as for occupations based on home economics skills.

The Family and Consumer Sciences Division of the American Vocational Association (1994) adopted the following vision statement for the field of Family and Consumer Sciences Education: "Family and consumer sciences education empowers individuals and families across the life span to manage the challenges of living and working in a diverse, global society. Our unique focus is on families, work and their interrelationships." It also adopted a mission statement identifying nine goals that provide a basis for curriculum development:

> The mission of family and consumer sciences education is to prepare students for family life, work life, and careers in family and consumer sciences by providing opportunities to develop the knowledge, skills, attitudes and behaviors needed for:
>
> 1. Strengthening the well-being of individuals and families across the life span.
> 2. Becoming responsible citizens and leaders for family, community, and work settings.
> 3. Promoting optimal nutrition and wellness across the life span.
> 4. Managing resources to meet the material needs of individuals and families.
> 5. Balancing personal, home, family, and work lives.
> 6. Using critical and creative thinking skills to address problems in diverse family, community, and work environments.
> 7. Successful life management, employment, and career development.
> 8. Functioning as providers and consumers of goods and services.
> 9. Appreciating human worth and accepting responsibility for one's actions and success in family and work life.

Family and consumer sciences programs are intended to serve a broad spectrum of youth and adults, including those considered at-risk (Redick and Vail 1992): pregnant teenagers, teenage parents, developmentally delayed students, physically impaired students, incarcerated persons, displaced homemakers, adults in transition, immigrants, and homeless youth, for instance. Enrollments include males and females of diverse racial and ethnic groups. Most educators in this field recognize that their classrooms are a microcosm of our global world. They know that they must meet the needs of diverse learners and thus embrace the concept of multicultural education as part of the family and consumer sciences program.

Family and consumer sciences programs also address the diverse needs of learners by offering both prevention programs (e.g., middle and high school family life programs) and intervention programs (e.g., pregnant teen programs). Programs are also typically categorized as useful programs or gainful programs. Useful programs are general or pre-occupational education, such as family life courses; gainful programs are occupational education, such as training in child care services or food production.

Curriculum Approaches

Which curriculum approach most effectively meets the mission and aims of home economics? Brown (1986) encourages moving away from the traditional technical approach (which involves teaching students expert ways to perform household tasks) and adopting instead a critical science approach: helping students learn to think, reflect, and take action through the study of perennial, practical family problems. She argues that the curriculum should empower individuals and families to examine recurring, persistent family issues like these: *What should I do to nourish myself and my family? What should I do to manage my resources? What should I do to nurture my children and family members?* In examining such issues, students have to analyze contextual factors, identify possible decisions, explain the consequences of those decisions, and explore the moral and ethical considerations inherent to each. Teachers encourage students to find solutions that provide for not only the well-being of the individual and family but also the well-being of society. Although teachers encourage students to find the best morally defensible solution, they do not advocate any predetermined outcomes.

Hultgren and Wilkosz (1986) conceptualize this method as a practical-problems approach to curriculum development. They define practical problems as questions of "what to do" or "what action to take" regarding critical concerns of the family that require reasoned thought, judgment, and action.

Not all family and consumer scientists, however, accept the critical science philosophy as an exclusive curriculum approach. Some argue that this approach may be suitable for family and consumer programs, but say it is inappropriate for other programs, such as those designed to prepare students for occupations in the home economics field.

Support for a more vocation-focused alternative grew out of the competency-based education movement. In a survey by Stout and Smith (1986), more than two-thirds of the state supervisors of family and consumer sciences reported that their states used or planned to use a competency-based approach for secondary family and consumer sciences programs. During the 1980s, Colorado, Kentucky, Georgia, Texas, and West Virginia produced curriculum guides using the competency-based approach, and most of these guides were directed to occupational home economics programming. Concurrently, some states, including Iowa, North Dakota, Texas, and West Virginia, continued to produce curriculum guides that focused on the development of concepts and generalizations. Smith and Morgan (1986) concluded that the concept-and-generalization approach was a viable option for family and consumer sciences and that many states were using this approach to curriculum development.

Some curriculum leaders embraced Brown's critical science philosophy and curriculum model, infused it with their own thoughts and interpretations, and began reconceptualizing the home economics curriculum. For each perennial practical problem, Brown (1978) recommended that curriculum planners include and make decisions about the following:

• Concepts of valued ends regarding the quality of life for the individual, the family, the culture, and society
• Concepts of personal and cultural context
• Concepts of means or actions for achieving the valued ends
• Concepts regarding the processes involved in decision making and action, interpersonal relations, and self-formation.

Although this reconceptualization process was fraught with political and intellectual turmoil, it gained support across the country during the 1980s and early 1990s. Minnesota, Nebraska, Ohio, Oregon, Pennsylvania, and Wisconsin were among the states that produced curriculum resources based on the critical science perspective. These states provided the initial impetus for reconceptualizing the home economics curriculum at the secondary level, and they continue to provide leadership in reconceptualizing the curriculum, developing resource materials, and conducting research. Essentially, they produced materials to guide teachers in creating *an emerging curriculum* with their students. The intent was that free of predetermined student outcomes and competencies, teachers could organize their teaching around the collaborative identification and analysis of perennial, practical problems of families, and thus help students develop the concepts and generalizations needed to take reasoned action to solve those family issues.

As proponents of the critical science perspective grew in number, discussions about which curriculum approaches to use continued. When the guidebook *Home Economics Concepts: A Base for Curriculum Development* was published in 1989 by the American Home Economics Association, three approaches to curriculum development were delineated: competency-based designs, concept-based designs, and process-based designs (American Home Economics Association 1989, Bobbitt 1989). Local and state planners use the design that best reflects their philosophical orientation.

A Knowledge Base and Essential Skills

According to Brown (1978, pp. 14–15), family and consumer sciences is a "problem oriented field in that . . . its knowledge base is generated by concern with an area of human problems. . . . The problems with which [the field] is concerned are practical problems of the home and family. . . . A practical problem is concerned with what to do, i.e., with action in situations for which reflective decision-making is required."

Hultgren and Wilkosz (1986, p. 145) note that "when conceptualizing home economics from a practical problem framework, the uniqueness of the knowledge base or curriculum content does not come from the uniqueness of the concepts, but rather from the formulation and ordering of knowledge for the problems which are to be solved." What becomes significant, then, are the questions themselves. Consequently, practical reasoning, "deciding what to do and believe about ill-structured everyday home and family problems using knowledge and cognitive skills available," is required for solving such practical, action-oriented questions (Laster 1987).

For good practical reasoning, students need knowledge related to the systems of action that families use to accomplish their work: that is, *family technical action,* where the family works to produce particular objects or achieve certain goals; *family communicative action,* where families share meanings and interpret information and where the focus is on clarifying meanings, uncovering assumptions, analyzing concepts, clarifying the validity of reasoning processes, and investigating the implications of ideas; and finally, *family emancipative action,* where family and social issues are examined and value decisions are made based on moral and ethical judgements (Wilsman 1986).

Those systems of action help define the collateral capacities that are to be developed through the curriculum—for example, self-reflection, the ability to develop perspectives, critical thinking, interpersonal relationship skills, communication, listening, creating and evaluating goals, decision making, and assuming responsibility (Thomas, Jax, Johnson, Kister, and Hultgren, personal communication, August 1994).

The knowledge base and essential skills for family and consumer sciences are recommended in *Home Economics Concepts: A Base for Curriculum Development* (American Home Economics Association 1989). This knowledge base is organized around the knowledge needed for action by family members and consumers as they resolve practical questions of the family in the following areas:

- Consumer and resource management
- Housing and living environments
- Individual, child, and family development
- Nutrition and food
- Textiles and clothing

Concepts and subconcepts involved in resolving questions for each of the major subject areas are structured around the following concept categories:

- Meanings
- Values, standards, and goals
- Information sources
- Factors affecting decisions
- The nature of concepts
- Decisions related to problem areas
- Public policy concerns in each problem area
- Cross-cultural and global issues

In home economics, says Johnson (personal communication, August 1994), the subject matter plus the processes equal the content of the curriculum. *Home Economics Concepts* includes recommendations for subject-matter concepts and for the concepts and subconcepts involved in the practical reasoning processes used to make private and public family, consumer, and work-related decisions. Figure 6.1 shows the conceptual framework used in the *Ohio High School Work and Family Life Curriculum Guide* to illustrate the inclusion of both processes and subject matter (Ohio Department of Education 1992–94).

Yet some say that to predetermine curriculum content defies the basic assumptions of a critical science philosophy. From a critical science perspective, content develops in response to the questioning; rather than being selected in advance, it emerges (Thomas and Hultgren, personal communication, August 1994).

Process-Oriented Teaching

The critical science approach to family and consumer sciences requires teachers to focus on process. In fact, this "process as content" curriculum paradigm demands new instructional processes: "critical analysis, problem solving, and democratic social processes" (Brown 1978, p. 32) and value reasoning, practical reasoning, and reflective dialogue. Innovative instructional strategies and materials have been developed for value reasoning (Hultgren 1986), practical reasoning (Brown and Paolucci 1979, Laster 1987), and reflective dialogue (Thomas et al. 1992).

As the movement toward a critical/practical science perspective in family and consumer sciences curriculum and instruction gained momentum, Laster (1985) noted that developments in cognitive psychology could contribute significantly to this approach. Although such developments played a major role in the process curriculum movement, some family and consumer sciences leaders believed an important aspect was missing. Laster (1987), Thomas (personal communication, August 1994), and Hultgren (personal communication, August 1994) believe that cognitive psychology did not provide for the ethical and moral dimension necessary to the solution of family problems. Both Laster's (1987) practical reasoning process and Hultgren's (1986) value reasoning process attend to this dimension.

The dimension of moral and ethical perspectives—that is, helping students develop a disposition to be ethically committed—is a critical component of the family and consumer sciences curriculum. By combining the cognitive process and social reconstruction orientations, as

FIGURE 6.1

Ohio High School Work and Family Life Conceptual Framework

Core Processes
(to be integrated into every core course area)

Managing Work and Family
Expanding the concept of work
  and family
Ongoing analysis of interaction of
  work and family roles
Managing work and family
  responsibilities

Problem Solving
Clarification of issues
Making decisions for the well-being
  of self and others

Interpersonal Skills
Positive, caring relationships
Effective communication
Conflict management
Using planning processes to
  achieve goals

Citizenship and Leadership
Citizenship at home and outside the
  home
Cooperation
Evaluation of social conditions

Core Course Areas
(minimum offering: one semester course per core course area)

Personal Development
Taking responsibility for self and
  others
Building self-esteem
Relationships with family and
  peers
Managing stress and conflict
Career planning
Responsible parenting

Nutrition and Wellness
Making choices to promote wellness
  for self
Relating psychological and social
  needs and food choices
Obtaining and storing food
Planning, preparing, and serving
  nutritious meals
Selecting and using equipment
Promoting optimal nutrition and
  wellness of society

Resource Management
Managing resources to achieve
  goals
Making consumer choices
Housing the family
Clothing the family
Feeding the family

Parenting
Exploring parenting roles and
  responsibilities
Assessing readiness and preparing
  for parenthood
Meeting the developmental needs of
  children
Using positive guidance and
  discipline
Nurturing positive parent/child
  relationships
Identifying and accessing parenting
  resources
Responsibilities of families and
  society for children

FIGURE 6.1—*(continued)*

Ohio High School Work and Family Life Conceptual Framework

Family Relations

Exploring roles and significance
   of family
Preparing for adult life, family life
Nurturing human development
   through the life span
Building healthy family
   relationships
Dealing effectively with family,
   stressors, conflicts, and crises
Managing work and family roles
   and responsibilities
Recognizing social forces that
   affect families

Life Planning

Developing a life management plan
Responsibility for self and others
Building interpersonal relationships
Establishing a lifelong career
   planning process
Managing resources to achieve
   goals and to meet food, clothing,
   and housing needs
Coordinating personal and career
   responsibilities

For more information, contact Family and Consumer Sciences Supervisor, Ohio Department of Education, Division of Vocational and Career Education, 65 S. Front St., Rm. 909, Columbus, OH 43215-4183. Telephone: (614) 466-3046.

---

discussed by Eisner (1985), educators in family and consumer sciences are moving from a subject-centered instructional approach to a process-oriented methodology. New process-oriented curricular materials that incorporate these strategies continue to be developed.

Applied to curriculum, the critical science perspective allows for relevancy, integration, and response to the unique needs of each student. The home economics curriculum is organized around the persistent, recurring practical problems of families. For example, using a process such as practical reasoning, students identify perennial problems of the family and examine current contextual factors to construct possible solutions to the problems under discussion. They then analyze these alternatives and identify possible consequences for each. Students are encouraged to consider the moral and ethical dimensions of alternatives before suggesting solutions.

Characteristics of constructivism are embedded in this type of curriculum: it is problem centered, it draws upon the context of the situation, and it helps students connect ideas so they can construct new solutions to real-world problems.

The Middle School Curriculum

The years between age 10 and age 14 are a critical time in human development, a time when emerging adolescents have significant needs that could be met by home economics programs (Lounsbury 1994). The question is which curricular approach helps us best meet these needs. During the early 1990s, dialogue that had centered on high school programs turned to the middle school level. Many curriculum leaders believed that the critical science approach was equally appropriate for emerging adolescents (Boggs and Kister 1994). The Ohio Department of Education (1990) curriculum guide for middle school, which followed this approach, has been widely accepted on the national level (see Figure 6.2). Other middle school guides include those developed by Colorado, Iowa, North Dakota, and West Virginia.

FIGURE 6.2

Ohio Middle School Conceptual Framework

Core Processes
(to be integrated in each course)

Problem Solving   **Management**

Interpersonal Skills   **Citizenship and Leadership**

Core Content Areas
(at least two per semester course, four per full-year course)

Creating a Self-Identity   **Relating to Others**
Concerns regarding: Concerns regarding:
  Self-formation   Communication
  Personal appearance   Family relationships
  Healthy lifestyle   Peer relationships
  Sexuality   Children
                                           Caring for others
                                           Global society

Becoming Independent   **Managing Resources**
Concerns regarding: Concerns regarding:
  Self-care   Personal resources
  Clothing   Economic resources
  Food preparation   Consumerism
  Careers   Living environment

For more information, contact Family and Consumer Sciences Supervisor, Ohio Department of Education, Division of Vocational and Career Education, 65 S. Front St., Rm. 909, Columbus, OH 43215-4183. Telephone: (614) 466-3046.

Fauske (1994), in sharing her vision of an ideal middle school home economics program, wrote that it would be developed through the "practical reasoning process." The curriculum itself would be focused on helping students address and solve the practical problems of families through the practical reasoning process. She further noted that the home economics program would include many activities:

> Classroom activities [will be] chosen to foster complexity in thinking, skills in practical reasoning, and practice in interpersonal communication. . . . Integration of curriculum from various school discipline areas with that of home economics may be an essential feature of an ideal middle school home economics program (Fauske 1994, pp. 206, 208).

Integration with Other Subjects

It is at the middle school level that family and consumer sciences is most frequently integrated with other subjects (Dohner 1994). The multidisciplinary approach, however, is used more frequently than an interdisciplinary or integrative approach in both middle schools and high schools.

Many family and consumer sciences curriculum guides focus on integrating the basic skills of math, science, reading, and writing into the family and consumer sciences curriculum. Colorado, Iowa, Kentucky, and Ohio are a few of the states that have developed such guides.

The critical science perspective promotes integration (Hultgren, Jax, Johnson, Thomas, Wyatt, personal communication, August 1994; Dohner 1994). By focusing on practical problems whose solutions require students to understand and examine contextual factors, the curriculum forces students to draw on information from a range of subject areas, not just from the family and consumer sciences curriculum.

The process-oriented curriculum's emphasis on relevance, integration, and response to individual needs may better enable teachers to fulfill the mission of home economics (as proposed by Brown and Paolucci) than would a content-oriented curriculum, but this approach also creates many challenges for educators.

Assessment

Besides internalizing the philosophy, understanding the new concepts, and developing the skills of process-oriented teaching, teachers need to face the demands of assessing student learning. Authentic assessment should be a natural fit with the critical science perspective. The notion of authentic teaching of authentic issues is paramount to the ideals of the critical science perspective. Why, then, not use authentic assessment?

During its many years of popularity, the technical-oriented home economics curriculum included laboratories in which authentic assessment was prevalent: Students performed the skills they were taught, and their performance was assessed using scorecards or rating scales. The process-oriented curriculum rose to prominence with its emphasis on problem solving and thinking skills, but appropriate authentic assessment instruments were not readily available for this curriculum. Furthermore, the requirements of grades for college entrance requirements, preparation for proficiency tests, and demands to fit assessment into the confines of a certain structure and organization of the school can be major barriers to its use (Jax, Thomas, Johnson, personal communication, August 1994).

Many states have presented inservice programs on authentic assessment, and most teachers see its merit, but few teachers of family and consumer sciences use it when implementing a process-oriented curriculum. Teachers who rely on the laboratory method of instruction, such as in occupational home economics programs (i.e., food service or child care services), are more likely to use authentic assessment.

Assessment of processes is a central issue in the movement toward the critical science curriculum. If the goal is to increase thinking skills, how can we best assess students' progress in this area? Thomas and Englund (1989, 1990) and Thomas (1988a, 1988b) have investigated both the teaching and assessment of thinking skills in vocational education. Laster (1987) and her students at Ohio State University studied alternatives for evaluating practical problem-solving skills. Today, researchers are still trying to determine the appropriate assessments for a process-oriented curriculum; the issue remains unresolved.

Factors Influencing the Home Economics Curriculum

Inservice Education and Research

Nobody fully understands just how to impel changes in curriculum orientation. We do know, however, that the typical one-day, one-shot inservice program is not effective in making such changes (Fedje 1992, Schultz 1994). The move to a critical science perspective requires teachers to have the courage to leave the tried and tested for new and uncharted horizons. The journey is slow and challenging because research is still needed on how best to bring about change in curriculum orientation and practice.

Hultgren (1990, 1992, 1994) provided leadership in using phenomenological approaches, including journal writing, to help teachers of family and consumer sciences articulate growth and change. Johnson (personal communication, August 1994) has been pursuing the question of how best to bring about curriculum change in research efforts at the University of Nebraska–Lincoln. Using Eisner and Vallance's (1974) categories of curriculum orientation, Cunningham (1992) and Johnson (personal communication, August 1994) developed an instrument to assess the curriculum orientation of family and consumer sciences teachers. They found that the predominant orientation of teachers in Nebraska was cognitive process. Johnson then developed inservice programming designed to move teachers to a critical science perspective. This long-term research agenda is ongoing.

Using the Cunningham and Johnson instrument, Wyatt (1994) and Laster (personal communication, August 1994) at Ohio State University examined the curriculum orientation of family and consumer sciences teacher educators (n = 177) and state supervisors (n = 35). They found that the predominant orientation for 77 percent of the teacher educators was cognitive processes; for 20 percent, critical consciousness/reconstructionist; for 5 percent, self-actualization; for 3 percent, technical; and for the remaining 1 percent, academic rationalism. The curriculum orientations of state, family, and consumer sciences supervisors were in the same rank order, with 68 percent scoring in the cognitive process category and 23 percent in the consciousness/reconstructionist category. I suspect that prior to Brown's writings, curriculum leaders would not have scored in these numbers in these categories (although no data are available to confirm my suspicions); it is far more likely that the technical category would have been one of the top two categories. Research is also needed to examine whether practice reflects a stated curriculum orientation.

Preservice and Graduate Education

Preservice and graduate education is a significant influence on curriculum orientation (Hultgren 1991; Wyatt 1994; Johnson, personal communication, August 1994). When students have opportunities to study with proponents of the critical science philosophy, they are more likely to later teach from a critical science perspective. When teacher educators at universities share the same philosophy with other curriculum leaders in the state, such as state and local supervisors, teachers also are more likely to embrace the critical science perspective (Hultgren 1989, 1992, 1994; Wyatt 1994).

Legislation

Beginning with the Smith-Hughes Act of 1917 and continuing through the 1968 Vocational Amendments to the current Carl D. Perkins Vocational Education Act, federal legislation has had a strong influence on the family and consumer sciences curriculum. Vocational family and consumer sciences programs follow the standards set by the legislation, which provides funding for state leadership, curriculum development, equipment, teacher education, and professional development. The current subject-matter mandates focus on preparing students for the work of the family and includes such topics as consumer education, parenting, balancing work and family, employability, and preparing for work in occupations related to family and consumer sciences.

It is important to recognize that not all family and consumer sciences programs are "vocational," especially middle school programs. In some states, however, the strength of the vocational family and consumer sciences programs has strongly influenced nonvocational programming; the curriculums of both programs can be very similar.

Most family and consumer sciences curriculum guides have been at least partially funded by federal dollars provided through vocational education legislation. Although the legislative directives come from the national level, curriculum development has occurred most frequently at the state and local levels.

Technology

Technology affects both the content and delivery of the home economics curriculum. Several states have developed curriculum guides that include or focus on technology. Iowa's *Scope and Sequence for Vocational Home Economics* recognized technology as a program component and stated, "One of the principal challenges will be to determine and create an awareness of the impact of technology on the family" (Iowa Department 1985). The Iowa materials encourage teachers to include technological advances in both the content and the delivery of the curriculum.

The Mid-America Vocational Curriculum Consortium, Inc. (1992), published the curriculum guide *Impact of Technology on the Family*. The purpose of this guide was to increase the awareness of new technological innovations and how they affect personal and family life. Teachers were encouraged to integrate technology information in existing units in all family and consumer sciences subject areas.

Similarly, the majority of family and consumer sciences curriculum guides produced in the late 1980s and early 1990s include a focus on technology. For example, in Wisconsin's *A Guide to Curriculum Planning in Home Economics* (Wisconsin Department 1987, p. 28), teachers are encouraged to develop and offer a course called Family and Technology that would "explore the profound effect technology has had on the way the family lives, thinks, feels, and perceives the world about them. The course challenges students to think about the technological future and its relationship to family and work life."

Technology also affects how the family and consumer sciences curriculum is delivered. Many teachers now have access to computers in their schools, and some classrooms are equipped with advanced computer technology. For example, in Ohio's Pickaway and Ross counties, all schools are equipped with interactive video, and a program for pregnant teenagers is delivered through this technology. Teachers are located at the Pickaway-Ross Vocational School, and pregnant teens in schools throughout the district are connected to them through interactive video for classroom instruction and interaction (Allenspach 1994).

The popularity of the Internet has led to the development of many resources for teachers. For example, teachers in Pennsylvania have created electronic "Teacher Pages" that are available to anyone with access to the World Wide Web. These pages provide current information on subject-matter topics and allow teachers to exchange strategies and techniques online (Brown 1994). Further, many teachers use computer programs as teaching strategies in the classroom. Computer programs are available for most family and consumer sciences subject areas, including nutrition, parenting, child development, housing, interior design, fashion, and family and consumer economics.

Current Issues

Current issues in home economics stem in part from Brown's writings. The question of which curricular approach or orientation to use remains unresolved, as does the question of how best to bring about the significant reexamination of thinking and the transformation needed to develop a new curriculum perspective. Also unresolved is the conflict between state mandates for competency-based education and educators' desire to develop a process-oriented curriculum. How best to assess growth and change in a process-oriented curriculum continues to be a concern. Translating the critical science perspective into teaching practice needs attention. Having professionals at various stages of professional growth and degrees of commitment to a curriculum perspective is both a blessing and a challenge. And the role of written curriculum documents continues to create controversy.

Questions about accreditation, national standards, and goals and outcomes for home economics continue to be the topics of dialogue and debate. Citing the guidelines of accrediting organizations, Love (1994) called for two related sets of standards, one to guide the nation's secondary family and consumer sciences programs and another for teacher education programs in family and consumer sciences. Hultgren and Thomas (personal communication, 1994) have questioned the usefulness of such standards. National standards developed in the 1970s proved to be less stringent than state standards and thus were not followed by many states.

The family and consumer sciences curriculum is currently driven by state mandates and influences rather than national efforts, with the exception of the Carl Perkins Vocational Education legislation, which provides content standards and funding for home economics curriculums. The Perkins legislation provides funding for leadership and curriculum development in family and consumer sciences education and has been a vital force in strengthening programs.

Economic conditions affecting all of education have created critical issues in family and consumer sciences because it is usually an elective area of study. Questions of what should have priority in our school systems and within family and consumer sciences curriculum continue to be debated.

The issue of where family and consumer sciences should be aligned in the school program (in the vocational or academic strand) continues to cause debate. Klein (1993) called for disassociating family and consumer sciences from vocational programs to create a new strand of studies for secondary schools to be known as "family studies." Kister (1994) has opposed this idea, saying the goals of family and consumer sciences could be met through alignment with vocational education, and noting that the focus of family and consumer sciences is the work of the family.

Family and consumer sciences education is also faced with community issues. Like some other subject areas, family and consumer sciences has received criticism from the Religious Right. Because many home and family life issues require ethical and moral decision making, some community members have taken the position that these topics are not the domain of the school (McQuaide and Pliska 1994, Kaplan 1994). Other community members have been avid supporters of the need for schools to address family issues and reinforce values such as respect, responsibility, integrity, and concern for others. Several states that attempted to include family or value issues in statewide directions for schools, such as Pennsylvania, Virginia, and Ohio, dropped references to values from their recommendations due to public criticism (Kaplan 1994). Most family and consumer sciences programs have addressed this issue at the local level. Building strong support for programs through local advisory committees, family involvement in programming, and positive visibility through community service learning are among the strategies that have led to strong community support of local family and consumer sciences programs.

Summary

Brown and her followers have brought about significant change in family and consumer sciences education. She called educators in this field to attention and challenged them to examine what was being done and what should be done. This call brought about reflection and renewal.

At its 96th annual meeting in June 1994, the American Home Economics Association changed its name to the American Association of Family and Consumer Sciences. Many home economics education programs across the country followed suit. In Ohio, Wisconsin, Nebraska, Iowa, and many other states, the secondary Home Economics Program is now called Family and Consumer Sciences. This change in name is not the essence of what has happened in family and consumer sciences over the past decade, but it is one very visible outcome of the substantial changes that have taken place in what was once known almost universally as home economics. One thing, however, has not changed: this field of study still retains its focus on the work of the family.

Family and consumer sciences education is moving to a process-oriented curriculum, emphasizing thinking and practical problem solving, communication, and interpersonal relationships as central processes around which to build the family-focused curriculum. The programs serve the needs of diverse audiences, including youth, adults, and at-risk populations. Enrollments in secondary programs are increasing, especially in states using a process-oriented curriculum (Kister, personal communication, August 1994).

There is much controversy about curriculum and programming in family and consumer sciences, but this controversy is viewed as a necessary and healthy part of the profession's move into the 21st century.

References

Allenspach, D. (September 1994). "High Tech in the Home Economics Classroom." *Vocational Education Journal* 69, 6: 52.

American Home Economics Association. (1989). *Home Economics Concepts: A Base for Curriculum Development*. Alexandria, Va.: Author.

American Vocational Association. (1994). *Home Economics Vision and Mission Statement*. Alexandria, Va.: Author.

Bobbitt, N. (1989). "Conceptualizing Curriculum in Home Economics." In *Home Economics Concepts: A Base for Curriculum Development*. Alexandria, Va.: American Home Economics Association.

Boggs, H., and J. Kister. (1994). "Helping Adolescents Solve Problems in Caring Ways." In *The Education of Early Adolescents: Home Economics in the Middle School,* edited by F.M. Smith and C. Hausafus. Home Economics Teacher Education Yearbook 14. Peoria, Ill.: Glencoe Division of Macmillan-McGraw Hill.

Brown, M. (1978). *A Conceptual Scheme and Decision-Rules for the Selection and Organization of Home Economics Curriculum Content*. Bulletin No. 0033. Madison: Wisconsin Department of Public Instruction.

Brown M. (1980). *What Is Home Economics Education?* St. Paul: Minnesota Research and Development Center for Vocational Education.

Brown, M. (1985). *Philosophical Studies in Home Economics in the United States: Our Practical-Intellectual Heritage,* Vols. I and II. East Lansing: College of Human Ecology, Michigan State University.

Author's Note: I am indebted to the following persons for agreeing to be interviewed and then reviewing this chapter, which is based in part on those interviews: Francine Hultgren, University of Maryland; Judy Jax, University of Wisconsin–Stout; Julie Johnson, University of Nebraska–Lincoln; Joanna Kister, Ohio Department of Education; Janet Laster, The Ohio State University; Ruth Thomas, University of Minnesota; and Marla Wyatt, Central Washington University.

Brown, M. (1986). "Home Economics: A Practical or Technical Science?" In *Vocational Home Economics Curriculum: State of the Field,* edited by J. Laster and R. Dohner. Teacher Education Yearbook 6. Peoria, Ill.: Bennett and McKnight Publishing, a division of Macmillan.

Brown, M., and B. Paolucci. (1979). *Home Economics: A Definition.* Washington, D.C.: American Home Economics Association.

Brown, R. (September 1994). "Teacher Pages: Open All Night." *Vocational Education Journal* 69, 6: 52.

Cunningham, R. (1992). "Curriculum Orientation of Nebraska Home Economics Teachers." Unpublished master's thesis, University of Nebraska, Lincoln.

Dohner, R.E. (1994). "Home Economics as Part of an Integrated Middle School Curriculum." In *The Education of Early Adolescents: Home Economics in the Middle School,* edited by F.M. Smith and C. Hausafus. Home Economics Teacher Education Yearbook 14. Peoria, Ill.: Glencoe Division of Macmillan-McGraw Hill.

Eisner, E. (1985). "Five Basic Orientations to the Curriculum." In *The Educational Imagination: On the Design and Evaluation of School Programs,* edited by E. Eisner. New York: Macmillan.

Eisner. E.W., and E. Vallance. (1974). *Conflicting Conceptions of Curriculum.* Berkeley, Calif.: McCutchan.

Fauske, I. (1994). "An Ideal Middle School Curriculum.

In *The Education of Early Adolescents: Home Economics in the Middle School,* edited by F.M. Smith and C. Hausafus. Home Economics Teacher Education Yearbook 14. Peoria, Ill.: Glencoe Division of Macmillan-McGraw Hill.

Fedje. C.G. (1992). "Toward a New View of Inservice Education." In *Lives and Plans: Signs for Transforming Practice,* edited by L. Peterat and E. Vaines. Teacher Education Yearbook 12. Mission Hills, Calif.: Glencoe Division of Macmillan-McGraw Hill.

Habermas, J. (1992). *Postmetaphysics Thinking: Philosophical Essays.* Translated by W.M. Hohengarten. Cambridge, Mass.: The MIT Press.

Hultgren, F. (1986). "Value Reasoning Design: Pennsylvania State University Curriculum Project." In *Vocational Home Economics Curriculum: State of the Field,* edited by J. Laster and R. Dohner. Teacher Education Yearbook 6. Peoria, Ill.: Bennett and McKnight Publishing, a division of Macmillan.

Hultgren, F. (1989). "Being Called by the Stories of Student Teachers: Dialogical Partners in the Journey of Teaching." In *Alternative Modes of Inquiry in Home Economics Research,* edited by F. Hultgren and D. Coomer. Teacher Education Yearbook 9. Peoria, Ill.: Glencoe Division of Macmillan-McGraw Hill.

Hultgren, F. (1990). "Bases for Curriculum Decision in Home Economics." *Illinois Teacher* 33, 5: 162–166.

Hultgren, F. (1991). "Stories, Standpoints, and Contradictions: Developing a Critical Orientation in Undergraduate Programs for Everyday Life." *People and Practice: International Issues for Home Economists* 3, 1: 1–23.

Hultgren, F. (1992). "The Transformative Power of 'Being With' Students in Teaching." In *Lives and Plans: Signs for Transforming Practice*, edited by L. Peterat and E. Vaines. Teacher Education Yearbook 12. Mission Hills, Calif.: Glencoe Division of Macmillan-McGraw Hill.

Hultgren, F. (1994). "Interpretive Inquiry as a Hermeneutics Practice." *Journal of Vocational Home Economics Education* 12, 1: 11–25.

Hultgren, F., and J. Wilkosz. (1986). "Human Goals and Critical Realities: A Practical Problem Framework for Developing Home Economics Curriculum." *Journal of Vocational Home Economics Education* 4, 2: 135–154.

Iowa Department of Public Instruction. (1985). *Scope and Sequence for Vocational Home Economics*. Des Moines: Career Education Division, Iowa Department of Public Instruction, p. 35.

Kaplan, G.R. (1994). "Shotgun Wedding: Notes on Public Education's Encounter with the New Christian Right." *Phi Delta Kappan* 75, 9: 1–12.

Kister, J. (1989). "Mission Statement." In *Home Economics Concepts: A Base for Curriculum Development*. Alexandria, Va.: The American Home Economics Association, pp. 1–3.

Kister, J. (1994). Letter to the Editor. *Journal of Home Economics* 86, 2: 3.

Klein, S. (1993). "Changing Roles at Home: Implications for Secondary Programs." *Journal of Home Economics* 85, 4: 19–26.

Laster, J. (1985). *Cognitive Psychology in Curriculum Planning*. Columbus: The National Center for Research in Vocational Education, The Ohio State University.

Laster, J. (1987). "Instructional Strategies for Teaching Practical Reasoning in Consumer Homemaking Classrooms." In *Higher Order Thinking: Definition, Meaning and Instruction Approaches*, edited by R. Thomas. Washington D.C.: The Home Economics Education Association.

Laster, J. (1989). "Practical Problem-Based Curriculum Design." In *Home Economics Concepts: A Base for Curriculum Development*. Alexandria, Va.: The American Home Economics Association.

Love, C. (February 1994). Presentation at annual meeting of National Council of Administrators in Home Economics, Greensboro, N.C.

Lounsbury, J. (1994). "The School Is a Teacher." In *The Education of Early Adolescents: Home Economics in the Middle School*, edited by F.M. Smith and C. Hausafus. Home Economics Teacher Education Yearbook 14. Peoria, Ill.: Glencoe Division of Macmillan-McGraw Hill.

McQuaide, J., and A. Pliska. (1994). "The Challenge to Pennsylvania's Education Reform." *Educational Leadership* 51, 4: 16–21.

Meszaros, P. (November 1981). "Toward the Year 2000: Directions for Home Economics Education." Paper presented at the Home Economics Future Committee meeting, Albany, N.Y.

Mid-America Vocational Curriculum Consortium, Inc. (1992). *Impact of Technology on the Family*. Stillwater, Okla.: Mid-America Vocational Curriculum Consortium, Inc.

Ohio Department of Education. (1990). *Ohio Middle School Resource Guide.* Columbus: Vocational Materials Laboratory, The Ohio State University.

Ohio Department of Education. (1992–94). *Work and Family Life Resource Guide.* Columbus: Vocational Materials Laboratory, The Ohio State University.

Redick, S., and A. Vail. (1992). *Motivating Youth at Risk.* Gainesville, Va.: Home Economics Education Association.

Schultz, J. (1994). "Family Life Education: Implications for Home Economics Teacher Education. *Journal of Home Economics* 86, 2: 30–37.

Smith, F.M., and J. Morgan. (1986). "Concepts and Generalizations Revisited." *Journal of Vocational Home Economics Education* 4, 2: 97–108.

Stout, B.L., and B.J. Smith. (1986). "Competency-Based Education: A Review of the Movement and a Look at the Future." *Journal of Vocational Home Economics Education* 4, 2: 109–134.

Thomas, R.G. (1986). "Alternative Views of Home Economics Education." *Journal of Vocational Home Economics Education* 4, 2: 162–188.

Thomas, R.G., ed. (1988a). *Thinking Underlying Expertise in Specific Knowledge Domains: Implications for Vocational Education.* St. Paul: Minnesota Research and Development Center for Vocational Education.

Thomas, R.G. (1988b). *The Tailored Response Test: An Approach to Assessing Higher Order Thinking Related to Work Roles and Contexts.* St. Paul: Minnesota Research and Development Center for Vocational Education.

Thomas, R.G., L. Anderson, B.D. Cooke, and L. Getahun. (1992). *Teaching for Transfer of Learning.* Berkeley: National Center for Research in Vocational Education, University of California at Berkeley.

Thomas, R.G., and M. Englund. (1989). *Instructional Design for Developing Higher Order Thinking Volume I: Knowledge Domain Development.* St. Paul: Minnesota Research and Development Center for Vocational Education.

Thomas, R.G., and M. Englund. (1990). *Instructional Design for Facilitating Higher Order Thinking Volume II: Instructional Design Model.* St. Paul: Minnesota Research and Development Center for Vocational Education.

Wilsman, M. (1986). "Modes of Rationality: Thinking About Curriculum." In *Vocational Home Economics Curriculum: State of the Field,* edited by J. Laster and R. Dohner. Teacher Education Yearbook 6. Peoria, Ill.: Bennett and McKnight Publishing, a division of Macmillan.

Wisconsin Department of Public Instruction. (1987). *A Guide to Curriculum Planning in Home Economics.* Madison: Wisconsin Department of Public Instruction, pp. 28–30.

Wyatt, M. (1994). "Curriculum Orientation of Home Economic Leaders and Characteristics of Recommended Home Economics Curriculum Documents." Unpublished doctoral dissertation, The Ohio State University, Columbus.

7

The School Mathematics Curriculum

Anna O. Graeber

Professional organizations have reached a relatively high degree of consensus about the K–12 goals of mathematics education. The *Curriculum and Evaluation Standards in School Mathematics*, issued by the National Council of Teachers of Mathematics (NCTM 1989), has the endorsement of numerous education associations, is widely cited, has reportedly sold over 180,000 copies, and is frequently hailed as a model for standards in other subject areas (Diegmueller 1994). Although many organizations and individuals have rallied behind the *Curriculum and Evaluation Standards in School Mathematics* (hereafter called NCTM Standards), such support must not be taken to mean that the mathematics curriculum as currently taught in schools, captured in commercial texts, and assessed by standardized tests reflects the curriculum outlined in the document. The NCTM Standards were written with the notion that they would be standard bearers for change. The shift to new goals, new curriculum, and new methods of teaching is detectable but slow.

Goals for Mathematics Education

Much of the current discussion of what the goals and content of school mathematics ought to be is driven by the NCTM Standards. This despite the fact that the document is already over a half-decade old and a commission is in place to consider revisions to it. Certainly, the NCTM Standards were influenced by prior calls for reform, such as those found in *A Nation at Risk* (National Commission on Excellence in Education 1983) and *Educating Americans for the 21st Century* (National Science Board Commission on Precollege Education in Mathematics, Sciences and Technology 1983). It also drew from goals proposed earlier, such as NCTM's (1980) *An Agenda for Action*, the Conference Board of the Mathematical Sciences' (1983) *New Goals for Mathematical Sciences Education*, The College Entrance Examination Board's (1985) *Academic Preparation in Mathematics*, and the National Council of Supervisors of Mathematics' (1988) *Essential Mathematics for the 21st Century*.

The NCTM Standards have also been used as a basis for the *Mathematics Framework for the National Assessment of Educational Progress* (NAEP) (United States Department of Education 1994), another potentially influential document in mathematics education. The fact that NAEP content strands are "intended to reflect NCTM's curricular emphases and objectives" (p. I) illustrates the extent to which the NCTM Standards have influenced other statements.

The overall goal identified by the NCTM Standards is the development of students who are mathematically literate or who have mathematical power (NCTM 1989, p. 5). Attainment of this overarching goal is believed to depend on ensuring that K–12 students (1) learn to value mathematics, (2) become confident in their ability to do mathematics, (3) become mathematical problem solvers, (4) learn to communicate mathematically, and (5) learn to reason mathematically (NCTM 1989, p. 5). This chapter deals primarily with the content standards, but readers should be aware that the mathematics education community recognizes that the attainment of these goals depends as much on how such curriculum is presented and assessed as it does on the content of the curriculum. This concern is reflected in the NCTM's publication of two companion documents to the NCTM Standards—*Professional Standards for Teaching Mathematics* (1991) and *Assessment Standards for School Mathematics* (1995).

The Need for New Goals

The NCTM Standards were developed to define criteria of excellence for assessing quality and to give direction for change. The momentum for establishing a new vision of the mathematics curriculum grew from a number of overlapping concerns, including (1) lower than desired student achievement; (2) less than positive student beliefs about mathematics; (3) questions about the adequacy of students' preparation (especially minorities and females) to compete in the world economic arena; (4) the rather pervasive and somewhat uniquely American belief that success in school mathematics requires a special ability possessed by only a few students; (5) the belief that higher-order thinking and problem-solving skills were displaced in the "back to the basics" movement of the '70s; (6) the perceived need for a better-educated citizenry that can make informed decisions about the increasingly technological and complex issues affecting society; (7) changing notions of what mathematics is critical, given the widespread availability of calculators and computers; (8) changes in the field of mathematics itself; and (9) new research findings and theories about children's learning.

The first six of these influences have been discussed in statements calling for general educational reform (see, for example, *Educating Americans for the 21st Century* [National Science Board Commission on Precollege Education in Mathematics, Science, and Technology 1983] and *A Nation at Risk* [National Commission on Excellence in Education 1983]) as well as in the mathematics education literature (e.g., Lapointe, Mead, and Phillips 1989; Mathematical Sciences Education Board 1989, 1990; Stigler and Barnes 1988). Therefore, there is little need to expound on those issues here. Some discussion of the last three issues, however, is necessary.

Influences of Technology and Changing Views of Mathematics

Mathematicians no longer consider mathematics to be confined to the study of numbers and shapes (Davis and Hersh 1981, Steen 1990). Rather, mathematics includes, among other ideas, the study of patterns, chaos, and uncertainty. Further, the subject of the patterns and logic studied is no longer tightly held to numbers and spatial relations. Recommendations for the K–12 curriculum now include many topics related to the study of probability and the collection and analysis of data. And an emphasis on students' justification of ideas is due to current learning theories that emphasize understanding and to mathematicians' involvement in probing the meaning and forms of "acceptable" proof.

The proliferation of affordable technology has influenced both what is considered important to teach and the techniques available for teaching the mathematics curriculum. The widespread availability of calculators has resulted in decreased attention to speed and accuracy, with examples involving numerous multidigit numerals. For example, column addition of five- and six-digit addends and division exercises involving four-digit divisors have virtually disappeared from mathematics textbooks, while additional emphasis is focused on place value, number sense, and estimation so that students can assess the reasonableness of machine-calculated answers. Decimal notation appears on four-function calculators, suggesting that decimal notation needs to be introduced to students earlier than in the past.

At the secondary level, graphing calculators make possible for students to study relationships modeled by quadratic and higher-powered expressions prior to learning algorithms for factoring such expressions or studying calculus. Even though calculus remains important in mathematics, computers that solve and explore problems have resulted in renewed interest in recursive methods and the use of other areas of mathematics associated with discrete mathematics (such as mathematics that deals with discrete or finite sets and topics such as graph theory, matrices, and iteration). The field of computer graphics has similarly influenced mathematical methods and objects of study. The art produced by the study of fractal geometry is but one "product" of this new way of viewing and doing mathematics.

Further, the very existence of some technologies for teaching can, in turn, influence what is taught and when it is taught. Calculators and computers that generate tables of data and graphs for given functions make the identification of roots, relative maximum, and relative minimum points available without factoring or calculus. Spreadsheet, function analyzer, and geometric tool programs make possible the exploration of multiple hypotheses in a short time. Such facility stimulates students to generate, test, and prove their own hypotheses rather than only re-prove classical theorems with centuries-old proofs (see Yerushalmy, Chazan, and Gordon 1987).

Influence of Learning Theory and Research on Learning

Understanding and personal construction of meaning are prevalent themes in almost all current discussions of learning theory. Student understanding of mathematics is not a new goal (e.g., Brownell 1935), though the emphasis given to it has varied over time. The present emphasis on personal construction of meaning is somewhat newer in mathematics education and is certainly linked to the ongoing interest in constructivism.

Postbehaviorist theories permit discussion of individuals' internal and external representation of ideas and the connections among them. These representations and their connections are currently seen as crucial to understanding; and facilitating children's construction of such connections through use of appropriate and worthwhile mathematical tasks is considered a critical teacher task. A major concern centers around students' understanding the use of symbol systems prior to being asked to use them. Consider, for example, the problem:

> *Shareen brought 3 markers to school. She found some more markers in her desk and now has 7 markers. How many markers did Shareen find in her desk?*

Students generally understand the equation $3 + \Delta = 7$ as an appropriate sentence for this word problem before they recognize $7 - 3 = \Delta$ as an equally valid representation. Allowing students to characterize the problem with an addition sentence rather than requiring them to use the subtraction sentence is one way to validate students' understanding. The longer-term goal, of course, is for students to understand that either sentence is appropriate and that the two are mathematically equivalent.

Another prevalent theme in research on mathematics learning is the influence of social interaction on cognitive development. Frequently traced to Vygotsky (1962), the theory that cognitive structures come about through social interaction finds support in studies of situated knowledge (Lave 1988, Saxe 1988) and "cognitive apprenticeships." In addition to raising the potential value of social interaction in the classroom, the theory highlights the need for learning activities relevant to each learner's culture. This view supports increasing emphases on beginning instruction with culturally relevant, meaningful problems and the value of discussion, writing, and other forms of communication in the classroom.

The emphasis on meaningful and culturally relevant activity is extremely important in school mathematics, which is all too frequently viewed by students as irrelevant or as a "male" or "white" activity (Fordham and Ogbu 1986, Meyer 1986). The importance of discourse is reflected in the NCTM Standards and the *Professional Standards for Teaching Mathematics* (NCTM 1991). In fact, Teaching Standard #2 in the 1991 document concerns "The teacher's role in discourse" (pp. 35–45).

Content Expectations

The NCTM Standards are organized into three grade levels—K–4, 5–8 and 9–12—with 13 or 14 standards at each level. In the following sections, I summarize the intent of the four standards that appear at each of the levels and discuss the remaining standards by grade level. These remaining NCTM standards are explored in clusters related to mathematics topics. This format highlights the essence of the topic areas and points out both significant differences from the past and areas currently under debate.

Across the Grades, K–12

Mathematics as Problem Solving, Mathematics as Communication, Mathematics as Reasoning, and Mathematical Connections are featured at each grade level in the NCTM Standards. NCTM believes these processes or themes should characterize instruction in all topics throughout the mathematics curriculum.

Mathematics as Problem Solving. Perhaps a major change in the role of problem solving in mathematics is the notion that problems should be the starting point, not the culminating activity, in learning mathematics. Beginning mathematics discussions with a problem meaningful to students provides motivation and purpose to the practice of mathematics and provides a context that helps support students' reasoning. For example, relatively simple word problems, such as the problem involving Shareen and her pencils, are now considered a starting point for knowledge of the basic addition and subtraction facts. Previously, students learned addition and subtraction facts and were then given an opportunity to apply them in word problems. Similarly, newer algebra curriculums give students variables to model situations (for example, the time it takes a skateboard to traverse a ramp of fixed length as a function of the height of the raised end) prior to teaching them to manipulate algebraic expressions.

Problems should be increasingly sophisticated in higher grades, but at every level, problem sets should include a variety of problems that are open ended, have no answer or more than one answer, involve significant investments of time (days), and are used in group settings. Students should also be encouraged to pose their own problems.

Although this "begin-with-problem-solving" perspective is widely though not universally shared, it represents a significant shift for mathematics teachers and is not faithfully reflected in many existing commercial textbooks.

Mathematics as Communication. The standard concerning Mathematics as Communication calls for relating and representing ideas through pictures, graphs, oral statements, or written discussions, with the form and sophistication of such communication becoming more advanced at each grade level. Communicating ideas prompts students to make new connections, clarify their thinking, and use mathematical language. Such communication within the classroom helps all students understand alternative methods and provides teachers with insights into students' understanding. Writing in the mathematics classroom; asking for more than "yes," "no," or a numeric answer; and asking students to justify correct and incorrect responses represent significant changes in practice for many mathematics teachers.

Mathematics as Reasoning. This standard encompasses the processes of conjecturing, testing, and proving. These processes underscore the reasons for doing things in mathematics and the importance of being able to explain one's thinking to others. Of course, the nature of the justification will be determined, in part, by the age and ability of the student. Traditionally, students were generally not required to justify their conclusions or processes until 10th grade geometry. However, the NCTM Standards suggest that early informal justifications based on models, illustrations, or simple logical reasoning precede more formal use of inductive and deductive logic in longer and more rigorous proofs.

Mathematics as Connections. This standard requires relating mathematical ideas to one another and to other fields. Understanding mathematics requires that procedures, or algorithms, be meaningful; that various representations (e.g., the equation, its graph, and a table of values) be understood to represent the same relationship; and that mathematics be linked to other subjects. A student who sees the connections among the square of a number, the geometric shape "square," and the expression $(a+b)^2$ has a much richer understanding of each. Also making connections to other subjects provides contexts for problems and illustrates the usefulness of mathematics outside the mathematics classroom.

Primary and Early Elementary Mathematics

Recommended for the K–4 level are an emphasis on understanding, the use of physical materials, the application of mathematics to everyday situations, and the appropriate use of calculators.

Numbers, Operations, and Computation. In the arena of numbers, primary attention at this level is given to number sense, the meaning of multidigit numbers, common fractions, and decimals. In computation, emphasis is on the meaning of the four operations (addition, subtraction, multiplication, and division), at least as they apply to whole numbers, estimation of results, and the use of mental arithmetic. The "basic facts" (facts involving addends or factors 0–9) are not ignored but prior to extensive drill or memorization of the facts, emphasis is given to the meaning of the operations, the use of facts in word problems, and the development of thinking strategies. Mathematical thinking strategies include schemes for building upon easy facts—usually doubles such as $5 + 5 = 10$. Students with flexible understanding of numbers can reason that $5 + 6$ is $5 + 5$ and 1 more. Research supports the belief that students given a rich variety of the many types of addition and subtraction problems learn their basic facts (Carpenter, Fennema, Peterson, Chiang, and Loef 1989). Evidence also suggests that textbooks generally include a very limited range of types of addition and subtraction word problems and that despite the absence of multiplication word problems in early grade level texts, students exposed to modeling, counting, or repeated addition strategies can solve such word problems (Fuson 1992). Students are encouraged to use calculators to solve problems with "large numbers" and to begin to make distinctions about the form of calculation (mental, paper and pencil, calculator) appropriate to different situations.

In the arena of operations, NCTM (1989) suggests that the development of standard algorithms "emphasize the meaningful development of these procedures" (p. 47). Experts in mathematics education disagree on the timing and extent to which instruction in "the standard algorithms" is appropriate. Some argue that the informal algorithms students develop (e.g., reasoning that $45 + 38 = 7$ tens and 13 ones or 8 tens and 3 ones or 83) be used and the standard algorithms not be taught (e.g., Kamii, Lewis, and Livingston 1993). Others suggest that once students have developed and understand their own algorithms, the standard algorithms be introduced as an efficient alternative. Still others argue that the "standard algorithms" are an important part of mathematics and should be taught relatively early.

Two other recommendations that deviate sharply from past practice in teaching computation are that (1) examples requiring regrouping should not be isolated from examples not requiring regrouping when teaching addition, subtraction, and multiplication algorithms, and (2) problems with and without remainders be used throughout the teaching of division.

Operations with decimals and common fractions are limited to addition and subtraction and should be related to models. Finding fractional parts of sets (e.g., $\frac{1}{3}$ of 12) can be modeled with sets and related to division.

Probability and Statistics. Even at these early elementary levels, the collection and analysis of data are suggested. Relative to past curriculums, less importance is attached to examining previously constructed graphs (traditionally limited to bar graphs) with more emphasis placed on having students begin with a question and then decide how to collect, display, and interpret the resulting data. Data displays may be simply organized lists or tables, Venn diagrams, tree diagrams, or even line plots and simple stem and leaf plots.

Experiences that lead to understanding of probability are also recommended. Such experiences are not intended to include quantitative formalizations of probability, but rather experience with coin tossing, dice, and spinners. Notions such as "more or less likely" and "fair chance" can be built on such experiences.

These topics can be found in most current commercial textbooks, but are frequently treated as peripheral and not developed from actual, hands-on, real-world experiences.

Geometry and Measurement. In the early grades, geometry is often neglected or reduced to the naming of geometric figures. Newer curriculum tasks in geometry are intended to help focus children's attention on the properties of common shapes (number of sides or angles, relative size of sides or angles, and symmetries) and the relationships among them. Reasoning is to be used and patterns explored in areas not directly involving number. Students are encouraged to investigate how shapes appear after rotation, enlargement, or reflection and how two-dimensional shapes can be partitioned or joined and replicated to form tessellations or three-dimensional objects.

In the realm of measurement, the focus on understanding calls for the use of nonstandard units and many experiences with counting repeated units, as opposed to merely using formulas to determine measures such as perimeter and area. Students are expected to have a sense of the "size" of various units and to make reasonable estimates of the dimensions of objects relevant to their experiences. Little is said in the NCTM Standards about the use of the metric or English systems of measurement, but the examples at all levels suggest parallel development and use of both systems.

Patterns and Relationships. The concept of pattern appears in the early levels and is carried through high school. Previously, patterns based on color and other qualitative characteristics were included in activities designed to develop students' classification, ordering, and seriation processes. Piagetian notions about cognitive development suggest that these processes are necessary for the understanding of number. Current recommendations, however, make less of these processes as prerequisites for understanding number. The search for and study of patterns is seen as a fundamental mathematical activity.

Tasks designed to develop the understanding of patterns and number are intertwined. Early on, patterns are applied to quantitative as well as qualitative notions. Number patterns encountered in counting, in the hundreds chart, in a multiplication table, or derived from use of a constant function on a calculator can be used in an activity involving the search for and description of patterns. In the middle elementary grades, these descriptions may even employ symbolic expressions, such as $\Delta = 3 + \square$.

A clear trend involves introducing algebraic ideas in earlier grades. This trend is the result of three movements. First, it relates to interest in having students come into contact with these ideas gradually, rather than facing all of the new forms and meanings (some of which contradict experience in arithmetic) in Algebra I. (See, for example, Booth 1988.) Second, it is a result of the belief that algebra is a fundamental part of mathematics, which can be useful at these levels. And third, it is a consequence of the "algebra for everyone" movement and the larger discussion of what should be taught in algebra.

Middle School Mathematics

Data from the Second International Mathematics Study (McKnight, Crosswhite, Dossey, Kifer, Swafford, Travers, and Cooney 1987) provide a critique of the traditional middle school curriculum. Teacher reports and studies indicated that textbooks at this level contained little new material, and the same topics reappeared each year with limited variation in treatment. Computation was a major topic, especially in early chapters of the texts, which were most likely to be covered. Eighth grade students in a number of other countries studied relatively more geometry and algebra than 8th graders in the United States. The NCTM Standards suggest a broad range of topics for all students and note that lack of mastery of computation with whole numbers should not prevent students from studying this range of topics.

Numbers, Operations, and Computation. The realm of numbers in grades 5–8 includes acquisition of meaning for rational numbers, the equivalence of forms (common fractions, decimals, percents, and numbers in scientific notation), the ordering of rational numbers, and the extension of the meanings of the four operations to rational numbers. New recommendations rebut the old adage, "Yours is not to question why, just invert and multiply." Instead, these recommendations emphasize a sense of the magnitude of results and use of estimation to verify results of operations with rational numbers. The understanding and applications of ratios and proportions are a major topic, but again, there is concern about how these notions are taught. The quick-fix, cross-multiplication method of solving proportions is shunned, at least initially, for methods more clearly linked to students' understanding of the meaning of ratio. In the arena of proportions, the generation of an equivalent unit ratio (with numerator of 1) helps make the ordering of two ratios or generation of equivalent ratios relatively easy and understandable.

A 6-ounce container of yogurt costs 44 cents. If the cost per ounce is the same, how much should an 8-ounce container of yogurt cost?

In the yogurt problem above, for example, students might use a unit ratio to find the cost of one ounce of yogurt (44/6) and then multiply by 8. Or, recognizing that both 6 and 8 are multiples of 2, students might use the technique dubbed "nice multiple"—i.e., find the cost of 2 ounces (44/3) and then multiply by four.

The study of whole numbers is extended to investigate multiples and factors and the composition of composite numbers from prime factors. Skill is expected in the selection of appropriate ways to compute (estimate versus exact, mentally versus paper and pencil, calculator, or computer) in given circumstances and with given numbers.

Geometry and Measurement. The trends noted in K–4 geometry and measurement continue in grades 5–8 (i.e., less emphasis on geometry as mastery of a vocabulary and on measurement as mastery of formulas, but more emphasis on relationships). Vocabulary is to be learned (e.g., *parallel*, *perpendicular*, *similar*, and *congruent*), and formulas are developed through experiences drawing figures and describing and characterizing geometric figures found in art and nature. Notions of perimeter, area, and volume are extended, and relationships among these measures are explored (for example, relationships between the area and perimeter of rectangles or the circumference and area of circles). Derived units are developed (e.g., speed, cost per unit, and miles per gallon).

Partitioning complex shapes to find total area and exploring relationships such as that embodied in the Pythagorean theorem provide experiences involving measurement and geometry. Selecting appropriate units for specific measurement tasks and using and estimating measures in hands-on settings are also recommended content.

Probability and Statistics. Statistics in the middle school continues to emphasize the use of data for addressing questions of interest or solving realistic problems. The decisions about what data to collect, from where, how, and how to display them, continue to be a part of the mathematics curriculum. The curriculum includes forms of display (including box and whisker plots, circle graphs, and tables in database computer programs) as formulation and analysis of arguments based on data become more involved with notions of central tendency (mean, median, and mode) and spread.

Probability is still to be rooted in real experiments, but now theoretical and empirical probabilities can be derived or calculated. Tables, tree diagrams, and area models are used to array possible outcomes. Students make predictions based on probability statements. The NCTM Standards emphasize the use of probability in "real-world contexts" (for example, weather reports).

Patterns, Functions, and Algebra. In the NCTM Standards, two of the 13 standards at the middle school level are devoted to the topics of patterns, functions, and algebra. The focus at this level becomes somewhat more symbolic. Even though patterns and functions are derived from real experiments or experiences, the expression of these patterns clearly extends beyond tables and graphs to the use of variables to express both a specific unknown (e.g., $x + 6 = 15$) and a generalized number (e.g., $3x$). Some topics associated with Algebra I are recommended, including the expression of relationships as linear equations and the solution of linear equations using informal techniques (guess and test, reading estimates from computer or calculator graphs) and more formal computational methods. Situations with relationships leading to inequalities and nonlinear relationships are also recommended for informal investigation. Emphasis is placed on connections among models, symbolic rules, and graphs.

High School Mathematics

At this level, NCTM makes a clear call for the elimination of the general mathematics track that frequently includes multiple repetitions of middle school arithmetic. The NCTM Standards propose that *all* high school students study, albeit to various depths, a three-year core curriculum that includes topics in algebra, geometry, trigonometry, probability, statistics, discrete mathematics, and the underpinnings of calculus. This core curriculum is meant to ensure that all students have an opportunity to learn the mathematics crucial for continued study, success at work, and effective citizenship. The NCTM Standards also identify additional topics and four years of mathematics for "college-intending students."

While it is assumed that students who have experienced the elementary and middle school curriculum based on the NCTM Standards will by and large possess the computational proficiency outlined therein, poor computational skills should not prevent students from studying the topics outlined in the core curriculum. Calculators and computers are expected to carry much of the computation. The discussion below emphasizes content in the core curriculum, although some attention is given to the topics for college-bound students.

Algebra, Functions, and Trigonometry. The topics of algebra, functions, and trigonometry involve many of the traditional concepts associated with these subjects. However, in each of these topics less attention is focused on algorithmic operations, especially early, with greater emphasis placed on motivating the use of algebra through the modeling of real-world phenomena. The use of graphing calculators and function analyzer software is considered central to the study of these topics.

In the NCTM core curriculum, trigonometry is confined to problem solving, using the trigonometry of the right triangle and the exploration of periodic functions such as those associated with sound waves and tides. More formal study of the trigonometric functions and their relationship to circular functions is suggested for college-intending students.

In algebra, college-intending students are expected to study the composition of functions, functions and their inverses, and functions involving two variables and to have greater skill in transforming algebraic equations and in using matrices to solve linear systems.

Geometry. Geometry is studied from synthetic (descriptive/deductive) and algebraic (coordinate geometry) points of view. Congruence, similarity, and transformations are recommended topics and lend themselves to connections between these two approaches. Current recommendations also call for greater emphasis on the visualization and representation of two- and three-dimensional shapes.

Two geometric topics likely to be less familiar to curriculum planners are translations (flips, rotations, dilations, etc.) and vectors. All students are expected to use vectors to model phenomena such as force, to analyze properties of translations, to deduce properties of figures using translations, and to relate translations to vectors. College-intending students are expected to have greater facility in using transformations and vectors in problem-solving settings.

All students should be competent with short, deductive arguments. The deeper understanding of axiomatic systems, which comes from the study of different sets of axioms, is recommended for college-intending students.

Probability and Statistics. At the high school level, statistical concepts are extended to include the following: understanding and application of measures of central tendency, variability, and correlation; the use of curve fitting for prediction from existing data points; the role of sampling in data collection and claim making; and the effect of data transformation on measures of central tendency and variability. All of these concepts are to be studied in the context of real-world reports and claims, with students expected to design, execute, and report on a statistical study. College-intending students should also engage in hypotheses testing and the transformation and analysis of data using statistics.

NCTM recommends that in addition to using experimental and theoretical probabilities, high school students use simulations to estimate probability and understand the notion of random variable. All students are to be able to calculate and interpret discrete probability distributions, describe the normal curve, and apply its properties to data taken as normally distributed. College-intending students are also to calculate and interpret specific probability distributions (e.g., normal, binomial, and chi-square).

Discrete Mathematics and the Underpinnings of Calculus. These topics are grouped together here because they both call upon concepts from algebraic and geometric topics. Two proposals embedded in these topics are among the recommendations furthest from current practice. The first is that ideas from both discrete mathematics and calculus be included in the curriculum for all students, not just those intent on going to college. The second is that the formal study of calculus be eliminated, "even for college-intending students" (NCTM 1989, p. 180).

Students are expected to model situations using such discrete mathematics structures as finite graphs, matrices, and recursion functions. Tree diagrams can be used in probability, with algebraic and geometric models of scheduling problems and route planning used for finite graphs. Possible applications for studying recurrence relations include situations in population growth and compound interest rates. All students are expected to engage in the design and analysis of algorithms used in various procedures they have studied (e.g., finding the greatest common factor of two numbers, solution of linear equations, and geometric constructions such as bisecting an angle). College-intending students should also solve problems involving linear programming and investigate the use and testing of computer algorithms.

In place of the formal study of calculus, students should systematically but informally explore ideas such as limit, area under a curve, rates of change, and slope of a tangent line. Students should also use graphs to determine maximum and minimum points and interpret these in problem-solving contexts. The notion of limit should be explored though investigations with infinite sequences and series and areas under a curve.

For college-intending students, study of the underpinnings of calculus includes understanding the slope of the tangent to a curve as a generalization of the slope of a line, applying the rate of change and area under a curve, and analyzing graphs of a variety of functions (polynomial, radical, etc.). All topics are expected to involve the use of graphing calculators and computer technology.

Issues

Some issues arise from differences between practice and recommendations; others reflect disagreement or uncertainty about what the recommendations ought to be. As noted below, they are not all entirely independent of each other.

The Use of Calculators and Computers and the Role of Computation

Guidelines from the *NCTM Standards* state that

 • appropriate calculators should be available to all students at all times.
 • a computer should be available in every classroom for demonstration purposes.
 • every student should have access to a computer for individual and group work.
 • students should learn to use the computer as a tool for processing information and performing calculations to investigate and solve problems (p. 8).

Despite such recommendations, the decreasing cost of calculators and computers, and the use of calculators on tests (such as the SAT and advanced placement tests), there are still debates about what technology is appropriate at what level. These debates involve disagreements about issues such as when the simple four-function calculator should be replaced by those that compute with common fractions, graph equations, solve equations, or calculate with matrices. A further barrier to implementation is the fact that we are just now beginning to see curriculum materials that integrate calculators and computers into experiences that promote conceptual understanding.

In part, such debates about use of technology reflect a larger issue in mathematics education: the role of computation in understanding. In the mathematics education research literature, the discussion of this question often appears in discussions about the roles of conceptual and procedural knowledge (see, for example, Hiebert and Carpenter 1992). While many questions remain, theory and some empirical evidence suggest that if students are to develop meaning for mathematical symbols and rules, conceptual learning should precede practice for efficiency.

Algebra Instruction

The algebra curriculum is under scrutiny for several reasons. First is the generally accepted belief that algebra encompasses a way of thinking essential to mathematics and should be available to all students. One rationale for making algebra available to all students comes from studies suggesting that minority students who have successfully completed algebra and geometry are as likely to succeed at the college level as nonminority students (Pelavin and Kane 1990).

The availability of technology and the effort to make school mathematics more useful have also spurred reconsideration of what ought to be part of algebra for everyone. The use of calculators and computers to graphically display functions and obtain approximations of roots and maximal and minimal points tends to minimize the need for extensive skill in factoring expressions, extracting roots of equations, or graphing equations by hand. The amount of time traditionally spent on topics such as factoring, simplifying rational expressions, and linear functions is also called into question because many phenomena are modeled by equations difficult to factor, critical values are only needed to some finite degree of accuracy, and relationships investigated are not primarily linear in nature. Questions about the extent to which symbol manipulation should be transferred from hand to machine center around the role of computation in understanding and the issue of college-level expectations. *Algebra for the Twenty-first Century* (NCTM 1993) contains a summary of discussions about what algebra should be taught.

Organization of High School Curriculum and Tracking

Although researchers agree that grouping by ability or by achievement at the elementary and middle school level is undesirable, recommendations for grouping at the high school level vary. Certainly, high school students exhibit vast differences in their achievement and interest levels. Current recommendations generally favor more years of mathematics for all students and the elimination of general mathematics, but no consensus exists on how courses based upon the NCTM core curriculum are to be organized in terms of student population or subject matter. Is the core taught to heterogeneous groups of students with college-intending students provided additional courses, or should courses be organized by achievement levels? Are the subjects to be delivered in the traditional slots of algebra, geometry, probability, and statistics; or should the organization be closer to that of the unified mathematics courses in which most or all of the strands in the high school curriculum are incorporated each year?

Though there is no clear answer to these questions, it is difficult to imagine making the connections called for in the NCTM Standards in single-subject courses. Further, descriptions of comprehensive high school curriculum development projects supported by the National Science Foundation (1993) clearly indicate a more unified approach.

Articulation of the High School and Collegiate Curriculum

The college-level mathematics curriculum and the expectations of college professors certainly influence what is taught in high schools. Recent discussions about reform at the collegiate level have highlighted the disjuncture between expectations for the existing calculus curriculum and a more conceptually based calculus curriculum. A discussion of the distinctions between these two sets of expectations, from the point of view of college and university mathematics instructors, can be found in Steen (1988).

Universities and colleges often institute their own placement tests. Expectations reflected on many of these placement tests are largely confined to symbol manipulation. From the point of view of the high school, it is relatively clear that until current efforts to reform calculus (and other college-level mathematics courses) bring about changes in entrance expectations, high school teachers of college-intending students will remain at least partially committed to goals not completely in line with the spirit of the recommendations for the high school curriculum.

The Role and Form of Assessment

NCTM's recommendations recognize the press for assessments that reflect the goals of the new curriculum. The NCTM Standards include standards on evaluation, which are expanded upon in *Assessment Standards for School Mathematics* (NCTM 1995). Performance-based assessments include longer, more complex, contextualized tasks than traditional mathematics tests. Several standardized test companies, known for their multiple-choice mathematics tests, are now publishing performance assessment forms. Even the SAT has moved to some constructed answers and allows limited use of calculators with specified characteristics. Additionally, portfolio assessment is under way in a number of states, with the New Standards Project heavily invested in the creation and evaluation of portfolios in mathematics and other areas (Resnick, Briars, and Lesgold 1992). Yet uncertainty and ambivalence remain on several fronts.

Technical issues of validity and reliability continue to be raised about performance assessments. Can the tests/tasks teachers use to make decisions in the classroom be used for external validation of learning? Is this approach affordable in terms of student time and scoring time? While these questions are being debated, both short-answer, multiple-choice, and performance-based tests are being given to students, sometimes in alternate years. Multiple-choice tests are still widely used and remain incentives and measures of students' and teachers' success. It is unclear whether these different forms of testing can drive a cohesive curriculum. Further discussion of this issue can be found in Webb (1992).

Resources

NCTM offers many curriculum resources. In addition to the *Curriculum and Evaluation Standards for School Mathematics* (1989), the *Professional Standards for Teaching Mathematics* (1991), and the *Assessment Standards for School Mathematic* (1995), the Council's *Addenda Series* includes grade level and activity books for grades K–6, and activity books for grades 5–8 and 9–12. *A Core Curriculum—Making*

Mathematics Count for Everyone (Meiring, Rubenstein, Schultz, de Lange, and Chambers 1992) may be of special interest to educators responsible for the high school curriculum. Recent NCTM yearbooks, such as *Discrete Mathematics Across the Curriculum* K–12 (Kenney 1991) and *Calculators in Mathematics Education* (Fey 1992) give insights into how NCTM recommendations can be implemented. These publications are available from NCTM (1906 Association Drive, Reston, VA 22091-1593) and through some commercial vendors.

The National Science Foundation supports a number of comprehensive K–6, middle, and high school curriculum development projects designed to reflect current thinking about the mathematics curriculum. Names and addresses for these projects are available from the National Science Foundation, Directorate for Education and Human Resources, Division of Elementary, Secondary and Informal Science Education, Instructional Materials Development Program, Arlington, VA 22230.

References

Booth, L. (1988). "Children's Difficulties in Beginning Algebra." In *The Ideas of Algebra, K–12: 1988 Yearbook of the National Council of Teachers of Mathematics*, edited by A. Coxford. Reston, Va.: National Council of Teachers of Mathematics.

Brownell, W. (1935). "Psychological Considerations in the Learning and Teaching of Arithmetic." In *The Teaching of Arithmetic. Tenth Yearbook of the National Council of Teachers of Mathematics*, edited by W.D. Reeve. New York: Teachers College, Columbia University, pp. 1–31.

Carpenter, T., E. Fennema, P. Peterson, C. Chiang, and M. Loef. (1989). "Using Knowledge of Children's Mathematics Thinking in Classroom Teaching: An Experimental Study." *American Educational Research Journal* 26, 4: 499–531.

College Entrance Examination Board. (1985). *Academic Preparation in Mathematics*. New York: Author.

Conference Board of the Mathematical Sciences. (1983). "New Goals for Mathematical Sciences Education." Report of a conference sponsored by the Conference Board of Mathematical Sciences in Warrenton, Virginia. Washington, D.C.: Author.

Davis, P.J., and R. Hersh. (1981). *The Mathematical Experience*. Boston: Houghton Mifflin.

Diegmueller, K. (September 28, 1994). "Standards-Setters Hoping to Publish Best Sellers." *Education Week*, pp. 1, 15.

Fey, J. (1992). *Calculators in Mathematics Education. 1992 Yearbook of the National Council of Teachers of Mathematics*. Reston, Va.: National Council of Teachers of Mathematics.

Fordham, S., and J. Ogbu. (1986). "Black Students' School Success: Coping with the Burden of 'Acting White.'" *The Urban Review* 18, 3: 176–206.

Fuson, K. (1992). "Research on Whole Number Addition and Subtraction." In *Handbook of Research on Mathematics Teaching and Learning*, edited by D. Grouws. Reston, Va.: National Council of Teachers of Mathematics, and New York: Macmillan, pp. 243–275.

Hiebert, J., and T. Carpenter. (1992). "Learning and Teaching with Understanding." In *Handbook of Research on Mathematics Teaching and Learning*, edited by D. Grouws. Reston, Va.: National Council of Teachers of Mathematics, and New York: Macmillan, pp. 65–100.

Kamii, C., B. Lewis, and S. Livingston. (1993). "Primary Arithmetic: Children Inventing Their Own Procedures." *Arithmetic Teacher* 41, 3: 200–203.

Kenney, M. (1991). *Discrete Mathematics Across the Curriculum, K–12. 1991 Yearbook of the National Council of Teachers of Mathematics*. Reston, Va.: National Council of Teachers of Mathematics.

Lapointe, A., N. Mead, and G. Phillips. (1989). *A World of Differences: An International Assessment of Mathematics and Science*. Princeton, N.J.: Educational Testing Service.

Lave, J. (1988). *Cognition in Practice*. Cambridge: Cambridge University Press.

Mathematical Sciences Education Board. (1989). *Everybody Counts*. Washington, D.C.: National Academy Press.

Mathematical Sciences Education Board. (1990). *Reshaping School Mathematics*. Washington, D.C.: National Academy Press.

McKnight, C., F. Crosswhite, J. Dossey, E. Kifer, J. Swafford, K. Travers, and T. Cooney. (1987). *The Underachieving Curriculum*. Champaign, Ill.: Stipes Publishing.

Meiring, S., R. Rubenstein, J. Schultz, J. de Lange, and D. Chambers. (1992). *A Core Curriculum—Making Mathematics Count for Everyone: Addenda Series, Grades 9–12*. Reston, Va.: National Council of Teachers of Mathematics.

Meyer, R. (1986). "Gender Differences in Mathematics." In *Results from the Fourth Mathematics Assessment of the National Assessment of Educational Progress*, edited by M. Lindquist. Reston, Va.: National Council of Teachers of Mathematics, pp. 149–159.

National Commission on Excellence in Education. (1983). *A Nation at Risk: The Imperative for Educational Reform*. Washington, D.C.: U.S. Government Printing Office.

National Council of Supervisors of Mathematics. (June 1988). "Essential Mathematics for the 21st Century." *National Council of Supervisors of Mathematics Newsletter*.

National Council of Teachers of Mathematics. (1980). *An Agenda for Action: Recommendations for School Mathematics of the 1980s*. Reston, Va.: Author.

National Council of Teachers of Mathematics. (1989). *Curriculum and Evaluation Standards for School Mathematics*. Reston, Va.: Author.

National Council of Teachers of Mathematics. (1991). *Professional Standards for Teaching Mathematics*. Reston, Va.: Author.

National Council of Teachers of Mathematics. (1993). *Algebra for the Twenty-First Century* (Proceedings of the August 1992 Conference). Reston, Va.: Author.

National Council of Teachers of Mathematics. (1995). *Assessment Standards for School Mathematics*. Reston, Va.: Author.

National Science Board Commission on Precollege Education in Mathematics, Science, and Technology. (1983). *Educating Americans for the Twenty-First Century*. Washington, D.C.: National Science Foundation.

National Science Foundation. (1993). *Mathematics Instructional Materials: Pre-school-High School*. Washington, D.C.: National Science Foundation, Instructional Materials Development Program.

Pelavin, S., and M. Kane. (1990). *Changing the Odds: Factors Increasing Access to College*. New York: College Entrance Examination Board.

Resnick, L., D. Briars, and S. Lesgold. (1992). "Certifying Accomplishments in Mathematics: The New Standards Examining System." In *Developments in School Mathematics Around the World, Proceedings of the UCSMP International Conference on Mathematics Education, 1991*, edited by I. Wirszup and R. Streit. Reston, Va.: National Council of Teachers of Mathematics.

Saxe, G.B. (1988). "Candy Selling and Math Learning." *Educational Researcher* 17, 6: 14–21.

Steen, L., ed. (1988). "Calculus for a New Century: A Pump, Not a Filter." Papers presented at a colloquium in Washington, D.C., October 28–29, 1987. MAA Notes Number 8. Washington, D.C.: Mathematical Association of America.

Steen, L., ed. (1990). *On the Shoulders of Giants: New Approaches to Numeracy*. Washington, D.C.: National Academy Press.

Stigler, J.W., and R. Barnes. (1988). "Culture and Mathematics Learning." In *Review of Research in Education*, edited by E. Rothkopf. Washington, D.C.: American Educational Research Association.

United States Department of Education. (1994). *Mathematics Framework for the National Assessment of Educational Progress*. Washington, D.C.: National Center for Educational Statistics.

Vygotsky, L. (1962). *Thought and Language*. Cambridge, Mass.: MIT Press.

Webb, N. (1992). "Assessment of Students' Knowledge of Mathematics: Steps Toward a Theory." In *Handbook of Research on Mathematics Teaching and Learning*, edited by D. Grouws. Reston, Va.: National Council of Teachers of Mathematics, and New York: Macmillan.

Yerushalmy, M., D. Chazan, and M. Gordon. (1987). *Guided Inquiry Technology: A Year-Long Study of Children and Teachers Using the Geometric Supposer*. Cambridge, Mass.: Center for Learning Technology.

8

Physical Education Curriculum

Robert P. Pangrazi and Charles B. Corbin

Physical education (PE, phys ed, gym) has many different meanings. The physical education professional describes it as an essential subject matter dedicated to learning in the psychomotor domain and committed to developing lifetime physical activity patterns. Some mistakenly consider physical education to be the same as athletics or competitive sports, while still others equate it with recess or play during free time.

The differences in perceptions of physical education are a result of the wide variety of experiences of different individuals. Though physical education professionals consider true physical education nothing less than a quality instructional program conducted by a physical education specialist, students do not always experience this kind of program. National statistics indicate that only half of the children in grades 1 through 4 receive physical education three or more days per week (Ross, Pate, Corbin, Delpy, and Gold 1987). In many schools that do offer physical education in the early grades, "specialists," many without valid credentials, teach the classes. In some schools, classroom teachers oversee physical education, varying the content according to their own interests and qualifications. Some schools even consider recess or free play adequate physical education.

As in grades 1 through 4, fewer than half of the students in grades 5 and 6 have physical education three or more days per week. And the odds of having a qualified specialist for instruction are no better than for grades 1 through 4. In grades 7 and 8, the picture improves somewhat. Approximately 70 percent of children at these grade levels have physical education three or more days per week, and qualified specialists are likely to teach these programs because of the large number of students involved (Ross, Dotson, Gilbert, and Katz 1985).

In high school, the number of students enrolled in physical education drops dramatically. Only 21.5 percent of high school students have physical education three or more days a week, and an astounding 47.8 percent do not have even one physical education class. Enrollment is highest in grade 9 and very low in grades 11 and 12 (Center for Disease Prevention and Control 1991). Specialists usually teach phys ed in high school, but there is still some concern about the quality of instruction. For example, does the curriculum meet the needs of today's students? Does it teach students skills they can use for a lifetime? Does it give them the knowledge requisite for maintaining personal fitness?

Unlike elementary and middle school students, many high school students are exempt from physical education requirements for a variety of reasons, such as participation in band, interscholastic sports, and ROTC.

This chapter outlines important physical education outcomes, objectives, perspectives, and curriculum models. The models are based on the assumption that physical education is most effective when taught by specialists in physical education. These specialists know how to develop and carry out curricular plans that help learners meet important physical education objectives.

Physical Education Outcomes or Objectives

Anyone involved in designing or evaluating physical education programs should read the booklet *Outcomes of Quality Physical Education Programs,* developed by the National Association for Sport and Physical Education (NASPE 1992), an organization associated with the American Alliance for Health, Physical Education, Recreation, and Dance (AAHPERD). The booklet lists 20 major outcomes for a physically educated person in categories covering the psychomotor, affective, and cognitive learning domains (see Figure 8.1). It also includes specific benchmarks for students in kindergarten and grades 2, 4, 6, 8, 10, and 12. The benchmarks are examples of types of learning that educators should evaluate. They are not all-inclusive, but they do provide teachers with a minimum standard of assessment and the grade levels at which

FIGURE 8.1
Definitions and Outcomes of the Physically Educated Person

A PHYSICALLY EDUCATED PERSON:

HAS learned skills necessary to perform a variety of physical activities.

(1) Moves using concepts of body awareness, space awareness, effort, and relationships.

(2) Demonstrates competence in a variety of manipulative, locomotor, and nonlocomotor skills.

(3) Demonstrates competence in combinations of manipulative, locomotor, and nonlocomotor skills performed individually and with others.

(4) Demonstrates competence in many different forms of physical activity.

(5) Demonstrates proficiency in a few forms of physical activity.

(6) Has learned how to learn new skills.

IS physically fit.

(7) Assesses, achieves, and maintains physical fitness.

(8) Designs safe, personal fitness programs in accordance with principles of training and conditioning.

DOES participate regularly in physical activity.

(9) Participates in health enhancing physical activity at least three times a week.

(10) Selects and regularly participates in lifetime physical activities.

KNOWS the implications of and the benefits from involvement in physical activities.

(11) Identifies the benefits, costs, and obligations associated with regular participation in physical activity.

(12) Recognizes the risk and safety factors associated with regular participation in physical activity.

(13) Applies concepts and principles to the development of motor skills.

(14) Understands that wellness involves more than being physically fit.

(15) Knows the rules, strategies, and appropriate behaviors for selected physical activities.

(16) Recognizes that participation in physical activity can lead to multicultural and international understanding.

(17) Understands that physical activity provides the opportunity for enjoyment, self-expression, and communication.

VALUES physical activity and its contributions to a healthful lifestyle.

(18) Appreciates the relationships with others that result from participation in physical activity.

(19) Respects the role that regular physical activity plays in the pursuit of lifelong health and well-being.

(20) Cherishes the feelings that result from regular participation in physical activity.

Reprinted from *Outcomes of Quality Physical Education Programs* with permission of the American Alliance for Health, Physical Education, Recreation and Dance, 1900 Association Drive, Reston, VA 22091.

various learnings can be evaluated. They represent reasonable levels of achievement and give direction to a planned, systematic approach to evaluation.

NASPE's major outcome areas provide the basis for describing the physically educated person. Generally, experts agree that these areas—plus social skills and positive self-concept—constitute the major objectives of physical education and thus should be prominent factors in determining the focus and direction of physical education programs. Although the area of social skills and positive self-concept might fit into the "values" outcome in the NASPE model, many experts believe it is a general objective worthy of the consideration given to the other five areas of the model.

Whatever the curriculum model used, experts agree on the following objectives (Pangrazi and Dauer 1995).

Objective 1: The student has skill (motor skills and movement competence)

The school years are an excellent time to teach motor skills, because youngsters have the time and predisposition to learn them. Youngsters should have opportunities to learn a wide variety of skills. Children's genetic endowments and interests vary, so each child needs opportunities to explore his or her own facility in different skill areas. The hierarchy of skill development in this area progresses through four stages: fundamental motor skills, movement concepts skills, rhythmic movement skills, and specialized motor skills.

Fundamental Motor Skills. Fundamental motor skills are utilitarian skills that people use to enhance the quality of life. They are "fundamental" because they are basic attributes that contribute to a fully functioning individual. These skills fall into three categories. *Locomotor skills* move the body from one place to another or project the body upward, as in jumping and hopping; they include walking, running, skipping, leaping, sliding, and galloping. *Nonlocomotor skills* are performed in place, without appreciable spatial movement; they include bending and stretching, pushing and pulling, raising and lowering, twisting and turning, shaking, bouncing, and circling. *Manipulative skills* are developed by handling objects. When we manipulate objects, we develop hand-eye and foot-eye coordination, skills that are particularly important for tracking items in space. Manipulative skills such as throwing, striking, kicking, catching, rebounding, and redirecting objects in flight are basic to many games.

Movement Concepts Skills. Physical education teaches youngsters about the classification of movement concepts such as body awareness, space awareness, qualities of movement, and relationships. Students develop an increased awareness and understanding of the body as a vehicle for movement and acquire a personal vocabulary of movement skills.

Rhythmic Movement Skills. Individuals who excel in movement activities possess a strong sense of rhythmic ability. Rhythmic movement involves motion in a regular and predictable pattern. The aptitude to move rhythmically is basic to skill performance in all areas. A rhythmic program that includes dance, rope jumping, and rhythmic gymnastics offers a variety of activities to help attain this objective.

Specialized Motor Skills. Specialized motor skills are used in various sports and other areas of physical education, including apparatus activities, tumbling, dance, and specific games. When developing specialized skills, students progress through planned instruction and drills. Many of these skills have critical points of technique and emphasize correct performance.

Objective 2: The student is fit (health-related physical fitness and wellness)

Physical education programs provide students with the opportunity to participate in regular physical activity. Proper development emphasizes participation in regular daily activity, which in turn results in fitness to the extent that student motivation and heredity allow. Most experts believe that health-related fitness should be the overriding goal; this definition of fitness includes cardiovascular fitness, muscular strength, muscular endurance and flexibility, and body composition. Recent test batteries focus on the development of criterion-related health standards associated with reduced health risks rather than skill-related elements based on normative standards (Cooper Institute for Aerobic Research 1992).

Students should have opportunities to comment on the fitness program and to choose activities. Students meet health-related physical fitness objectives when they learn to accept responsibility for participating in regular activity, whether at school or at home. In high school, students should also meet higher-order objectives, such as fitness and activity problem solving and decision making.

Objective 3: The student has knowledge (human movement principles)

The school years should be years of opportunity—opportunity to experience many different types of physical activity. The curriculum should be expansive rather than restrictive, allowing students to better understand their strengths and limitations and to learn what types of activities they prefer. Related to this experience is the opportunity to learn basic concepts of movement. Students should leave school knowing about stability, force, leverage, and other factors related to efficient movement. Learning basic principles and concepts of physical activity, particularly how physical activity contributes to good health and wellness, is an important part of this knowledge objective.

Learning how to assess personal fitness and activity levels, how to plan activity programs, and how to make informed decisions about physical activity and fitness are also important objectives in this domain. Because each individual has unique needs, and because programs must be developed according to those needs, an understanding of genetic diversity among people (i.e., differences in muscle type, cardiorespiratory endurance, and motor coordination) helps students evaluate their physical capabilities.

Related to understanding principles of human movement is knowing how to safely participate in activity. Schools have the legal and moral obligation to provide a safe environment, which means actively teaching and modeling safety during activities. Instructional procedures in any activity include attention to safety factors, and active supervision is necessary to guide students in safe participation.

Objective 4: The student is active (lifetime participation in activity)

Many factors affect lifetime activity patterns. Sallis (1994) classifies the factors influencing people's lifetime activity patterns as psychological, social, physical environmental, and biological. A major role of physical education is to foster these four factors.

Psychological determinants are extremely powerful. Students must derive enjoyment from an activity if they are to regularly participate in it. Real enjoyment comes when we do not have to think about *how* to do something, but can just do it. If we want students to remain active throughout their lifetime, then we must help them become proficient in a variety of motor skills, for as adults, they may not be able to find the time to learn and practice new skills. Many adults will not participate in an activity unless they believe their skills are good enough for them to do so without embarrassment. Unfortunately, the hectic schedule that many adults keep leaves them little time to practice skills, so they may never reach what they believe is an adequate level of competence.

Another factor is the need for play. This can be established through activity orientations transferable to other situations. Such activities should include a variety of games suitable for small groups and sport activities adapted to local situations.

Social influences also affect lifetime activity patterns. These factors include having family and peer role models, encouragement from significant others, and opportunities to participate in activity with others in one's social group. Physical environmental factors include adequate programs, facilities, equipment, and supplies; safe outdoor environments; and opportunities for physical activity near home and at school. Opportunities at school include recess, physical education, intramurals, recreation programs, and sports.

Biological factors include age, gender, ethnicity, and socioeconomic status. For more details concerning determinants of physical activity, see Sallis 1994.

Objective 5: The student has social skills and a positive self-concept

Social skills and positive self-concept, though not among NASPE's categories of physical education outcomes, do appear under several major outcomes. Additionally, many physical educators believe that social skills and positive self-concept are high priorities for physical education. Most experts agree that physical education classes should offer an environment for effective social living.

Youngsters need to internalize and understand the merits of participation, cooperation, competition, and tolerance. Through empathetic listening and guidance, teachers can help students develop an awareness of how they interact with others and how the quality of their behavior influences others' responses to them. Through modeling, teachers can also help students differentiate between acceptable and unacceptable ways of expressing feelings. Teachers must establish reasonable limits of acceptable behavior and enforce those limits consistently.

Higher-Order Physical Education Objectives

Like any curriculum, a high-quality physical education program is designed to meeting higher-order educational objectives (Corbin 1994). When children come to school, they depend on teachers to provide them with meaningful learning experiences. As grade levels increase, so does the need to help learners become independent problem solvers and decision makers. Teacher-directed experiences are appropriate in the early grade levels, but high schools students should be involved in self-directed activities that help them meet higher-order objectives defined in the curriculum.

A major goal of physical education is to help students achieve lifetime physical activity patterns. Meaningful educational experiences within each of the major objectives help students become less dependent on others and more able to independently plan personal activity programs and to be informed participants in physical activity.

Perspectives Influencing Physical Education

Though physical education programs vary widely across the United States, most endorse similar goals and objectives greatly influenced by current social and professional perspectives. Most curriculum models are based on a variety of goals and objectives emanating from a variety of perspectives and theories. Nevertheless, some programs orient their programs more closely to one perspective than another. An understanding of these perspectives provides a better understanding of the different curriculum models presented later in this chapter.

Social/Historical Perspective

Early physical education in the United States was dominated by European gymnastics and highly organized and disciplined calisthenics programs. Many early leaders were European immigrants who brought these formal programs to the United States, implementing them first in colleges and then in the public schools (which were far more prevalent in the United States than in the immigrants' homelands).

In the late 1800s and early 1900s, a major shift began. As education in general was altered by the perspectives and teachings of Dewey and others, physical education shifted as well. Jesse F. Williams' text (1927), published in numerous editions, was one of several that changed the view of U.S. physical education. Williams championed democratic ideals and concepts of sportsmanship and teamwork. Thus, physical education's recent history is one of learning "through the physical." This perspective did not negate the importance of physical fitness and "education of the physical," but did place a strong emphasis on social development through physical education. This perspective continues to have currency in the field of physical education today.

Cultural/Sports Perspective

Since the turn of the century, sport has become not only a diversion for millions of American participants, but also for millions of American spectators (Eitzen and Sage 1986). Youth sports are now highly organized and have high rates of participation. Collegiate and professional sports have become big business. In 1972, Title IX provided girls and women even greater access to sports.

With the shift from formal gymnastics to more "American" activities, sport became central to many programs of physical education. Because sport had become part of the American culture, people naturally accepted the development and appreciation of sports skills as part of American education. This perspective accounts for the emphasis placed on sports in the expanded curriculum, which includes interscholastic and intramural programs.

Public Health Perspective

In the 1950s, President Eisenhower established the President's Council on Youth Fitness because of concern about the fitness of American youth. The next decade saw the beginnings of the fitness boom that continues to this day.

Recent studies suggest that physical inactivity among adults is a primary risk factor for heart disease and a major contributor to other diseases as well. In the first chapter, *Healthy People 2000* (U.S. Department of Health and Human Services 1990) recommends physical activity. And McGinnis (1992) says that convincing sedentary people to become more active is the most effective step we can take to reduce disease and premature death in the United States. Data show that an active childhood provides health benefits that extend later in life; moreover, active children are likely to be active later in life (Raitakari, Porkka, Taimela, Telama, Rasanen, and Viikari 1994).

Based on the evidence, several public health experts have called for the use of physical education as a public health tool (Sallis and McKenzie 1991; Simons-Morton, O'Hara, Simons-Morton, and Parcel 1987). They suggest that school programs designed to promote lifetime physical activity will produce important public health benefits, including reduced morbidity and mortality from "hypokinetic" conditions such as heart disease, back pain, obesity, diabetes, high blood pressure, and cancer.

The public health perspective has had considerable impact on instruction in physical education and strongly influenced the *Healthy People 2000* recommendation that students participate in more physical education by the year 2000. A statement by the Centers for Disease Control (CDC in press) provides guidelines for increasing physical activity in schools and communities and supports the public health perspective.

Movement Perspective

Some physical educators feel that movement is a broad area encompassing much more than sport and the formal activities commonly associated with physical education. The movement perspective suggests that students need effective instruction in a variety of areas, including dance, play, and creative movement. Effective movement is a means of expression and communication as well as a source of joy and understanding. Movement has meaning in and of itself, but it is also a means to accomplishing other things.

Arnold (1979) explains the potential for movement as follows:

> The world of movement for the agent or the moving being is a world of promise towards self-actualization. It can expand his/her conscious horizons. It is a world in which the mover can come to understand an aspect of his/her social-cultural world and in doing so discover more perfectly him/herself and his/her existential circumstances. To deny this world of bodily action and meaning because of prejudice or neglect is to deny the possibility of becoming fully more human (p. 179).

The movement perspective is very broad as it relates to all types of movement experiences.

Curriculum Models in Physical Education

Curriculum models provide an overall philosophy that guides the design and content of the physical education curriculum or program. Models include sets of beliefs and goals that evolve from a value base and provide a framework for selecting and organizing content, structuring and sequencing activities, and evaluating the yearly curriculum plan. The following models are most often identified in physical education.

Multi-Activity Model

The multi-activity model is by far the most common curriculum model. This approach draws from all of the physical education perspectives and uses a variety of activities, each selected for its value in accomplishing important goals and objectives in physical education. The multi-activity model is also a multigoal model designed to help learners accomplish all of the important goals, outcomes, and objectives of physical education. The multi-activity model is widely used at the elementary level and provides broader experiences there than at higher levels. Activities typically fall into the following categories:

- Team sports (e.g., basketball, softball, and soccer);
- Individual or lifetime sports (e.g., gymnastics, tennis, and Frisbee);
- Dance (e.g., folk, square, modern, and country swing);
- Physical conditioning activities (e.g., jogging, weight training, and aerobics);
- Recreational games (e.g., horseshoes, shuffleboard, and table tennis);
- Outdoor adventure activities (e.g., bicycling, skiing, and orienteering); and
- Aquatics (e.g., swimming, skin diving, and water sports).

The multi-activity curriculum usually includes activities from all these categories. Such factors as student and community interest, teacher interest and expertise, class size, facilities, equipment, and climate determine which activities become part of the phys ed program. Activities in the curriculum generally follow the activity preferences of society, usually with a significant time lag, as evidenced by the inclusion of "new" activities reflecting the fitness renaissance, the wellness movement, the interest in outdoor adventure activities, and the Eastern influence in the martial arts and yoga.

Instruction in these activities proceeds from introductory lessons to advanced and specialized courses. Students are usually grouped by grade level rather than by ability or developmental level. In most situations, students proceed through a sequence of required physical activities each year. A modification of this model is the elective (or selective) format, which allows students to choose activities in which they would like to participate. Students sometimes must choose from the various categories of activities in the curriculum by taking a certain number of team sports, lifetime sports, or physical conditioning units. This choice format helps increase students' and teachers' interest, enthusiasm, and motivation.

The use of activities or movement forms in this model is based on the idea that such activities contribute to the goals of general education—developing the total person socially, emotionally, intellectually, and physically. The popular "education through the physical" philosophy emphasizes the use of physical activities for personal development in the areas of physical fitness, motor abilities, mental abilities, and social abilities. The multi-activity model has remained popular because of its diversity and flexibility in meeting students' changing interests. It provides novelty and excitement as the students explore, experiment with, and experience a variety of physical activities. Many curricular opportunities for students to compete with other students, with the environment, or with themselves add to the model's popularity.

Fitness Education Model

The fitness education model, commonly called the Fitness for Life approach (Corbin and Lindsey 1993a) or competency-based physical education (Brynteson and Adams 1993), is the most consistent with the public health perspective of physical education. This model is most likely to be implemented as a significant part of the curriculum at the upper middle or secondary school level (Corbin 1994, Johnson and Harageones 1994). The underpinning idea is that at some point in children's education it is appropriate to devote one large block of time to learning concepts related to the physical fitness objectives: Is Active, Has Knowledge, Values Activity, and Is Fit. Such programs at the first-year college level are effective in promoting knowledge, improving attitudes about activity, and altering lifestyle activity patterns later in life (Brynteson and Adams 1993; Slava, Laurie, and Corbin 1984).

The Fitness for Life approach originated in colleges and universities. The approach is based on the HELP philosophy, which suggests that good

Health and reduction in health risk can result from participation by Everyone in Lifetime physical activity of a Personal nature. Lessons focus on teaching students facts about fitness and physical activity and ways to become good physical fitness consumers, program planners, and problem solvers.

Students participate in both classroom and gymnasium sessions. Students do self-testing to establish a fitness profile on which they base their personal program planning. They perform various physical activity experiments and learn a variety of personal fitness activities that they can use for a lifetime. In a Fitness for Life class, students find answers to these central questions:

• Why is physical activity important to every person? (learning the facts about exercise)

• What are my personal activity and fitness needs? (learning to self-assess)

• How do I perform personal lifetime activity? (learning how to exercise properly)

The program provides information and activities related to such topics as cardiovascular fitness, strength, endurance, flexibility, fat control, skill-related fitness, correct ways to exercise, and how to plan an exercise program. Students also learn to diagnose and solve various physical fitness problems. Five states require this type of course. The province of New Brunswick in Canada and the Department of Defense Dependents' Schools worldwide also have such a requirement, and this type of program is becoming popular in several European countries (Watson, Sherrill, and Weigand 1994).

The Fitness for Life program is most often a one-semester course provided at one grade at the secondary level, but other options are available for incorporating it into a school curriculum. One has students take a 6- or 9-week Fitness for Life unit. Many curriculum and instructional materials are available to teachers, including books for students, lesson plans, slides, dittos, overhead transparencies, review questions, laboratory experiments, and test materials (Corbin and Lindsey 1993b).

Another similar approach at the secondary level includes a focus on the components of human wellness. A wellness program provides a preventive approach to achieving good health and expands on the fitness concepts model. A healthy lifestyle for all students is the major objective of this model.

Advocates of this model point to the many health problems in our society and assert that students need information and skills pertinent to human wellness. The model is more comprehensive than the fitness concepts theory. Units of instruction include stress management, alcohol and drug abuse, nutrition, weight control, physical fitness, coping skills, personal safety, environmental awareness, behavioral self-control, and problem-solving skills related to these topics.

Both fitness education approaches focus primarily on knowledge and understanding of physical fitness and wellness. People who advocate these models find that the emphasis on knowledge adds credibility to the program. But it is important to understand that an increase in time spent on lecture and analysis means a reduction in time spent learning physical skills. Students need information, but they also need successful encounters with physical activity; and that means time allotted for practicing and performing physical skills. Determining exactly how much time should be spent on knowledge acquisition and how much on physical skill development is difficult. The bottom line is getting students to incorporate physical activity into their lifestyles.

Most schools using this "knowledge concepts approach" offer a balance of physical activity and knowledge concepts. An effective approach is to offer several units on wellness activities (including fitness) to supplement or complement the physical education curriculum.

Movement Analysis Concept Model

This model is primarily associated with the movement perspective of physical education. Curriculum models using an application of movement analysis concepts have primarily affected elementary physical education, although some junior and senior high school programs have been influenced by Rudolf Laban's (1963) movement concepts of time, space, force, and flow. Curriculum content in this model focuses on teaching movement elements, which serve as the basic organizing center. The units focus on such elements as force, balance, striking, motion, stability, and leverage, which are part of many sports skills.

This model also emphasizes terminology, knowledge, and analytical abilities. Instructional emphasis is on indirect methods, such as problem solving or guided discovery. For example, students might spend time analyzing various levels of movement for dribbling a basketball or playing defense in basketball. Students studying racquetball might use a discovery approach in exploring court position and relationships with opponents in racquetball.

Personal Meaning Model

This model is highly influenced by the social-historical perspective of physical education as well as the movement perspective. The personal meaning model (Jewett and Mullan 1977) is appropriate for use at any grade level. It is a purpose-process curriculum framework based on students' motives or purposes for participating in physical activity. The model focuses on three major purposes shared by all people: individual development, environmental coping, and social interaction. These three major purpose concepts are made up of 23 purpose elements, including circularespiratory efficiency, catharsis, challenge, awareness, teamwork, competition, and leadership. The content of the curriculum provides experiences related to all of the purpose elements.

A curriculum based on student motives devotes time to discussing values, motives, and knowledge concepts; highlighting the value of the individual in society; and emphasizing social responsibility and the development of the cooperative skills necessary for social change.

Sports Education Model

The sports education curriculum model, developed by Siedentop, Mand, and Taggart (1986), allows all students, regardless of ability level, to experience the positive values of team sports that are common to most interscholastic sports programs. This model, which has strong ties to the cultural-sports and social-historical perspectives, emphasizes outcomes such as working to reach deferred goals, teamwork, loyalty, commitment, perseverance, dedication, and concern for other people. It highlights the importance of teams, leagues, seasons, championships, coaches, practice, player involvement, formal records, statistics, and competitive balance—characteristics typically emphasized in sports programs but not in the physical education program. This model purports to give all students a chance to experience a quality competitive sports program organized and supervised by an unbiased physical educator who protects the important values of sport. Students learn to compete and to be good competitors.

Siedentop, Mand, and Taggart point out at least six characteristics that make the sports education model different from the more traditional approaches to physical education:

1. Sports education involves seasons rather than units.
2. Students quickly become members of teams.
3. There is a formal schedule of competition.

4. There is usually a major culminating event.

5. Records are kept and publicized.

6. Teachers assume the role of coaches.

Each season starts with time for instruction and the development of team strategies according to teams' strengths and weaknesses. Students are placed on teams, elect a student captain, and provide feedback to the team members about skill development. Team members must organize practice, decide on players' positions, and choose strategies for playing other teams. Students can take on more responsibility as the program evolves and they begin to understand its goals.

Social Development Model

Hellison (1978, 1985) originated a social curriculum model for physical education at the high school level. The model focuses primarily on the development of social competence, self-control, responsible behavior, and concern for others. To accomplish the primary goal of social competence, the model reduces the emphasis on fitness and the development of sport skills.

This model is closely allied with the social-historical perspective, and its supporters view it as a necessary remedy for many problems in society and the home. Proponents assert that society offers adolescents many choices but little opportunity to develop control over their lives. They also believe that students have become more disruptive and difficult to manage.

The social development model has been field-tested successfully with troubled and alienated youth as well as with the general student population. Students proceed through six developmental levels of social competence, with different students entering at different levels:

Level 0: Irresponsibility. Students do not participate and are totally unmotivated and undisciplined. They interrupt and intimidate other students and teachers. They make excuses and blame others for their behavior. Teachers find it difficult to manage or accomplish much with these students.

Level 1: Self-Control. Students at the self-control level can control themselves without the direct supervision of the teacher and do not infringe on the rights of other students or the teacher. They can begin to participate in class activities and enhance their learning.

Level 2: Involvement. Level 2 involves student self-control and desired involvement with the subject matter of fitness, skills, and games.

Students are enthusiastically involved in the program without the constant prompting or supervision of the teacher.

Level 3: Self-Responsibility. Students at Level 3 begin to identify their interests and start to make choices within the parameters of the program. Motivation and responsibility are characteristics of these students, who start to take more responsibility and explore options for their lives outside the program. At this stage, students begin to develop their own identities.

Level 4: Caring. The caring stage has students moving outside themselves and showing concern for other students and the teacher. Students are cooperative and helpful and show a genuine interest in the lives of others and real concern about the world around them.

Level 5: Going Beyond. The highest level is characterized by student leadership and additional responsibility for program decisions. Students become coworkers with teachers as they get involved in decisions that affect all the students in the program.

The social development model is implemented in different ways depending on the specifics of the school situation and the students. Hellison (1985) suggests using a daily program, with each week arranged so that two days are spent on sport skills and game activities, two days on individual physical fitness routines, and one day on cooperative and sharing activities focused on social development. Each day, teachers begin or end a class with a "self-control" activity or strategy that reminds students of the important social goals of the class (self-control, involvement, self-responsibility, and caring).

Many strategies are available to the teacher for each of the social development levels, including teacher talk, modeling, reinforcement, reflection time, student sharing, the talking bench (where two students go to work out a problem), student checklists, student achievement records, and behavior contracts between the student and the teacher.

The Structure of the Curriculum

The K–12 curriculum in physical education contains many repetitive elements, because much of physical education involves previously learned skills. For example, in the primary grades, students learn to throw, but they continue to refine and practice this skill throughout their school years. Therefore, two major components of structure are important.

The first structural component involves the outcomes of the curriculum: what is to be learned in the psychomotor, cognitive, and affective domains. These outcomes cut across all ages and developmental levels and imply practice and the refinement of skills. In the early grades, teachers introduce youngsters to new skills. In the later grades, students then learn to use the skills in competitive situations, in cooperative situations, and in activities they pursue in their leisure time.

The second structural component involves how and when to implement the curriculum. Figure 8.2 outlines the curriculum for the elementary, middle/junior high, and senior high school years. The emphasis of the program varies dramatically, depending on the age of the learners.

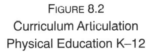

FIGURE 8.2
Curriculum Articulation
Physical Education K–12

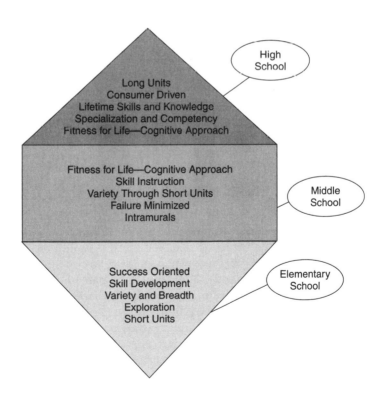

Elementary School Years

Teachers in the elementary school introduce students to new skills and help them practice and refine those skills. To ensure that students master skills, teachers may have to modify lessons and equipment and provide many opportunities for one-to-one instruction in a noncompetitive setting. Students should properly learn skills before using them in competitive situations because once caught up in an activity, people tend to concentrate on achieving certain outcomes rather than using skills properly. For example, if a teacher tells students to make a basket without first teaching the individual skills involved in basket making, then students will likely concentrate on completing the basket, not on mastering the skills involved. Teachers can choose to reinforce either the completion of the basket or the learning of basket-making skills.

Instructional emphasis at the elementary level is on variety and breadth. These years are a time when students explore the myriad activities available to them, learning about genetic limitations, personal likes and dislikes, and the benefits of different types of activities. Units of instruction are relatively brief to ensure variety and take advantage of students' natural curiosity.

Elementary physical education curriculums should allow students to experience success because children develop attitudes toward physical activity that often last throughout adulthood. Typical activities in the primary grades focus on exploration and learning through movement. Sports, games, and individual and dual activities receive greater emphasis as students move into the intermediate grades. Instruction becomes more structured, and students focus more on developing correct performance techniques.

Middle/Junior High School Years

Students at the middle school level are developmentally diverse. A number of personal problems, including those created by puberty, must be taken into account in physical education programs. Physical performance differences become much greater, and youngsters are keenly aware of such differences. The drive to be part of a peer group makes it difficult for youngsters to accept failure; therefore, the program must place students in situations that minimize failure and losing. Many students feel a loss of self-esteem if they are asked to perform (and fail) in front of peers. The challenge is to allow participation in a nonthreatening atmosphere.

Variety is still a keyword in curriculum implementation. Middle school youngsters have short attention spans and a high level of curiosity. They want more than five or six units of instruction during the school year. Shorter units also ensure that students who dislike a unit or do not perform well at certain tasks will be unhappy for only a short time. These units continue to emphasize proper skill technique, and students practice skills in a variety of lead-up games (modified sport activities that minimize the number of skills used) that ensure greater success for students.

Middle school teachers should be aware that the rapid growth spurts of adolescence usually interfere with students' ability to learn new motor skills. Teachers need to be patient and adjust the pace of learning to the various abilities and developmental levels of students.

During the final year of middle/junior high school or the initial year of high school, the Fitness for Life program (Corbin and Lindsey 1993a) is taught in many schools.

High School Years

The physical education program for high school students differs dramatically from elementary and junior high school programs. The focus of the high school program is on specialization and competency. An overriding objective is for students to graduate from high school with competency in one or two activities. Competency implies both the skill and confidence to enter an activity setting and feel comfortable about participating. Too often, phys ed merely introduces learners to activities; students then remain perpetual beginners, repeatedly confronting their own incompetencies and limitations. Students need units of at least one semester or year to develop competency in a sport.

Units of instruction in high schools should be consumer driven. Students have learned the basic skills in the elementary and middle school years. They have learned about their strengths and deficiencies and their personal likes and dislikes. High school should allow them to learn skills in areas they enjoy and want to master.

A forward-thinking view of the high school program sees it as a comprehensive fitness and exercise club. Students choose from among aerobics, weight training, water aerobics, racquetball, tennis, and many other activities. The number of students who participate determines the success of the program, and teachers use creative programs and activities to attract new participants. Participation in a Fitness for Life course prior to this type of experience gives students a sound base for planning their activities. Students who do not participate in a Fitness for Life course at the middle school level should be offered such a course at the high school level.

Issues That Divide Experts

Comprehensive School Health

During the 1990s, some educators have worked with social agencies to develop comprehensive school health programs. The goal of such programs is to integrate all of the health programs within a school and provide comprehensive programs for all people associated with the school, including students, teachers, staff, and even families of students and staff. When implemented successfully, these efforts consolidate a multitude of different program areas. These programs have been successful in some schools, but division of responsibility remains a major issue. People are reluctant to give up their "turf."

Although most people acknowledge that a combined effort is desirable, questions invariably arise over who is responsible for what. Many educators fear that comprehensive programs allow others to invade their territory and threaten their job security. Problems concerning division of responsibility are one reason that physical education and health education still remain separate programs in most schools.

Skill Development Versus Fitness Development

As noted previously, two major outcomes for the physically educated person are skill development and fitness development. The debate over emphasis has continued for years. Time is central to the problem because so little time is available for physical education instruction, which has such ambitious objectives. Those favoring skill or fitness development really favor more time for teaching skills or for working on fitness. Much of the skill/fitness conflict could be resolved if more time were available for teaching physical education, because most physical educators acknowledge the importance of both outcomes.

Clearly, even with additional time, physical education cannot make every child skillful in every sport, nor can it provide enough activity to guarantee fitness for every child. For this reason, many educators now advocate an emphasis on skill development in the early school years followed by students' own choice of skills to be learned in the later grades. They also acknowledge the importance of taking time to teach students about active lifestyles, particularly in the upper grade levels (see the preceding section on the Fitness Education Model). By teaching children to be active, physical educators help them remain fit even when teachers are not present.

Fitness for All or High-Level Fitness

In 1958, the American Association for Health, Physical Education, and Recreation (now the American Alliance for Health, Physical Education, Recreation, and Dance) introduced the first physical fitness test for youth after early research suggested that U.S. children were less fit than children in other countries (see Corbin and Pangrazi 1992 for a complete review). Within a few years, the President's Council on Physical Fitness and Sports (PCPFS) developed and sponsored fitness awards for students who scored at the 85th percentile on all tests in a multi-item battery. Over the years, the national test has been modified many times, but very few children meet the standards for these demanding awards.

In fact, fewer than 1 percent of all children achieve high-level fitness awards. Many current experts (Corbin, Whitehead, and Lovejoy 1988) have argued that such awards do not motivate students to be fit, but instead detract from such motivation. They argue that fitness should be for all children and favor the use of criterion-referenced health standards and health-related fitness test items for assessing appropriate levels of fitness for children (Cooper Institute for Aerobic Research 1992). This group believes that all children can achieve these standards with appropriate physical activity and that the standards are consistent with the most recent national health goals (U.S. Department of Health and Human Services 1990) and recent epidemiological evidence concerning physical activity and health (Blair 1993, McGinnis 1992). Further, they assert that because heredity and maturation play major roles in the fitness performance of children, the achievement of high-level performance awards is impossible for many children (Bouchard 1993).

Others argue that because high-level performance is rewarded in other areas of the curriculum, it should be rewarded in the physical domain. Further, they believe there is nothing wrong with recognizing excellence. In recent years, there has been more agreement between the two sides of this controversy, but the debate is likely to continue for some time.

Evidence (Corbin and Pangrazi 1992) suggests that our children are not less fit than children in past decades; most children do meet the minimal fitness standards associated with good health. The bad news is that children tend to become less active as they grow older. And those who are inactive as youngsters are likely to remain inactive when they become adults (Raitakari et al. 1994).

Fitness Versus Physical Activity

The fitness boom has been going on for more than 25 years. The emphasis in our culture became so strong that *Megatrends* author John Naisbitt (1982) declared it a fitness "trend" rather than a fad. But for many of the past 25 years, the focus, especially in schools, has been on getting children physically fit, despite recent evidence that the relationship between fitness and physical activity levels is not particularly strong among children (Pate, Dowda, and Ross 1990). This is true for several reasons. First, children are the most active segment of the population (Rowland 1990) and are much more homogeneous in their activity than adults. In other words, even the least active children get some fitness benefits; this is not true of adults. Second, maturation often overrides activity in its effect on fitness. Older children do better than younger children, as do those youngsters who are physiologically more mature than others their age. Third, heredity has a strong controlling effect on fitness performance.

Accordingly, many experts now place less emphasis on fitness and greater emphasis on lifestyle physical activity, believing that if they can get children to be active, fitness will take care of itself (Corbin, Pangrazi, and Welk 1994). On the other hand, a focus on fitness may discourage many slow maturers or those who lack hereditary predisposition. Such individuals prefer activity over fitness. Still, many believe that physical fitness should be a major objective of physical education and that students should be assessed in this area.

Coaching and Physical Education Teaching

Few disagree with the notion that physical education, particularly at the secondary level, has suffered because of its relationship to varsity athletics. Although many people agree that varsity sports programs are an important part of the cocurriculum, particularly as a program for gifted students, conflicts surrounding coaches' instructional duties have arisen.

Research shows that athletic coaches are often subject to role overload and role conflict. Many coaches teach physical education classes and other classes. When overload and subsequent role conflicts exist, the role that receives emphasis is the role of coach. The role of teacher is often underemphasized because it offers fewer rewards. Coaches, for example, typically must attend clinics, workshops, and meetings to stay on top of their duties. As a result, secondary coaches seldom attend professional meetings in physical education, even when phys ed is their primary teaching responsibility.

Innovations in athletics are much more likely in high schools than innovations in physical education. At issue is how physical education can be at the cutting edge when those most responsible for its success are overloaded and rewarded for roles other than teaching. Some have argued for professional coaching positions so that physical educators dedicated to innovative teaching can be in charge of physical education programs. This issue has existed for many years and has not yet been resolved.

Qualifications for Professional Physical Educators

College graduates, including future teachers, are taught by college professors who now must have advanced degrees. Prior to the 1970s, this was not typically the case. In physical education, many of the faculty held master's degrees and were hired based on their competencies in specific sports areas. After the 1970s, the doctorate became a requirement for faculty status in most universities and specialty areas such as exercise physiology, biomechanics, sports psychology, pedagogy, and fitness and health promotion. Further, professors were expected to establish ongoing research programs to advance within the university.

Over time, many professors in the "subspecialty areas" have distanced themselves from teacher education and now consider themselves exercise scientists or kinesiologists with a dedication to the discipline rather than to a specific profession, such as teaching. As a result, many large research universities have dropped teacher education programs. Those that have retained them may have few professors with experience in teaching and thus often are not dedicated to the goal of educating professional educators.

The American Academy of Kinesiology and Physical Education recently identified the subject matter of physical education as the discipline and designated physical education as a professional area that is based on this subject matter. At issue is the responsibility of universities concerning the discipline and the profession of physical education teaching. Many programs previously dedicated to physical education have now aligned themselves almost exclusively with the discipline. Fewer major research universities prepare graduate students with doctorates that are designed to place them as faculty members in teacher preparation.

In the years ahead, as the issue is debated, we will no doubt see changes in who prepares teachers of physical education (major research universities versus smaller universities and colleges) and who prepares the future teacher educators. Those with a disciplinary emphasis, especially in major research universities, often do not value the scholarly efforts of those in teacher education. This attitude causes role conflicts. And people in teacher education often feel that chances for success are small in universities that emphasize the discipline.

At any rate, fewer and fewer programs prepare people with doctoral degrees in professional physical education. Some schools have developed separate departments or programs for the discipline (kinesiology) and the profession (physical education) to resolve the issue. Other institutions have dropped or deemphasized one of the programs. Only the future will tell how this issue will be resolved.

Competition for Academic Time

Healthy People 2000 recommends physical education for all children. So why do schools minimize physical education? While some suggest that program quality is the culprit, competition for academic time is the more likely problem. To gain more time for math and science instruction, administrators often cut physical education. Many phys ed teachers tell of being assigned several free periods rather than classes because students cannot schedule physical education. This practice continues despite research like the Three Rivers study, which showed that elementary children who took more time in physical education at the expense of time in the classroom learned as much in the classroom, while demonstrating higher achievement in areas associated with physical education objectives (Shephard 1984).

As mentioned earlier, evidence shows that active children choose an active lifestyle later in life (Raitakari et al. 1994). Active children and adults are healthier than those who are inactive, yet many school administrators believe time spent on physical education during the schoolday is time wasted. High school students who are required to take as many as 20 academic units for graduation now find it almost impossible to fit in physical education. Thus, the limitation on time is imposed by other requirements, despite the fact that most adults acknowledge that they themselves benefit from an exercise break during the day. Studies have shown that companies with fitness and health promotion programs have fewer absences, more job satisfaction, and better production rates (Opatz 1994). We have every reason to believe the results in schools would be similar if students (and teachers) participated in similar programs.

This issue crosses subject-matter lines. For it to be resolved, school administrators, school boards, legislators, and parents must be convinced that the national goal of increasing students' physical activity is important enough to warrant time in the already crowded schoolday.

References

American Association of Health, Physical Education, and Recreation. (1958). *Youth Fitness Testing Manual.* Washington, D.C.: Author.

Arnold, P.J. (1979). *Meaning in Movement, Sport, and Physical Education.* London: Heinemann.

Blair, S.N. (1993). "C.H. McCloy Research Lecture: Physical Activity, Physical Fitness, and Health." *Research Quarterly for Exercise and Sport* 64, 4: 365–376.

Bouchard, C. (1993). *Physical Activity and Fitness Research Digest* 1, 4: 1–8.

Brynteson, P., and T.M. Adams. (1993). "The Effects of Conceptually Based Physical Education Programs on Attitudes and Exercise Habits of College Alumni After 2 to 11 Years of Follow-up." *Research Quarterly for Exercise and Sport* 64,2: 208–212.

Center for Disease Prevention and Control. (1991). "Participation of High School Students in School Physical Education—United States, 1990." *Morbidity and Mortality Weekly Report* 40, 607: 613–615.

Center for Disease Prevention and Control. (In press). "Guidelines for Promotion of Physical Activity and Reduction of Sedentary Lifestyles in Youth." Atlanta: Center for Disease Prevention and Control.

Cooper Institute for Aerobic Research. (1992). *Fitnessgram Test Administration Manual.* Dallas: Cooper Institute for Aerobic Research.

Corbin, C.B. (1994). "The Fitness Curriculum: Climbing the Stairway to Lifetime Fitness." In *Health and Fitness Through Physical Education*, edited by R.R. Pate and R.C. Hohn. Champaign, Ill.: Human Kinetics.

Corbin, C.B., and R. Lindsey. (1993a). *Fitness for Life.* 4th ed. Glenview, Ill.: Scott, Foresman and Company.

Corbin, C.B., and R. Lindsey. (1993b). *Fitness for Life Teacher's Resource Book.* 4th ed. Glenview, Ill.: Scott, Foresman and Company.

Corbin, C. B., and R.P. Pangrazi. (1992). "Are American Children and Youth Fit?" *Research Quarterly for Exercise and Sport* 63, 2: 96–106.

Corbin, C. B., R.P. Pangrazi, and G. Welk. (1994). "Toward an Understanding of Appropriate Physical Activity Levels for Youth." *Physical Activity and Fitness Research Digest* 2, 2: 1–8.

Corbin, C. B., J.R. Whitehead, and P.Y. Lovejoy. (1988). "Youth Physical Fitness Awards." *Quest* 40, 3: 200–218.

Eitzen, D.S., and G. Sage. (1986). *Sociology of North American Sport.* Dubuque, Iowa: W.C. Brown.

Hellison, D.R. (1978). *Beyond Balls and Bats.* Reston, Va.: American Alliance for Health, Physical Education, Recreation, and Dance.

Hellison, D.R. (1985). *Goals and Strategies for Teaching Physical Education.* Champaign, Ill.: Human Kinetics Publishers.

Jewett, A., and M. Mullan. (1977). *Curriculum Design: Purposes and Processes in Physical Education Teaching-Learning.* Reston, Va.: American Alliance for Health, Physical Education, Recreation, and Dance.

Johnson, D.J., and E.G. Harageones. (1994). "A Health Fitness Course in Secondary Physical Education: The Florida Experience." In *Health and Fitness Through Physical Education*, edited by R.R. Pate and R.C. Hohn. Champaign, Ill.: Human Kinetics.

Laban, R. (1963). *Modern Educational Dance.* 2nd ed. (Revised by L. Ullman). New York: Praeger Publishers.

McGinnis, J.M. (1992). "The Public Health Burden of a Sedentary Lifestyle." *Medicine and Science in Sport and Exercise* 24 (supplement): S196-S200.

Naisbitt, J. (1982). *Megatrends.* New York: Warner.

National Association for Sport and Physical Education. (1992). *Outcomes of Quality Physical Education Programs.* Reston, Va.: American Alliance for Health, Physical Education, Recreation, and Dance.

Opatz, J.P., ed. (1994). *Economic Impact of Worksite Health Promotion.* Champaign, Ill.: Human Kinetics.

Pangrazi, R.P., and V.P. Dauer. (1995). *Dynamic Physical Education for Elementary School Children.* 11th ed. Boston: Allyn and Bacon.

Pate, R.R., M. Dowda, and J.G. Ross. (1990). "Associations Between Physical Activity and Physical Fitness in American Children." *American Journal of Diseases in Children* 144: 1123–1129.

Raitakari, O.T., K.V.K. Porkka, S. Taimela, R. Telama, L. Rasanen, and J.S.A. Viikari. (1994). "Effects of Persistent Physical Activity and Inactivity on Coronary Risk Factors in Children and Young Adults." *American Journal of Epidemiology* 140, 3: 195–205.

Ross, J.G., C.O. Dotson, C.B. Gilbert, and S.T. Katz. (1985). "What Are Kids Doing in School Physical Education?" *Journal of Physical Education, Recreation, and Dance* 56, 1: 31–34.

Ross, J.G., R.P. Pate, C.B. Corbin, L.A. Delpy, and R.S. Gold. (1987). "What's Going on in the Elementary Physical Education Program?" *Journal of Physical Education, Recreation, and Dance* 58, 9: 78–84.

Rowland, T.W. (1990). *Exercise and Children's Health.* Champaign, Ill.: Human Kinetics.

Sallis, J.F. (1994). "Influences on Physical Activity of Children, Adolescents, and Adults or Determinants of Active Living." *Physical Activity and Fitness Research Digest* 1, 7: 1–8.

Sallis, J.F., and T.L. McKenzie. (1991). "Physical Education's Role in Public Health." *Research Quarterly for Exercise and Sport* 62, 2: 124–137.

Shephard, R.J. (1984). "Physical Activity and 'Wellness' of the Child." In *Advances in Pediatric Sport Sciences*, edited by R.A. Boileau. Champaign, Ill.: Human Kinetics.

Siedentop, D., C. Mand, and A. Taggart. (1986). *Physical Education—Teaching and Curriculum Strategies for Grades 5–12.* Palo Alto, Calif.: Mayfield Publishing Co.

Simons-Morton, B.B., N.M. O'Hara, D.G. Simons-Morton, and G.S. Parcel. (1987). "Children and Fitness: A Public Health Perspective." *Research Quarterly for Exercise and Sport* 58, 4: 295–303.

Slava, S., D.R. Laurie, and C.B. Corbin. (1984). "Long-term Effects of a Conceptual Physical Education Program." *Research Quarterly for Exercise and Sport* 55, 2: 161–168.

U.S. Department of Health and Human Services. (1990). *Healthy People 2000.* Washington, D.C.: U.S. Government Printing Office.

Watson, E.R., A. Sherrill, and B. Weigand. (1994). "Curriculum Development in a Worldwide School System." *Journal of Physical Education Recreation and Dance* 65, 1: 17–20.

Williams, J.F. (1927). *The Principles of Physical Education.* Philadelphia: W.B. Saunders.

9

Redefining the Content of the Science Curriculum

Andrew Ahlgren

In 1985, when the American Association for the Advancement of Science (AAAS) designed and launched Project 2061, the nation was just beginning to respond to reports of the failure of schools to educate our children, particularly in science and mathematics. Since then, several reform initiatives have tried to identify reasons for this failure and to bring about the necessary changes in science and mathematics education. Approaches to reform have been varied: Some reformers have called for changes in the curriculum, others have focused on teaching methods, and still others on assessment. Some have emphasized more hands-on experiences in the classroom; others have promoted a theme-oriented approach. Some have recommended only slight changes, while others have recommended sweeping changes in the way we teach science and math. Most reformers have acknowledged, however, that serious reform takes a long time and that there are no quick fixes that will do the job.

Author's Note: Ann Cwiklinski, Project 2061 Staff Writer, and Mary Koppal, Project 2061 Communications Manager, assisted in the preparation of this chapter.

In the area of science, there have been two comprehensive efforts to specify the goals of science education over the past decade: the National Research Council's (NRC) *National Science Education Standards,* published in draft form in 1994, and the science literacy goals established by AAAS' Project 2061 and published in *Science for All Americans* (1989) and *Benchmarks for Science Literacy* (1993). A third, large-scale enterprise, the Project on Scope, Sequence, and Coordination of Secondary School Science of the National Science Teachers Association, is a loose collection of diverse curriculum developments, mostly for middle school, that emphasizes a parallel course structure rather than any particular set of learning goals.

Although Project 2061 uses the single term "science" in its titles, its recommendations go well beyond traditional school science to include social as well as natural science, mathematics, technology, and the interconnectedness of these content areas. This breadth results from the belief that understanding any one of these areas is so closely related to understanding the others that conceptualizing goals for one requires parallel work for the others. There need not, however, be any inference of turf infringement in the actual curriculum—Project 2061's treatment of "science literacy" is about *what* everyone should learn and approximately *when,* not about the curriculum divisions in which that learning should occur.

On many of the most essential reform principles, there is a high level of consensus among these initiatives, perhaps an indicator of the strength and effectiveness of the science education reform movement. For example, those involved in this reform movement generally agree that

• The first priority is basic science and mathematics literacy for all students so that as adults they can participate fully in a world that is increasingly being shaped by science and technology.

• Science literacy consists of knowledge of certain important scientific ideas and habits of mind and an awareness of the nature of science, its connections to mathematics and technology, and its relation to society.

• Education for science literacy will create a larger and more diverse pool of students who seek further education in scientific fields.

• The sheer amount of material that today's curriculum tries to cover must be significantly reduced so that students (who now often only memorize and forget without understanding) will have the time to acquire essential knowledge and skills.

• Instruction should exist as much as possible in real-world rather than abstract context, with students frequently and actively exploring nature and the world around them in ways that resemble how scientists themselves go about their work.

• The involvement of families and communities is essential for real reform to take place.

Given these broad areas of agreement, what are the distinguishing features of each major reform initiative and, in particular, how do they relate to the work of Project 2061?

National Science Teachers Association Focuses on Changing Curriculum Structure

Whereas *Science for All Americans (SFAA)*, published by AAAS, was entirely about *learning goals*, the National Science Teachers Association (NSTA) undertook the invention of a new *curriculum* plan. In 1989, NSTA began its Scope, Sequence, and Coordination curriculum project (SS&C), which proposes to reform science education at the secondary level by advocating carefully sequenced, parallel, well-coordinated instruction in all the sciences. SS&C is designed to replace the traditional "layer-cake" approach to science courses—often earth science in 9th grade, biology in 10th grade, chemistry in 11th grade, and physics in 12th grade—with a curriculum in which students study the physical, biological, and earth and space sciences every year—eventually from junior high school through 12th grade.

As part of its initiative, SS&C has published a general collection of reprinted papers about research on learning, *Relevant Research* (1992), and also *The Content Core* (1993), which speculates on how topics might be organized in a model science curriculum. Different state SS&C sites have taken diverse tacks, mostly at the middle school level, holding in common only the parallel-sciences principle. The newest SS&C enterprise, for grades 9–12 only, is multistate. Claiming commitment to NRC's less-is-more standards, it is taking on the very real practical difficulties of escaping the traditional more-is-more curriculum. Perhaps most significant, NSTA was instrumental in getting the National Research Council, the operational wing of the National Academy of Sciences, to take responsibility for the development of national science education standards. NSTA hopes to play a major role in promulgating the NRC standards when they emerge.

Building a Consensus for Standards

In 1991, the U.S. Department of Education, at the urging of NSTA, asked NRC to take the lead in developing political support for a broad set of standards for effective science education. Drawing on the experience and expertise of numerous educators, scientists, and other scholars—and the already completed *SFAA* and *Benchmarks*—NRC released in November 1994 a draft National Science Education Standards (NSES) for a final round of reviews. Following this review process, the current schedule calls for a final version to be published by the end of 1995.

The draft NSES provides recommendations for fundamental ideas and abilities to be learned in the natural sciences, but not in the social sciences, mathematics, or technology, as does Project 2061's *SFAA* and *Benchmarks*. In addition to its content recommendations, NSES includes much shorter recommendations concerning teaching and assessment practices, school science programs, professional development, and the overall educational system. In a similar spirit, Project 2061 began in 1991 to commission a dozen expert task forces to examine and report on most of these same noncontent areas and on other important aspects of the education system: how to encourage the development of new instructional materials and technology, the role of family and community in reform, how to foster partnerships between education and business, making connections across the entire school program, the financial implications of reform, among others. Publication of a volume integrating these reports (*Blueprints for Reform*) is scheduled for 1997.

Differences in Organization of Content

Besides differences in the scope of their initiatives, NRC's content standards and project 2061's *Benchmarks* are organized quite differently. The NRC's are organized by grade range, with somewhat varying content areas cycling through each. *Benchmarks* takes the opposite approach: Each of 12 chapters deals with a single content area, and grade ranges appear as subsections of each chapter. The grade ranges for recommendations are also somewhat different. The science standards divide K–12 into three bands (K–4, 5–8, and 9–12). Project 2061, on the advice of its school district collaborators, has chosen to use four bands (K–2, 3–5, 6–8, and 9–12) to provide more differentiation between early and late elementary. Moreover, there are frequent differences in how concepts are sorted, so the ideas in a single science standard item might be distributed among several benchmarks. It is important to remember, however, that the organization of either set of content recommendations is designed specifically to catalog goals for learning and is not meant to prescribe how curriculum and instruction should be organized. Differences in goal organization may be inconvenient for users of both but carry no importance otherwise.

Similarities in Content Recommendations

Where they address common areas—learning goals in the natural sciences—NRC science standards and the work of Project 2061 overlap extensively in their content recommendations. And, in fact, Project 2061's *Benchmarks for Science Literacy* was the principal outside source for NRC as it drafted the content portion of NSES, as stated in the NSES introduction:

> The content standards sections of the *National Science Education Standards* have drawn extensively on and have made independent use and interpretation of the statements of what all students should know and be able to do that are published *in Science for All Americans* and *Benchmarks for Science Literacy* (November 1994 draft NSES, p. I–2).

A detailed study of the content portion of NRC standards and their relationship to Project 2061's *SFAA* and *Benchmarks* shows the similarities to be large and the differences small.[1]

Both visions of what is essential for everyone to know exclude a host of topics that congest the traditional science curriculum, topics such as Ohm's law, series and parallel circuits, geometric optics, phyla of plants and animals, and cloud types. And both visions vigorously avoid a preoccupation with memorizing details and vocabulary at the expense of understanding. Although the SS&C project has released *High School Framework for National Science Education Standards*, a document that includes under the NSES headings at least three times more content than what is recommended by either NRC or Project 2061, presumably that content would be learned only by science majors, not by all students.

Taking the widely accepted principle of "less is more" seriously is not easy. It requires painstaking effort to examine and select for the curriculum only those concepts and skills that will clearly contribute to a basic level of science literacy for all students. Such effort means not giving in to the familiar temptation to use new content goals merely as

---

[1]*Comparison of Content between the November draft of National Science Education Standards and Benchmarks for Science Literacy/Science for All Americans*, prepared by Project 2061 and endorsed by NRC, is available from Project 2061.

topic headings under which all the current excesses of the science curriculum can be restuffed (such as might be suspected of some state frameworks and perhaps even SS&C's *High School Framework*). For its part, Project 2061 plans to provide ongoing advice and assistance to help educators in studying science literacy goals and in designing curriculum that is derived from a careful study of those goals.[2]

Yet, content is treated differently in a few categories. The greatest apparent difference is the treatment of "inquiry." Both visions agree that students should understand some important things about scientific investigation, but NSES goes further by specifying that all students should learn and retain an ability to plan and carry out complete scientific investigations. While Project 2061 considers the ability to conduct scientific research highly desirable for students who will specialize in science-related careers, it considers the ability to react critically to reports of research, such as those that commonly appear in the media, to be an appropriate goal for adult science literacy. (To reach that understanding, students would, of course, have to carry out investigations of their own *along the way*. Project 2061 considers long-term *retention* of the skill to be too ambitious.)

The science standards place a similar emphasis on having all students learn how to carry out design projects as adults, whereas *SFAA* and *Benchmarks* emphasize understanding the problems and considerations of design proposed or carried out by others. The NSES emphasis on ability to *do* investigation or design as a *goal* may arise from NRC's desire to ensure that students will have enough hands-on investigation experiences to understand what these activities entail.

With this overview of major reform efforts, this chapter will now try to capture issues by focusing more intensively on Project 2061. This project's work continues to evolve in response to the efforts of other reform initiatives and to the ever-changing education reform environment, yet its focus and its organizing philosophy remain the same: science literacy for all Americans. This chapter focuses on Project 2061's science literacy goals for student learning and some implications of those goals for the curriculum. It also highlights key concerns that have been—and still have to be—addressed in pursuing reform.

---

[2]Project 2061's *Resources for Science Literacy* will be published by the end of 1995 and *Designs for Science Literacy* at the end of 1996.

Project 2061's Vision of Science Literacy[3]

The 1988 ASCD yearbook contained a chapter on Project 2061's early efforts to rethink the science curriculum, a year before the publication of *Science for All Americans*. Since that 1988 chapter, the principles underlying our reform efforts have remained intact, and we have produced several sets of tools to help school districts design and assemble their own curriculums to promote science literacy among their students.

From the beginning, we took a long-term, comprehensive approach to curriculum reform. Rather than recommend another well-intentioned but ultimately ineffectual quick fix for just one piece of the curriculum, we chose to reconceptualize the entire K–12 science, mathematics, and technology curriculum domain from scratch. To further increase the likelihood of successful and lasting reform, we also decided to look at all aspects of the education system with the potential to support or constrain curriculum content, instruction, and assessment; business and industry; curriculum connections; educational policy; educational research; equity; finance; higher education; materials and technology; family and the community; school organization; and teacher education.

Science Literacy Goals: *Science for All Americans* and *Benchmarks for Science Literacy*

Central to our reform efforts is the premise that curriculum design should be based on carefully considered, clearly defined learning goals—not on the historical aggregation of miscellaneous goals implicit in existing curriculums. Our first task, therefore, was to define what science, mathematics, and technology we wanted all high school graduates to know—and remember—as a result of their 13 years in school. To this end, we convened panels of experts in science, mathematics, or technology to help us identify the knowledge, skills, and ways of thinking that all high school graduates would need to be science literate—that is, to be able to make sense of how the world works, to think

---

[3]Project 2061 defines "science literacy" as including science, mathematics, and technology. The term spares us the inconvenience of repeating more meticulous and unwieldy phrases such as "deep and lasting knowledge and skills in the natural, social, and mathematical sciences and technology." We believe that science, mathematics, and technology are so closely interwoven that learning any one of them requires learning about the others.

critically and independently, and to lead interesting, responsible, and productive lives in a culture increasingly shaped by science. As they debated the substance of science literacy, panel members had to defend their positions to their colleagues in terms of both scientific and educational significance. After almost two years of deliberations, the panels produced recommendations in five areas: biological and health sciences, social and behavioral sciences, physical and information sciences and engineering, mathematics, and technology.

These recommendations were integrated into *SFAA*'s coherent set of learning goals in science, mathematics, and technology for all high school graduates. *SFAA* first draws portraits of science, mathematics, and technology, which emphasize their roles in the scientific endeavor and reveal some of the similarities and connections among them. It goes on to recommend not only specific, interconnected facts and concepts in these three domains, but also habits of mind essential to science literacy and some general principles of teaching and learning. *SFAA* specifies literacy in the following areas:

• *The Scientific Endeavor.* Chapters 1–3 describe the nature of science, mathematics, and technology as related endeavors, including their similarities, connections, and differences. "The Nature of Science" focuses on three major subjects: the scientific worldview, scientific methods of inquiry, and the nature of the scientific enterprise. "The Nature of Mathematics" describes connections and creative processes involved in both theoretical and applied mathematics and the cycle of abstraction and modeling. "The Nature of Technology" describes elements of design and how technology both shapes and is shaped by science and society.

• *Scientific Views of the World.* This second section (Chapters 4–9) presents views of the world as depicted by current science. "The Physical Setting" describes overall contents and structure of the universe on astronomical, terrestrial, and submicroscopic levels and the physical principles on which it seems to run. "The Living Environment" delineates basic ideas about how living things function and how they interact with one another and their environment. "The Human Organism" discusses our species as one that is in some ways like other living things and in some ways unique. "Human Society" considers scientific findings about individual and group behavior, social organizations, and the process of social change. "The Designed World" reviews principles of how people shape and control the world through different areas of technology and some basic issues related to those technologies. "The Mathematical World" presents basic mathematical ideas of number, form, relationships, uncertainty, and reasoning, which together play a key role in almost all human endeavors.

Chapters 7–9 extend the notion of science literacy to include understandings in the social sciences, technology, and mathematics.

A few examples of goals from these latter chapters will help convey a sense of just how broadly the Project construes science literacy. *SFAA* discusses computer technology in its section on information processing:

> Mechanical devices to perform mathematics or logical operations have been around for centuries, but it was the invention of the electronic computer that revolutionized information processing. One aspect of mathematical logic is that any information whatsoever—including numbers, letters, and logical propositions—can be coded as a string of yes-or-no bits (for example, as dots and dashes, 1's and 0's, or on/off switches). Electronic computers are essentially very large arrays of on/off switches connected in ways that allow them to perform logical operations. New materials and techniques have made possible the extreme miniaturization and reliability of no-moving-parts switches, which enable very large numbers of connected switches to be fitted reliably into a small space. Very small size also means very short connections, which in turn means very brief travel time for signals; therefore, miniaturized electronic circuits can act very quickly. The very short times required for processing steps to occur, together with the very large number of connections that can be made, means that computers can carry out extremely complicated or repetitive instructions millions of times more quickly than people can (p. 120).

> An important potential role for computer programs is to assist humans in problem solving and decision making. Computers already play a role in helping people think by running programs that amass, analyze, summarize, and display data. Pattern-searching programs help to extract meaning from large pools of data. An important area of research in computer science is the design of programs—based on the principles of artificial intelligence—that are intended to mimic human thought and possibly even improve on it in some ways (p. 122).

Symbolic relationships are also discussed:

> Numbers and relationships among them can be represented in symbolic statements, which provide a way to model, investigate, and display real-world relationships. Seldom are we interested in only one quantity or category; rather, we are usually interested in the relationship between them—the relationship between age and height, temperature and time of day, political party and annual income, sex, and occupation. Such relationships can be expressed by using pictures (typically charts

and graphs), tables, algebraic equations, or words. Graphs are especially useful in examining the relationships between quantities.

Algebra is a field of mathematics that explores the relationships among different quantities by representing them as symbols and manipulating statements that relate the symbols. Sometimes a symbolic statement implies that only one value or set of values will make the statement true. . . . More generally, however, an algebraic statement allows a quantity to take on any of a range of values and implies for each what the corresponding value of another quantity is. . . .

There are many possible kinds of relationships between one variable and another. A basic set of simple examples includes (1) directly proportional (one quantity always keeps the same proportion to another; (2) inversely proportional (as one quantity increases, the other decreases proportionally); (3) accelerated (as one quantity increases uniformly, the other increases faster and faster); (4) converging (as one quantity increases without limit, the other approaches closer and closer to some limiting value); (5) cyclical (as one quantity increases, the other increases and decreases in repeating cycles); and (6) stepped (as one quantity changes smoothly, the other changes in jumps (pp. 132–133).

Chapter 10, "Historical Perspectives," illustrates the scientific enterprise with 10 historical examples that are of exceptional significance in the development of science. These examples deal with the moving earth, universal gravitation, relativity, geologic time, plate tectonics, the conservation of matter, radioactivity and nuclear fission, the evolution of species, germs as a source of disease, and the industrial revolution. All these historical episodes provide concrete examples of how the scientific enterprise operates. Consider, for example, this *SFAA* passage on Copernicus, which illustrates the important notions that new scientific ideas are limited by the context in which they are conceived and often rejected by the scientific establishment:

Shortly after the discovery of the Americas, a Polish astronomer named Nicolaus Copernicus, a contemporary of Martin Luther and Leonardo da Vinci, proposed a different model of the universe. Discarding the premise of a stationary earth, he showed that if the earth and planets all circled around the sun, the apparent erratic motion of the planets could be accounted for just as well, and in a more intellectually pleasing way. But Copernicus' model still used perfect circular motions and was nearly as complicated as the old earth-centered model. Moreover, his model violated the prevailing commonsense notions about the world, in that it required the apparently immobile earth to spin completely around on its axis once a day, the universe to be far larger than had been imagined, and—worst of all—the earth to become commonplace by losing its position at the center of the universe. Further, an orbiting and spinning earth was thought to be inconsistent with some biblical passages. Most scholars perceived too little advantage in a sun-centered model—and too high a cost in giving up the many other ideas associated with the traditional earth-centered model (pp. 147–148).

Chapter 11 presents "Common Themes" that cut across science, mathematics, and technology. These themes—systems, models, stability, constancy and change, and scale—can serve as tools for scientific thinking about diverse phenomena and provide insights into how the world works. Take, for example, this excerpt from *SFAA*'s section on models, germane to several disciplines:

> The most familiar meaning of the term "model" is the physical model—an actual device or process that behaves enough like the phenomenon being modeled that we can hope to learn something from it. Typically, a physical model is easier to work with than what it represents because it is smaller in size, less expensive in terms of materials, or shorter in duration.
>
> Experiments in which variables are closely controlled can be done on a physical model in the hope that its response will be like that of the full-scale phenomenon. For example, a scale model of an airplane can be used in a wind tunnel to investigate the effects of different wing shapes. Human biological process can be modeled by using laboratory animals or cultures in test tubes to test medical treatments for possible use on people. Social processes, too, can be modeled, as when a new method of instruction is tried out in a single classroom rather than in a whole school system. But the scaling need not always be toward smaller and cheaper. Submicroscopic phenomena such as molecular configurations may require much larger models that can be measured and manipulated by hand (pp. 168–169).

Chapter 12, "Habits of Mind," sketches the attitudes, skills, and ways of thinking that are essential to science literacy. These include values inherent in the practice of science, mathematics, and technology; informed, balanced beliefs about social benefits of the scientific endeavor; computation and estimation, measuring accurately, observation and manipulation, communication and critical-response skills; and using ordinary tools and instruments (including calculators and computers).

This chapter recommends, for example, that education foster openness to new ideas—tempered by informed skepticism:

> The purpose of science education is not exclusively to produce scientists, it should help all students understand the great importance of carefully considering ideas that at first may seem disquieting to them or at odds with what they generally believe. The competition among

ideas is a major source of tension within science, between science and society, and within society. Science education should document the nature of such tensions from the history of science—and it should help students see the value to themselves and society of participating in the push and pull of conflicting ideas.

Science is characterized as much by skepticism as by openness. Although a new theory may receive serious attention, it rarely gains widespread acceptance in science until its advocates can show that it is borne out by the evidence, is logically consistent with other principles that are not in question, explains more than its rival theories, and has the potential to lead to new knowledge. Because most scientists are skeptical about all new theories, such acceptance is usually a process of verification and refutation that can take years or even decades to run its course. Science education can help students to see the social value of systematic skepticism and to develop a healthy balance in their own minds between openness and skepticism (pp. 185–186).

SFAA's supplemental Chapters 13–15 lay out some principles of effective learning and teaching and offer some observations on education reform.

In addition to the specific recommendations offered in Chapters 1–12, *SFAA* conveys several broad implications for the content of the curriculum.

First, the curriculum content should be shaped by a vision of the lasting knowledge and skills we want all students to acquire by the time they become adults. Accordingly, the recommendations in *SFAA* do not constitute a curriculum, but rather a coherent picture of the understandings individuals should retain after leaving school.

Second, the curriculum should provide all students with a common base of knowledge and skills. *SFAA* concentrates on a common core of learning that would contribute to the science literacy of all students, but does not spell out all science, mathematics, and technology goals that belong in the K–12 curriculum. This common core can provide a solid basis for additional learning that addresses the particular needs, talents, and interests of individual students.

Third, the core curriculum should focus on less, rather than more, content. If we want students to learn science, mathematics, and technology well, we must radically reduce the amount of material now being covered. An overstuffed curriculum places a premium on the ability to commit terms, algorithms, and generalizations to short-term memory, leaving less time for students to acquire deeper understanding of important concepts. *SFAA* omits content that does not contribute to science literacy to focus on content that does.

Fourth, the common core of learning in science, mathematics, and technology should center on the connected knowledge from many disciplines that constitute science literacy, rather than on preparation for specifically disciplinary careers. *SFAA* describes knowledge about the physical setting and the living environment, reveals similarities between the natural and the social sciences, and reflects the interdependency of science, mathematics, and technology. When *SFAA* was published in 1989, it informed the national reform discourse, provoking serious and widespread discussion about key substantive and strategic issues such as science literacy, science for all, the overburdened curriculum, and goal-directed reform. In addition, specific science literacy goals from *SFAA* were discussed, and other national reform initiatives and standards developers adopted many of them. At the state level, prepublication drafts of *SFAA* were used in formulating the California Science Framework, which in turn served as the model for frameworks in many other states. Subsequently, dozens of states have drawn directly on *SFAA* in shaping their science education reform efforts. A large number of school districts, large and small, urban and rural, are using *SFAA* as a focus for their reform initiatives.

The positive response to the document by educators and scientists over the past five years indicates that the *SFAA* recommendations offer a sound and durable basis for designing curriculums in science, mathematics, and technology. In fact, when recently reprinting *SFAA*, we found it necessary to make only a half dozen small changes to the content in response to cumulative suggestions from the science and education communities since the book's publication.

A set of learning goals defining the science literacy expected from high school graduates only begins to define the content of an entire K–12 curriculum in science, mathematics, and technology. A curriculum designer or teacher for the early grades certainly could not make decisions about the content of the 2nd grade curriculum based on *SFAA* alone. Once we had satisfactorily answered the question of what all high school graduates should know and be able to do in science, mathematics, and technology, myriad questions remained. Two big ones were (1) *What* can students learn *in what sequence* and *at what approximate grade levels* during their 13 years in school to arrive at the science literacy goals described in SFAA? and (2) *How* must schooling change to ensure that K–12 education fosters that learning? Our next publication, *Benchmarks for Science Literacy* (1993), was an attempt to answer the first question and to begin suggesting some answers to the second.

Benchmarks arose from the work of school district teams of teachers and administrators who Project 2061 engaged to come up with thoughtful new curriculum ideas to satisfy the goals in *SFAA*.[4] While working on K–12 curriculum models to meet their local needs and the goals in *SFAA*, the teams immediately confronted the problem of how to sequence student understanding from rudimentary ideas intelligible to kindergartners toward the more sophisticated goals in *SFAA*. Based on their own classroom experiences and on education research, team members began to map out such sequences for many sections of *SFAA* and to collaborate with Project 2061 central staff on laying out a common set of expectations for students at various grade levels.

The resulting AAAS publication, *Benchmarks for Science Literacy,* translates *SFAA*'s view of literacy into benchmarks, or specific learning goals, for the ends of grades 2, 5, 8, and 12. (Though checkpoints for 4th, 8th, and 12th grades had been popularized by organizations such as the National Assessment of Educational Progress and the National Council of Teachers of Mathematics, all Project 2061 team members felt strongly that the developmental difference between a kindergartner and an 8th grader demanded more than one checkpoint.) The benchmarks represent learning thresholds that *all* students are expected to reach on their way to becoming science literate. These benchmarks are carefully sequenced to ensure that difficult benchmarks for later grades are anticipated by earlier-grade, precursor benchmarks that contribute to each later concept. For example, the following sample benchmarks from *Benchmarks for Science Literacy* (pp. 116–117) illustrate the K–12 progression of ideas for a single topic, Interdependence of Life:

Kindergarten through Grade 2
By the end of 2nd grade, students should know that
• Animals eat plants or other animals for food and may also use plants (or even other animals) for shelter and nesting.
• Living things are found almost everywhere in the world. There are somewhat different kinds in different places.

Grades 3 through 5
By the end of 5th grade, students should know that
• For any particular environment, some kinds of plants and animals survive well, some survive less well, and some cannot survive at all.

---

[4]We carefully selected the six teams to represent urban, suburban, and rural U.S. school districts and other demographic differences among U.S schools. Each team included elementary, middle, and high school teachers of science, mathematics, technology, social studies, and the humanities, as well as principals and curriculum specialists.

• Insects and various other organisms depend on dead plant and animal material for food.

• Organisms interact with one another in various ways besides providing food. Many plants depend on animals for carrying their pollen to other plants or for dispersing their seeds.

• Changes in an organism's habitat are sometimes beneficial to it and sometimes harmful.

• Most microorganisms do not cause disease, and many are beneficial.

Grades 6 through 8
By the end of 8th grade, students should know that

• In all environments—freshwater, marine, forest, desert, grassland, mountain, and others—organisms with similar needs may compete with one another for resources, including food, space, water, air, and shelter. In any particular environment, the growth and survival of organisms depend on the physical conditions.

• Two types of organisms may interact with one another in several ways: They may be in a producer/consumer, predator/prey, or parasite/host relationship. Or one organism may scavenge or decompose another. Relationships may be competitive or mutually beneficial. Some species have become so adapted to each other that neither could survive without the other.

Grades 9 through 12
By the end of 12th grade, students should know that

• Ecosystems can be reasonably stable over hundreds or thousands of years. As any population of organisms grows, it is held in check by one or more environmental factors: depletion of food or nesting sites, increased loss to increased numbers of predators, or parasites. If a disaster such as flood or fire occurs, the damaged ecosystem is likely to recover in stages that eventually result in a system similar to the original one.

• Like many complex systems, ecosystems tend to have cyclic fluctuations around a state of rough equilibrium. In the long run, however, ecosystems always change when climate changes or when one or more new species appear as a result of migration or local evolution.

• Human beings are part of the earth's ecosystems. Human activities can, deliberately or inadvertently, alter the equilibrium in ecosystems.

It is important to remember that benchmarks are goals for increasingly sophisticated understanding—not specifications for courses, units, or lessons by which students would learn. An immense amount of creativity and insight is still required for sketching curriculum and instruction. In addition to the sequential K–12 connections among benchmarks, there are many cross-subject connections in keeping with

Project 2061's emphasis on the interconnectedness of knowledge. To encourage curriculum designers to build important connections into units and materials, some of these connections are made explicit— through essays and a cross-reference feature—in *Benchmarks*. (The Translating Learning Goals into Curriculum section that follows will further discuss connections among the benchmarks.)

All of the teacher-recommended benchmarks underwent systematic examination in light of available cognitive and developmental research. For example, though the term "atom" appears in some science curriculums as early as 3rd grade, research shows that the idea of atoms—as invisibly small particles whose activities account for chemical and physical changes—is not likely to be grasped before grades 7 or 8, and not very well even then. And by middle school, students typically have some fixed misconceptions about atoms that must be overcome. Taking this into account, the relevant benchmarks recommend a variety of preliminary experiences and ideas through grade 5, which anticipate an introduction to atomic theory in grades 6–8 and a more thorough treatment of the topic in high school. Sometimes the research corroborated the teams' initial recommendations; other times it indicated that a benchmark should be moved to another grade level, or that some additional early-grade benchmarks had to be created to prepare students for a later, difficult benchmark.

Benchmarks Chapter 15, "The Research Base," provides a survey of all such research bearing on the substance and grade-level placement of the benchmark statements. For example, this excerpt supports the content and placement of benchmarks dealing with the universe and the earth:

4A The Universe

Research available on student understanding about the universe focuses on their concepts of the sun as a star and as the center of our planetary system. The ideas "the sun is a star" and "the earth orbits the sun" appear counter-intuitive to elementary school students (Baxter 1989, Vosniadou and Brewer 1992) and are not likely to be believed or even understood in those grades (Vosniadou 1991). Whether it is possible for elementary students to understand these concepts even with good teaching needs further investigation (p. 335).

4B The Earth

Shape of the earth. Student ideas about the shape of the earth are closely related to their ideas about gravity and the direction of "down" (Nussbaum 1985, Vosniadou 1991). Students cannot accept that gravity is center directed if they do not know the earth is spherical. Nor can they believe in a spherical earth without some knowledge of gravity to account for why people on the "bottom" do not fall off. Students are likely to say many things that sound right even though their ideas may be very far off base. For example, they may say that the earth is spherical, but believe that people live on a flat place on top or inside of it—or believe that the round earth is "up there" like other planets, while people live down here (Sneider and Pulos 1983, Vosniadou 1991). Research suggests teaching the concepts of spherical earth, space, and gravity in close connection to each other (Vosniadou 1991). Some research indicates that students can understand basic concepts of the shape of the earth and gravity by 5th grade if the students' ideas are directly discussed and corrected in the classroom (Nussbaum 1985).

Explanations of astronomical phenomena. Explanations of the day-night cycle, the phases of the moon, and the seasons are very challenging for students. To understand these phenomena, students should first master the idea of a spherical earth, itself a challenging task (Vosniadou 1991). Similarly, students must understand the concept of "light reflection" and how the moon gets its light from the sun before they can understand the phases of the moon. Finally, students may not be able to understand explanations of any of these phenomena before they reasonably understand the relative size, motion, and distance of the sun, moon, and the earth (Sadler 1987, Vosniadou 1991) (pp. 335–336).

Not surprisingly, the development of *Benchmarks* exposed some of the current limitations of available education research, however. For some topics, especially those in the life and social sciences and technology, learning research is scant. Project 2061 hopes to encourage more research in these uncharted areas. Another problem is that any measure of how well students learn a particular concept from instruction specially contrived for research purposes may not indicate how well students would fare with the same concept in a typical classroom. And, of course, research cannot adequately predict what sort of learning can be expected from students of the future, whose understanding of science has been cultivated from kindergarten by exemplary teachers, who themselves have been schooled to science literacy in exemplary schools. But by taking into account both formal research and the recommendations of classroom teachers, *Benchmarks* provides a reasonable picture of what students—with the right kind of instruction—can be expected to know at various grade levels. *Benchmarks* will undergo periodic revisions as more research on learning becomes available[5] and as we see

[5]We hope researchers refer to *Benchmarks* to identify important topics for investigation. Such topics might include studies on the grade-level placement of benchmarks, the relationship between benchmarks and their precursors, effective ways to group benchmarks into instructional units, how to assess student progress toward science literacy, and how to evaluate learning materials and techniques used in support of the benchmarks.

how *Benchmarks* is being used in curriculum design and with what results.

Rather than get into a lengthy summary of the content of *Benchmarks*, which essentially elaborates on the same topics as *SFAA*, it may be more helpful to look at what a curriculum built around *Benchmarks* might be like.

Translating Learning Goals into Curriculum

By adopting the goals in *Benchmarks*, curriculum designers ensure themselves of a coherent rationale on which to base a K–12 science, mathematics, and technology curriculum. Because *Benchmarks* deliberately avoids prescribing a detailed program of instruction or specific materials, it leaves curriculum designers free to construct a curriculum that makes sense locally—one that reflects, for example, state and district requirements, student backgrounds and interests, teacher preferences, and local resources.

Our hope is that state framework groups and local curriculum designers will use *Benchmarks* in the spirit in which it was intended: that they will form K–12, cross-discipline committees to redesign or create a curriculum that reflects the K–12 continuity and cross-subject connections in *Benchmarks* and that they will design instruction to promote deep and lasting understanding of important ideas.

First, on the subject of curriculum connections, all the benchmark statements in *Benchmarks for Science Literacy* have implicit connections to other benchmarks and ultimately contribute to specific adult science literacy goals from *Science for All Americans.* But the reader may not immediately discern, for example, which K–2 learning goals contribute to later ideas in high school, or how ideas from the *Benchmarks* Chapter 4 section, Forces of Nature, complement ideas from the Chapter 8 section on Materials and Manufacturing. Only considerable familiarity with and extensive use of this 400-page book and its cross-reference feature reveal such connections. To illustrate for curriculum designers some of the important connections in *Benchmarks,* the Project has identified sample benchmark "strands," or webs of benchmarks that trace student progress from early-grade understandings toward particular adult science literacy goals from *Science for All Americans.* The sample strands, which are available in map form on the computer disk version of *Benchmarks,* cover a wide range of topics, including Centrality of Evidence, Feedback and Control in Technological Systems, Water

Cycle, Flow of Matter in Ecosystems, The Idea of Evolution, Culture and Heredity Influence Behavior, World Markets, and Sampling.

Figure 9.1 shows the way ideas from across *Benchmarks* chapters converge to represent a sophisticated idea from *SFAA:*

> However complex the workings of living organisms, they share with all other natural systems the same physical principles of the conservation and transformation of matter and energy. Over long spans of time, matter and energy are transformed among living things, and between them and the physical environment. In these grand-scale cycles, the total amount of matter and energy remains constant, even though their form and location undergo continual change (*SFAA*, p. 66).

Note that the particular phenomena covered by the early-grade benchmarks relate directly to the more abstract ideas reserved for grades 6–8. The map includes benchmarks from several chapters and sections within chapters, illustrating that the prerequisites for later ideas often come from more than a single subject-matter domain. (Of course, the organization for presenting *goals* in *SFAA* and *Benchmarks* is not meant to constrain the possible organization of ideas in the *curriculum.*)

The sample strand maps can be used in the analysis and planning of a K–12 curriculum or, we hope, can inspire curriculum designers to map additional strands for other *SFAA* goals. Curriculum designers can also consult or develop maps as they consider how to incorporate, at a particular grade level, connections across subject-matter domains—which leads to the often debated question of curriculum integration. The connections among ideas in *SFAA* or *Benchmarks* decidedly imply connectedness in the curriculum. But Project 2061 does not prescribe how the connections should be learned. Consistent with our emphasis on science literacy that spans the natural and social sciences, mathematics, technology, and the history of science, some curriculum designers may choose to build a thoroughly integrated curriculum around projects or social issues, drawing in mathematics, science, or social science content as it is needed to advance understanding. Yet Project 2061 does not necessarily endorse such vigorous integration of various disciplines. Another alternative is coordination of more traditional courses as in the original SS&C notion, so that students have their attention directed to ideas they learn in one subject that relate to ideas they encounter in other subjects. For example, when math teachers introduce the idea of probability, they can also demonstrate its usefulness in the study of heredity. Or geology, technology, and social science teachers can coordinate their instruction on various aspects of the energy consumption and fossil fuel story. Many curriculum designers will no doubt prefer the middle

FIGURE 9.1

Benchmarks Chapters Representing Idea from SFAA: Flow of Matter in Ecosystems

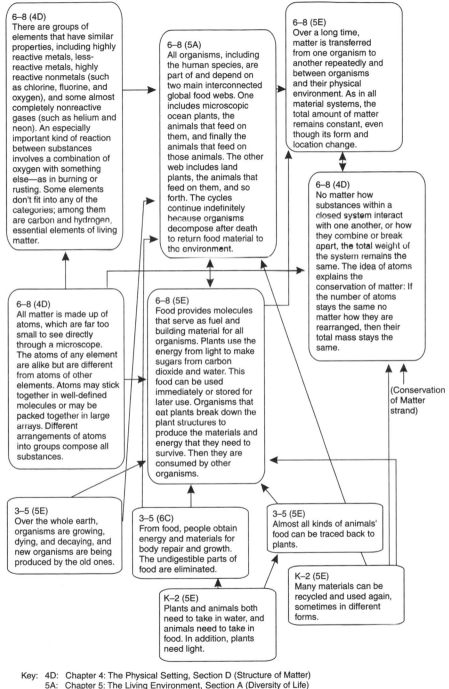

Key: 4D: Chapter 4: The Physical Setting, Section D (Structure of Matter)
5A: Chapter 5: The Living Environment, Section A (Diversity of Life)
5E: Chapter 5: The Living Environment, Section E (Flow of Matter and Energy)
6C: Chapter 6: The Human Organism, Section C (Basic Functions)
Source: Project 2061 Draft April 10, 1995.

ground when it comes to integration, working some integrated activities into a curriculum that also allots time to the separate disciplines. For example, "capstone" courses could make explicit the relatedness of subjects previously treated in separate courses. The cross-reference feature in the *Benchmarks* book and the strands available on the *Benchmarks* disk lend themselves to this full range of approaches.

Project 2061 does advocate, however, the importance of comprehensive planning across grades and subjects. Unless educators from various disciplines and grade levels work together to plan a K–12 curriculum for science literacy, any curricular connections are liable to be superficial. As our own school district teams have shown us, cross-discipline planning can result in different degrees of curriculum integration. Though all six teams devised abstract curriculum models that tended to favor integration, only a few of the teams have found circumstances in their districts favorable to implementing an integrated curriculum. For example, the San Francisco team, managed, among others, to implement a 3-week project on "Cardboard Kayaking," which incorporated ideas and skills from mathematics, science, technology, history, geography, language arts, drawing, and poetry. Because other teams have found their local school districts resistant to some of their grander schemes for curriculum integration, they have begun to promote curriculum connections by getting mathematics and science teachers together to discuss *Benchmarks*.

Earlier, we mentioned our hope that curriculums designed around *Benchmarks* would result not only in K–12 and cross-subject connections, but also in instruction that promotes deep and lasting understanding. This latter goal is easy to declare but difficult to accomplish. Curriculum designers will need a wide variety of curriculum materials to flesh out any K–12 curriculum based on *Benchmarks* and *SFAA*. Unfortunately, the Project's ongoing survey of curriculum resources reveals that materials and activities that adequately address benchmarks are scarce. Some benchmarks are quite difficult for students to learn well and seem to require more or different kinds of activities than are available in any single resource we have seen. And some very popular science and mathematics resources recommend activities that serve no benchmarks, addressing instead content that is different from or more sophisticated than the content of *Benchmarks'* threshold learning goals. It is understandable that the first priority for science education may be that students become engaged in and favorably disposed toward science, even if what is actually learned is not very important. It is to be hoped, however, that materials developers will be able to produce activities that teach important ideas as well as engage students. There is surely a place for "aerobic science education" (it does not matter what you learn as long as you are breathing hard), but we can try for more payoff.

To make a larger pool of suitable curriculum materials available to curriculum designers, Project 2061 is actively moving toward three goals: (1) identifying resources that in their current form might serve benchmarks, (2) encouraging creative thinking by educators about how to enhance existing resources to meet benchmarks, and (3) fostering the development of new materials around benchmarks. Our efforts toward these goals raise a number of complicated issues related to assessment and the organization of the curriculum. For example, how can 13 years of learning experiences be configured within the curriculum to ensure that all the benchmarks are met? And when is a benchmark "met"? Can we expect students to adequately grasp a benchmark after a single learning experience, or must they encounter the idea several times in diverse contexts over several years? If the latter is the case, how will this approach further complicate the organization of learning experiences over 13 years? How will students demonstrate that they have "learned a benchmark"? To answer these questions, we are examining the experiences of our school district teams and others engaged in translating the goals of *SFAA* and *Benchmarks* into curriculum models and frameworks, local curriculums, and even individual activities. Our findings will appear in a forthcoming Project 2061 publication, *Designs for Science Literacy,* which will show educators how to work through many of the issues involved in designing a curriculum around goals for science literacy. We hope further that *Designs* will eventually provide help to structure dialogue between still more diverse areas of the curriculum— including the humanities and arts—to encourage the overall planning of coordinated reform that will be necessary for sustained improvement in schooling.

References

American Association for the Advancement of Science. (1989). *Science for All Americans.* New York: Oxford University Press.

American Association for the Advancement of Science. (1993). *Benchmarks for Science Literacy.* New York: Oxford University Press.

American Association for the Advancement of Science. *Blueprints for Reform.* Manuscript in preparation.

American Association for the Advancement of Science. *Designs for Science Literacy.* Manuscript in preparation.

Baxter, J. (1989). "Children's Understanding of Familiar Astronomical Events." *International Journal of Science Education,* 11: 502–513.

National Research Council. (1994). *National Science Education Standards* (draft). Washington, D.C.: National Academy Press.

Nussbaum, J. (1985). "The Earth as a Cosmic Body." In *Children's Ideas in Science,* edited by R. Driver, E. Guesne, and A. Tiberghien. Milton Keynes, UK: Open University Press.

Project on Scope, Sequence, and Coordination of Secondary School Science. (1993). *The Content Core.* Vol. I. Washington, D.C.: National Science Teachers Association.

Project on Scope, Sequence, and Coordination of Secondary School Science. (1992). *Relevant Research.* Vol. II. Washington, D.C.: National Science Teachers Association.

Sadler, P. (1987). "Misconceptions in Astronomy." In *Proceedings of the Second International Seminar Misconceptions and Educational Strategies in Science and Mathematics,* edited by J. Novak. Vol. 3. Ithaca, NY: Cornell University.

Sneider, C., and S. Pulos. (1983). "Children's Cosmographies: Understanding the Earth's Shape and Gravity." *Science Education,* 67, 2: 205–221.

Vosniadou, S. (1991). "Designing Curricula for Conceptual Restructuring: Lessons from the Study of Knowledge Acquisition in Astronomy." *Journal of Curriculum Studies* 23: 219–237.

Vosniadou, S., and W. Brewer. (1992). "Mental Models of the Earth: A Study of Conceptual Change in Childhood." *Cognitive Psychology* 24: 535–585.

10

Social Studies: The Study of People in Society

Donald H. Bragaw and H. Michael Hartoonian

The 21st century will bring us face-to-face with the information-electronic-biotechnological age. A new set of issues, together with persistent problems, will confront us and tax our intellectual and moral fiber, making it even more difficult to realize the fundamental democratic ideals of our society (Cleveland 1985). Demographic and statistical data speak clearly to the rapidly changing nature of our families; the reconceptualization of work; the distribution of justice and poverty; the securing of human rights for all; the conditions of illiteracy; and the age, class, and ethnic makeup of our citizens. The world is diverse, globally interdependent, and ethically challenged, and the task of "bringing the American dream to all" calls for citizens with a new sense of purpose. It is within this context that social studies takes a leading role in helping students understand their social world—how it came to be, how it relates to natural systems, and how to constructively and actively engage themselves in its development (Boulding 1985, Task Force for Global Education in the U.S. 1987). Robert Bellah and his associates (1986) have described it well:

> Citizenship is virtually coexistent with getting involved with one's neighbors for the good of the community. . . . One of the keys to the

survival of free institutions is the relationship between private and public life, the way in which citizens do, or do not, participate in the public sphere (p. 200).

What we are advocating is a social studies program based on the notion of policymaking—both personal and public. Inspired by the social interactive inquiry philosophy of Charles S. Peirce (1956); John Dewey (1916, 1927, 1938), Charles Beard (1932, 1934), and L.S. Vygotsky (1978); and the work of social studies theorists Erling Hunt and Lawrence Metcalf (1968), Newmann, Bertoucci, Landness (1975), Shirley Engle and Anna Ochoa (1988), and Freeman Butts (1989), we seek to make comprehensible the intensely social nature of the operating world as students will come to know it. Schools must help students understand this very real world so they can cope with the pressures of their own existence, while at the same time giving them the tools by which to understand, analyze, and promote policy at all levels in society.

Many people think of policies concerning health care, welfare, refugees from Haiti, or AIDS as being national or state-level governmental concerns and make little or no connection between policy actions or statements and the values, beliefs, and habits that guide an individual's decision to act in certain ways on key personal issues that affect that individual's daily life. In truth, such personal policies have a significant effect in a number of different ways because

- No decision, personal or public, is ever made in isolation.
- Individual policy decisions have personal and social dimensions.
- There are multiple explanations and/or interpretations for people's beliefs and actions.
- A single decision may have a rippling effect beyond the policy statement.

Personal policy decisions occur in much the same fashion that national policies are considered and rejected or enacted into operational law. Policy studies provide students with a set of analytical tools by which to consider major issues and problems in their own lives, the lives of others, and at all levels of governance—past and present. They also create frames of deliberation in which students' personal values can be juxtaposed with the values and beliefs of others and the larger societies of which they are members. Such studies provide a content or knowledge vehicle by which students can connect their real lives to the world around them by investigating and evaluating past and present situations through historical and social science data.

Present Issues in Social Studies

Although social studies is regarded as an important part of any academic program in all 50 states and all U.S. possessions, there is often disagreement among educators about the purpose and nature of the social studies curriculum. Over the past 10 years, serious efforts have been made to define or redefine the field of social studies by persons within the professional field and well-meaning reformers from without (Bragaw 1986b). Unlike mathematics or science, social studies is an area of the school's program about which *everyone* has an opinion concerning what should be addressed in the curriculum. The Bradley Commission (1988) decried what they referred to as the decline of history and made recommendations to improve that subject (history) K–12 while assigning the social sciences a much lesser role. The National Commission on Social Studies in the Schools (NCSSS 1989), taking a similar tack in emphasizing history and geography, made few significant changes in the overall design of the traditional social studies program. NCSSS did, however, propose for grades 9–11 a radical adjustment in the study of history that blends the story of the United States into the total fabric of world history over a three-year span of time. During this same period, the National Council for the Social Studies (NCSS), the professional social studies association, has been reexamining the nature of the subject. Their most recent effort at providing a definitional position has won the support of the field, as well as other educational associations. This support is for an inclusive definition statement for social studies that stresses the importance of subject matter knowledge, curriculum integration, and the central goal of civic competence. NCSS (1994) asserts:

> Social studies is the integrated study of the social sciences and humanities to promote civic competence. Within the school program, social studies provides coordinated, systematic study drawing upon such disciplines as anthropology, archaeology, economics, geography, history, law, philosophy, political science, psychology, religion, and sociology, as well as appropriate content from the humanities, mathematics, and natural sciences. The primary purpose of social studies is to help young people develop the ability to make informed and reasoned decisions for the public good as citizens of a culturally diverse, democratic society in an interdependent world (p. 3).

The work of the social studies professional community has always been to bring the scholarship of the social sciences (including history and geography) to pedagogical life. During the past three decades, research and logic have suggested new configurations to the study of people in society. This newer scholarship suggests that greater attention be paid to broad ideas and patterns of human and social change across cultures; to the emerging and challenging variations in social systems and political economies; to involvement in the formulation, implementation, and appraisal of personal and public policies and choices; and to bringing into the mainstream those whose lives and heritage have been excluded by previously prescribed versions of "truth." The call is for greater intensity in fewer topics, more student involvement in the construction of their own learning, and the development of values that uphold and secure a democratic way of life.

Content Standards in Social Studies

The last decade of the 20th century seems to be a time of establishing standards, developing assessment designs, and limiting curriculum experimentation. These activities seem curious and, perhaps, contradictory, given the fact that the reform topics of "restructuring schools" and "site-based management" are but two contemporary and important educational thrusts encouraging teachers themselves to become standards setters. Indeed, the problem in social studies has never been a lack of content; the problem has been one of overload. The multiplicity of standards being developed in each of the social sciences threatens, once again, to overwhelm teachers and students and confuse a public already dismayed by the inability of educators to agree on programs that deal with the problems confronting society.

At the time this chapter went to press, several academic areas either have or will have developed standards to guide the selection of content to be included in the social studies curriculum. To bring some semblance of order and coherence to these efforts, the National Council for the Social Studies (1994) has developed 10 standards statements that address the separate social science disciplines *and* their integration. These statements provide a vehicle for helping educators use the separate standards being developed, in that the NCSS standards provide a content umbrella—for seeing relationships among the social sciences—under which content specificity can be achieved using the separate standards developed in the areas of history, geography, civics, and so forth. For example, one of the NCSS standards for history—time, continuity, and change—states that the learner will, in the 4th grade, be able to "demonstrate an ability to use correct vocabulary associated with time, reading and constructing simple time lines, identifying examples of change, and recognizing examples of cause and effect" (p. 34). In the 8th grade, the learner will be able to "identify and use key concepts such as time, chronology, causality, change, conflict, and complexity to explain, analyze, and show connections among patterns of historical change and continuity" (p. 34).

The importance of these standards across the grade levels is in their attention to the essence of historical knowledge and historical processes and their inescapable connections to the other social sciences. As teachers and others involved in curriculum design develop the specificity for a history class, for example, they should use the NCSS standards to establish a broad K–12 social studies curriculum design into which the history standards can be placed. Similar relationships have been established between the content umbrella provided by the NCSS standards and in-depth attention being given to specific content areas by standards developed in geography, civics, economics, and so forth. Thus, as specific topics and time periods are considered for inclusion in the curriculum, teachers are encouraged to study and draw from the several social science discipline standards themselves. In this way, teachers and curriculum developers have a more inclusive picture of the scope of social studies programs. The NCSS standards are a very real way to avoid the dilemma of content overload, as so often occurred in the past, and encourage greater thematic organizational focus for content integration.

The Nature of Knowledge in Social Studies

Almost everything about the social world is more complex than we have allowed students to understand. Allowing students to discover how the world works always involves the dilemma of the proper relationships among information, knowledge, and reality. It is extremely important to recognize that there is a significant difference between information and knowledge. Information is one-dimensional—linear or horizontal, fragmented, and quite useless in and of itself. On the other hand, students gain knowledge about regions, for example, when they can take information about places on the earth, structure it to show relationships among those pieces of information, and use it to construct their own concept of region. Once formed, the students' concept of region can be enhanced and refined and used again and again, each time with greater clarity and analytical power. The process of structuring and using information develops knowledge. Information provided by a teacher or textbook is generally, and wrongfully, perceived as knowledge. Such collections of information, structured according to frameworks designed by textbook writers, or preconstructed by adults, remains information, not knowledge. Knowledge is something *created* through a process of personal involvement that allows for complex relationships between the learners (including the teacher), the materials of instruction, and the context of the classroom, even when that classroom includes the larger community (Raskin and Bernstein 1987, Brooks and Brooks 1993).

The challenge for teachers is to design varied experiences that promote the use of information from the several areas of the social sciences, as well as from the humanities, science, and mathematics, to help students create knowledge for themselves. For this creative process to work with integrity, the most powerful content-based concepts must be used, for they are the best ideas available for helping students formulate personal and public policy decisions. Big ideas such as justice, equality, freedom, and diversity become powerful content containers when students grasp principal connections within and across subject areas and use these ideas to conceptualize reality, deal with causality and validity, and create meaning.

It is important to select information and knowledge from the humanities and mathematics and science, but this type of interactive social studies curriculum is grounded in history and the social sciences because students can use information across the span of historical time to analogize and reflect on the larger meanings of their concepts. The nature of this knowledge, however, must be seen from the vantage point of two interrelated questions: (1) What content should be selected to best serve students in their efforts to understand the human condition? and (2) What abilities should students develop to engage in this search?

Integrated Nature of Content

Life is, and always has been, integrated. And knowledge is culturally and historically determined and interpreted by its seekers. Unless we construct school programs upon these truths, we put our students at risk of misinterpreting, or falsely analyzing, the world around them. For example, the sciences of the 20th century are quite different from 16th century science and, no doubt, will differ from 21st century science. Thus, separating our science or our tools from our culture, or separating our several bodies of organized knowledge from one another and from the issues and problems they help us to investigate, leads us to half-truths and disillusionment.

A curriculum that attempts to address authentic abilities and issues, then, must be based upon an integrated and coherent structure of meaning. And, because meaning is rooted in culture, the quality of that curriculum will be determined by how completely and accurately our models of knowledge reflect the reality of culture. A model for the integration of knowledge is useful to the degree that it provides a framework for observing, describing, analyzing, evaluating, and making policies about society that lead to a more holistic understanding of how the world works (Toepfer 1990, 1994; Banaszak, Hartoonian, and Leming 1991; Beane 1990; Wronski and Bragaw 1986; Boulding 1985; Goodlad 1984).

Our present technological ability to generate data—raw information—and to manipulate it in manifold ways, forces everyone concerned with education to realize that the learning process must be based on inquiry, problem solving, and decision making. The sheer volume of data can no longer be committed to memory; only the ability to conceptualize enables students to separate and efficiently use all the information available to them.

Research in cognition points to the need for a major shift in teachers' epistemological assumptions. It explains that learning occurs only when students are involved in making their own meaning by adding to or revising previously established foundations. The teacher's role is to provide those opportunities for adding and revising and to assist in clarifying or suggesting new dimensions of knowledge not yet determined by the student. Those opportunities should not be restricted by artificial discipline walls but rather generated by major concepts or big ideas with mind-expanding or global power.

Operational Abilities

Social studies content should help students study, learn, and use the powerful ideas and skills from history and the social sciences. Whatever the program—whether it focuses on history, expanding horizons, themes, or concepts—the significant question is what students will be expected to achieve. Those expectations should center around the following abilities:

1. *Students need to be able to develop an information base in history and the social sciences and to make connections among previously learned and new information.* The most important attribute of this ability is the idea of "connections." A necessary condition of making informational connections that move one toward knowledge and wisdom is a

sound information base. But the more significant condition comes with the extension of this information to areas new to the learner. Learning the facts about the needs people have in various societies, for example, is a necessary condition to learning about the connections between needs and social institutions in any society. It may well be, as Hunt and Metcalf (1968) observed, that "there is only one role which facts can play in meaningful learning—to function as data in conceptualization. If they do not, they may, perhaps, be memorized and retained for awhile, but their meaning and future usefulness will be slight." This ability to conceptualize is, basically, knowing how to use data to make meaning. Marilyn Ferguson (1976) summed it up nicely:

> In most lives, insight has been accidental. We wait for it as primitive man awaited lightning for a fire. But making mental connections is our most crucial learning tool. This is the essence of human intelligence: to forge links; to go beyond the given; to see patterns, relationship, and context (p. 71).

The task of the curriculum leader, then, is to make sure that a dynamic factual base is built into each social studies program. The most worthy facts help students build connections and deal with orders of magnitude. For example, knowing the number of farmers in the United States is not as important as knowing the percentage of farmers in the economy and their contribution to the gross national product. Knowing the size of the national debt, in and of itself, is not as powerful as knowing the magnitude of the national debt in relation to national worth.

Orders of magnitude also have historical and geographical worth. Curriculum designers can address the factual base of the social studies by introducing materials that raise questions about connections. For example: How have income levels changed over the last 75 years in the United States? Where is the population center of the United States today? Where was it 75 years ago? Why has it changed? The factual base that helps children best see relationships and connections in their own lives is the one to use; but students must realize that facts are constantly changing. Each grade level should stress different orders of magnitude and different fact clusters, always seeking to reveal connections.

2. *Students need the ability to think using different logical patterns and perspectives obtained through the study of history and the social sciences.* The content areas of the social studies can help students see, understand, and use different logical patterns and identify cause/effect relationships. Causality means dealing with questions of explanation, evidence, and bias. For example, older students can be provided with information that helps them explore the political, geographic, economic,

and historic rationales for active U.S. involvement in Central and Caribbean-American affairs. From this, they can construct arguments for and against such involvement in ways that reflect the patterns of thought and world views of the actors on all sides of the issue. This ability involves using inductive, deductive, and analogical forms of logic. At the lower elementary level, this ability might be developed by asking a class to establish reasons why schools and communities have rules.

Logical patterns and perspectives of history and the social sciences must be understood within the time-space continuum in which we live. In this sense, history and geography are parts of the same whole. What does a map of the world look like with China at its center? What was going on in China or in North Africa compared with activities in Western Europe in the 9th or 10th century A.D.? The answers to these questions suggest that time and place orientations provide frameworks for thinking about issues, problems, and possibilities.

Logical patterns and perspectives also have to do with the analysis of the social systems in which we live. This means attending to how reality is conceptualized by various societal populations; how these conceptions are explained and validated; and how new concepts, generalizations, and laws are created given altered circumstances. Students who grasp the essential meaning of the humanistic nature of the 15th and 16th century Renaissance (rather than memorizing the names of painters or writers) will be more significantly served when they encounter the Harlem Renaissance in American history or the term "urban renaissance" in their daily newspapers. Thus, the ideas of perspective (time and space) and logic (the analysis of social and other systems) provide criteria for content selection by suggesting questions such as Does this content and learning material enable students to "travel" to different times (past, present, and future) and places (near and far) in a way that allows them to see multiple connections? Does this content allow students to analyze institutions and systems in these times and places as a way of finding out how their own world works? Does this content allow students to "see" this multicultural, multiethnic, interdependent world through "different eyes"—as well as their own?

3. *Students need to be able to recognize that new knowledge is created by their interaction with new information from history or the social sciences.* Creating new knowledge means developing and designing new stories, explanations, models, pictures, dramas, music, or other modes of communicating extensions of previously learned knowledge to new settings, questions, and issues. In this context, students may design and build new model communities in the 3rd grade, write dramas

about social institutions in different cultures in the 6th grade, and prepare a position paper on changes in fiscal policy that could reflect serious thought about the economic health of the country in the 12th grade.

The most important element in the process of helping students become more creative in their ability to develop useful knowledge is the "pairing" of facts and ideas—that is, the bringing together of different thoughts, points of view, or rationales to form a reflective, new synthesis. For example, as 3rd graders consider the traffic patterns in a community, talk with police and city planners, look at traffic patterns in other communities, and discuss the issue with people who drive cars and use other means of transportation, they can propose a new design to move people and goods. Students who pursue a study of peace or conflict resolution over the vast span of history (e.g., the Trojan War to the Camp David Accords) might be able to develop some basic generalizations, principles, or axioms that appear to be useful in settling disputes. Such principles might then be tested by students using current conflicts to make judgments about the lessons of history.

Learning such as this must be based on major ideas and many different types of materials and experiences. Curriculum leaders, including teachers, therefore, need to provide settings and resources that help students consider different ideas and develop and express their own.

4. *Students need to be able to learn to communicate with others about the data and interpretations of history and the social sciences as applied to their studies and to the real world.* Communication skills such as reading, writing, listening, and speaking should enable students to convey and receive knowledge from history and the social sciences in ways that communicate meaning and a rationale for civic behavior. Students must be given opportunities to recognize different perceptions and to learn and practice ways to negotiate positions with respect for different perspectives. Additionally, they need to recognize that some people operate from an ignorant or irrational base, for whatever reason, which makes it difficult to either communicate or negotiate with them.

What strategies and settings allow for the study of problem solving, bargaining, and the reluctant use of force in human decision making? Historical examples are frequently found in the causes of war or in major economic, political, or social policy debates such as health care, welfare, or gays in the military. When using communication/negotiation as a criterion for content selection, curriculum leaders must take into account two notions of human interaction. One obvious idea is that communication/negotiation is a matter of skill development in reading, writing, listening, and speaking. These skills are important to all school subjects, and the content selection criterion here simply involves permitting enough time and practice for students to write and teachers to guide them in their communication skill development process at appropriate learning levels within the social studies program. A less obvious notion is the appreciation of the nature and necessity of transcending personal experiences, sampling ideas from the past as well as from contemporary societies, which help us carry on a human dialogue. Such a dialogue brings meaning to persistent questions such as What is a good citizen? Can an individual be just in an unjust society? What is the proper relationship between positive and natural law? Can virtue be taught? How should minority rights be protected? What is justice? What is happiness? Understanding these and other questions demands good communication and negotiation skills.

It is important that students deal with representative ideas that connect certain themes across the ages. It is equally important that they know how to sample the totality of information in the first place. Thus, learning materials should use or have students use sampling and other methodological techniques, including those used by historians and social scientists, to collect, organize, interpret, and communicate information and knowledge.

5. *Students need to be able to learn how to make enlightened personal and public policy decisions based on their knowledge of history and the social sciences and participation in meaningful civic activities.* Making personal and public policy decisions requires that students can conceptualize a problem or issue, create a plausible sequence of cause/effect relationships between events and consequences, create and evaluate alternative sequences, and implement a decision that has as its base concern the value of democratic society and individual well-being. These abilities can be discussed from the point of view of a series of questions such as Were people less concerned with environmental issues in the 18th and 19th centuries? What is your evidence? What should we learn about the social ecosystems in which we all live? How can we learn to become better inhabitants of the earth?

By policymaking, we also mean that students, through formal and informal learning and social relationships, begin to develop self-governance abilities that extend into the various publics in which students find themselves. Creating civic actors requires that the social studies program from the early years on include contemporaneous, historical, and literary elements that help students increase their critical thinking capacity about all types of people making personal decisions and public policies.

Such an orientation calls for developing social participation activities focused on democratic, individual, and cooperative policymaking such as

- developing classroom and school rules (fairness);
- dealing with classroom and school incidents that call for adjudication through negotiation (justice);
- agreeing on and carrying out tasks related to projects (responsibility);
- reading and discussing stories that pose dilemmas for their characters (equality); and
- giving students opportunities for vicarious policy decision making (values examination).

* * *

Curriculum leaders should include each of these five abilities in their instructional designs. Consider, for example, the issue of whether or not a state should build a new maximum security prison versus passing antigun legislation. An instructional unit that addresses the five operational abilities could first develop factual background on the issue and stress those data among which connections can be drawn. For example, what is the relationship between incarceration, gun use, and state crime rates? How much will the prison cost? How will the money for the prison be raised? What trade-offs will have to be made in the state budget? Will antigun laws reduce the amount of crime?

Students could look at the issue from different political orientations. They could then role-play the different positions through a series of "public hearings" that provide opportunities for practicing communication and negotiation skills. Public policy positions could then be formulated based on the results of research and discussions. And student participation in government, business, or other internships could provide practical experience in observing how policy is derived. Thus, the unit helps students develop, extend, and refine all five operational abilities.

Abilities into Knowledge

The successful learning of these five abilities demands content and materials that deal with significant intellectual concepts and involve an examination of public and private issues of importance in an integrative manner. For example, discussion of the New Deal, the New Frontier, the location of a new school, or welfare programs becomes important when students can see the major ideas that underlie these topics, when they are able to consider the nature of the policies involved, and when these events are related in some real way to their own lives. Content selection criteria must initially be concerned with "big ideas" and should address settings and materials that help students develop problem-solving skills from hypothesis formation to using probability and statistics. These ideas, settings, resources, and materials should also include opportunities to engage in scenario development, case study analysis, philosophical reasoning, and the use of documents and stories (literature) that illuminate the lives of people—their intellectual, moral, physical, and spiritual courage as well as their corruptibility (Dewey 1927, Newmann and Oliver 1970, Bragaw 1986a).

When this content is used as a basis for the interactions between teachers and students, the result is social studies knowledge. By definition, then, the quality and self-correcting features of this knowledge are functions of the quality of the interactions among teachers, students, and content resources within the bureaucratic and ideological constructs of school. When considering knowledge in this way, it is possible to more accurately develop a logical and fair evaluation system. The five abilities can be considered not only as criteria for content selection but also for student and program evaluation. Students achieve more, and program evaluation is easier when the focus of learning is clear.

Again, the purpose is to refocus curricular questions away from the coverage of information and toward helping students construct frameworks of meaning consistent with the nature of knowledge in the social studies. This means letting go of some information now being taught and reallocating time to deeper inquiries that help learners build intra- and interdisciplinary connections. The challenge of such a constructivist approach is not to teachers alone, but places much greater responsibility on the student and the entire professional school support system, which must be attuned to this dramatic change.

Program Design

The curriculum design suggested here is based upon the interaction between single discipline and integrated knowledge configurations as they exist in schools today. The present curriculum and some present trends in social studies are similar to trends found in other content fields. That is, integrated programs have and will continue to increase in importance in elementary schools and in the middle schools, while high schools will continue to be university-discipline oriented, with the possible exception of programs in the last years of the sequence when such courses as humanities, science and society, global studies, and contemporary issues will continue to exist as long as district budgets permit.

In the new century, children must learn to grapple with two major forces that suggest a more integrative approach to learning: (1) the irrevocable global interdependence of all people and nations, and (2) the creation of knowledge patterns that no longer fit neatly into Aristotelian and Germanic discipline structures (Boyer and Levine 1981, Raskin and Bernstein 1987, Brady 1989). Both of these forces make it essential that education provide better opportunities for students to learn how to study ideas in different ways and participate in the decisions that will affect their destinies. While the emphasis on citizenship is not new to social studies, the emphasis on policy studies within the total program is new (Beard 1934, Newmann and Oliver 1970).

Along with the five operational abilities, an emphasis on policy studies must take into account some "constants"—themes essential to the perpetuation of our humanity—as well as new phenomena brought about by advances in science, technology, and new thought in history and the social sciences. Themes that help us recognize the powerful ideas that motivate and shape the world around us will help students focus their learning.

There have been many suggestions over the years as to which major concepts offer the most powerful organizing framework for the school program called social studies. The following are eight possible themes for a policy studies focus K–12. They should not be considered absolute. Given the dynamic quality of the social sciences, curriculum choices should be made on the basis of age appropriateness, curriculum significance, and societal relevance.

Cultural Diversity and Unity

At the turn of the century, it was a prevalent belief that hyphenated Americans should discard their cultural heritages and melt together in the crucible of American society, thus forming a new race of people (Zangwill 1975). Such thinking has been replaced by a growing consciousness of the value of each individual's heritage, and recognition that we are unified by our geography and a wide-ranging democratic society. Cultural pluralism, people living side-by-side from different backgrounds, is a reality in our own country and the world. This should not suggest that separatism or particularism should prevail; rather that all perspectives are compatible and should all contribute to preserving the unity of the democratic republic we all share.

Change and Continuity

People, events, and ideas change. History records the struggles between people and groups who favor and oppose change. While it is seldom a clear or smooth process, change is, nevertheless, continuous and currently shows signs of accelerating. But as important as change is in our lives, the human experience is continuous and interrelated. Continuity is also a fact of life. People are inevitably a product of all of the changes that have occurred before. Students must learn how change and continuity constantly influence their lives and the world in which they live.

Global Perspective

Notions of "global community," "spaceship earth," "the shrinking globe," and "global interdependence" abound in current literature. Every society struggles with the ongoing conflict between the desire for independence and the realities of interdependence. The world is becoming more crowded, more interconnected, and more volatile. While political boundaries may confine, cultural boundaries tend to disappear with rapidly expanding economic, social, technological, and human interaction patterns that transcend political lines.

Place

The study of area distribution, the examination of particular places, and the delineation of regions help students understand how earth species are organized. People use similar earth space or areas in different ways. People move themselves, messages, and goods and services over interconnecting transportation and communication routes. Their lives are governed by a variety of spatial arrangements. The study of geography not only includes people and almost all their activities but also the earth and earth processes. Consequently, geography links the social and the natural sciences and provides the spatial perspective necessary for understanding culture and human behavior.

Technology and Science

Technology and science constitute an inclusive set. That is, the line between these notions is not always clear. As humans modify nature for their purposes, they engage in both science and engineering. Technology can also be understood as one of our "tools." We use these tools in utilitarian as well as aesthetic ways to bring comfort, meaning, enjoyment, and danger to our lives. Given the facts of the Information Age, data and technologies are so pervasive in our lives and the lives of most of the world's people that we, indeed, do see and understand the natural and social worlds only within the frameworks of the tools we use. Social studies education must help students understand the role of technology in their lives and alert them to both its promises and its potential dangers.

Production and Consumption

Every society faces four fundamental choices: (1) What and how many goods and services should be produced? (2) How much and in what way are natural resources, human resources, and capital (tools) to be used for production? (3) Should the goods and services be used for immediate consumption or further production? and (4) How shall the total output of a society be divided among its members? These four questions constitute a fundamental conflict between unlimited economic needs and wants, and limited natural and human resources. The basic economic problem of scarcity confronts all societies in different ways and to different degrees. Even though the problem is economic, its solutions involve political and cultural decisions.

Governance

Governments are established to provide security, protection, and essential public services. Authority is legitimate power, recognized as such and sanctioned by custom, institutions, laws, constitutions, or morality. In a democracy, authority is sanctioned by the consent of the governed at all levels of the society's political structure. The exercise of democratic political authority should be guided by social justice and fairness. Political authority should work to ensure the greatest amount of individual freedom under law and seek a fair distribution of privileges and resources to all citizens. Every social studies student should understand the function and role of government and authority in a democratic society.

Citizenship

Citizenship in a democracy involves both obligations and privileges. Students need to understand how government and the political system actually work. In social studies classes, students should have opportunities to develop the knowledge and skills required to be effective citizens in a democratic society. They need to understand the underlying purposes and values of government in a free society, which requires opportunities for them to practice their roles, rights, and responsibilities as citizens. One focus should be on helping students understand the necessary distinctions between private and public interest, and that, as Pericles enjoins us, a democratic society demands that they participate in its deliberations. The all-important notion of public service should also be built into programs.

Again, it should be stressed that although these are highly recommended as guiding concepts for social studies programs, they are suggested as a beginning place for social studies professionals, selecting the major ideas that govern their content decisions at the elementary, middle, and secondary school levels.

Elementary Programs

Early elementary programs naturally tend to be integrative. Teachers are generalists at this level, and students are open and eager to explore—uncrushed yet by overwhelming content—and are beginning to emerge from protective home environments. A major concern is mastery of reading, writing, and computational basics. The challenge is to allow those basics to develop in a variety of contexts that promote problem-solving and decision-making capacities. Social studies provides the ideal context.

Whether the program is focused on the "expanding horizons" or another curriculum design, geography, history, and the other social sciences provide a cauldron of information and ideas (in the eight content themes) that allow children to explore the worlds around them—present, past, and future. Any such program includes multiple occasions to examine the very critical questions of diversity and conflicting values between and among individual experiences (ethnic conflicts, group migration decisions, national immigration policies, and increased diversity among new U.S. citizens). Each of the examples in the eight content themes provides a rewarding context for the combination of all of these factors.

Undertaking historical investigations (such as historical preservation, archaeological digs, family roots, and personal time lines), economic simulations (such as The Mini-Society), and the solving of geographic location problems within the context of community studies are but some ways in which children's problem-solving skills can be challenged. State and local governance can best be studied by examining the local issues that consistently beset communities—and invariably require some type of intervention or other action. Mediation programs that help reinforce interactive communication skills are now being introduced in many elementary school programs. The entire scope of conflict resolution has taken on a new life as violence begins to infiltrate the elementary school. It is not too early for students to study, discuss, and act upon issues such as environmental dangers, hunger, poverty, racial equality, civil rights, and other issues that recur in history and to which people have responded with a variety of policy actions over the years.

Civic involvement and responsibility are also developed through the establishment of democratically operated classrooms, which provide students with opportunities to participate in the choice of curriculum directions. Developing simple but worthy classroom, school, and community service projects encourages early student recognition of personal decisions and public policy outcomes. School improvements, antilittering, and safety campaigns can be organized and carried out by students (Saxe 1994).

The Middle Grades

The middles grades are an area where, while it has taken some 20 or more years—changes in school structure appear to be making headway (George and Alexander 1993; George, Stevenson, Thomason, and Beane 1992; Vars 1987; Toepfer 1994). Principles of adolescent development suggest that the organization and presentation of subject matter disciplines in the middle grades address the intellectual growth of students and their ability to construct meaning. In an attempt to deal with the nature of adolescence, which is a time of uneven and sporadic intellectual, physical, and emotional development, it is recommended that learning occur "in its natural state," which is clearly a call for the integration of knowledge. Designing such learning requires an examination of the way in which teachers, courses, and students are organized. Grade-level interdisciplinary teaming; integrative or interdisciplinary curriculum; heterogeneous grouping; and the use of cooperative learning strategies are becoming standard middle school practices (Stevenson and Carr 1993). The recommendation described earlier for the elementary grades is the foremost premise upon which middle grades curriculum is now built. Themes govern an entire school's program, or thematic units help students grasp the notion that knowledge is not naturally separated into university-dictated compartments, but rather is holistic and integrated by natural forces.

James Beane (1990), a foremost proponent of the reform of middle grades curriculum, suggests two areas of curriculum concern—issues of a personal nature (personal changes, identity, social status, friendships, etc.) and issues of a wider, more global and community-conscious focus (the changing world, cultural diversity, interdependence, the environment, effects of the media, etc.). These concerns suggest to Beane some fundamental unifying curriculum themes largely derived from the social sciences. Four such themes are interdependence, justice, conflict resolution, and transitions.

Using this paradigm, Beane suggests that traditional schooling, governed as it is (in a majority of schools) by traditional university research agendas, has little to do with the lives of students of this age group—perhaps the most critical age group in terms of future development and decision making (Toepfer 1990). Beane's program also makes headway in melding Gardner's (1991) "frames of mind"—positing at least seven student intellectual entry points for ideas and information processing.

Some innovative middle schools have put together classroom- and school-tested integrated curriculums built around major themes (Ross and Olsen 1993). The major thrust is on designing an entire middle school (whether grades 5–8 or 6–9), focused on integrating knowledge. An additional question in all of this, which has portent for the future, is why not look upon the middle school as a continuous experience by creating a nongraded situation in which students progress according to both their interest and their ability to master the processes of learning?

In this way, students would have mastered—for their age, experience, and mental maturity—the five basic abilities seen as key to any well-prepared individual. The fact that the themes are all oriented in the social sciences clearly points to the power of social studies as the major integrative force for all curriculum.

This idea of integrated knowledge as the core of the middle grades program fits well with several ideas advanced by the various social science disciplines—each separate from the other, and not originally for the purpose of advancing integrated or thematic curriculum. The Bradley Commission on History in the Schools (1989), for example, recommended that history be focused around several major themes—conflict and cooperation; civilization, cultural diffusion, and innovation; human interaction with the environment; values, beliefs, political ideas, and institutions; comparative history of major developments; and patterns of social and political interaction. These themes have strong implications for use as centralizing ideas for grade-level investigation in all subject areas.

Geographers, in like manner, have suggested that curriculum in social studies be constructed around five major geographic themes—place, location, people's interaction with their environment, people's migratory nature over time, and regionalism (as opposed to looking upon political boundaries as being sacred). Again, while initially confining these themes to the social studies, the geographers provide major ideas in which the entire school curriculum might be centered.

In a major advance in thinking, the National Commission on Social Studies in the Schools (1989), in an otherwise sterile report, suggested a three-year sequence of courses that integrate the U.S. historical experience into the larger scope of global history. Although NCSSS specifically suggested a chronological order (sometimes thought of as the binding chains of historical thinking) to this design, no firm or fast time frame should restrict the integrative imagination of both the teacher and the students in dealing with this major reconceptualization of content organization. While primarily oriented for grades 9–12, the NCSSS sequence reflects a position with clear implications for revising intellectual frameworks at all levels.

The Secondary Experience (Grades 9–12)

Secondary schools are still primarily defined as grades 7–12. The changeover to middle schools, while progressing, has not been accomplished either administratively or curricularly in the majority of school districts. This has meant that when social studies programs are defined, there will be at least two years of American history at grades 8 and 11; a geography, civics, or world cultures course at grade 7; and, usually a world history course when social studies is offered at grade 10. Only a few states require a 12th grade course, while some permit a wide variety of electives. Perhaps more than any other part of the K–12 social studies curriculum, this university-oriented organizational structure most nearly matches the design of the late 19th and early 20th century schools.

In the secondary years, students should receive a good grounding in the history and government of their own nation, and the cultures of other areas of the world, including Europe, Asia, Africa, and Latin America. The program should involve geography and the undergirding notion of global interdependence. It should also allow students to explore and use the various social sciences. The placement of these topics and their instructional treatment should be based upon sound developmental and learning theory, the expertise of teachers, and community consultation. In addition to history, geography, and culture studies, the program should consistently involve personal decision making and public policy issues that ask students to use historical and social science data. With the trend toward four years of social studies, a final year of public policy—domestic and global—would provide a worthy capstone for a well-designed program. However, decision making and public policy should be governing ideas throughout the 7–12 program because it cannot be guaranteed that all students will complete a full secondary experience.

To expand their civic memory and social conscience, students must have a firm foundation in the cultural values of U.S. democracy. In one interpretation, the history of the United States is the history of personal and public policymaking at all levels of government and in private life. For example, Susan B. Anthony chose a personal policy of persistent pursuit of public recognition of women's rights. Her work resulted in public policy discussions that eventually led to enactment of public law.

A major policy study might focus on constitutional development. Specific projects might include constitutionality of laws, child welfare, slavery, mental hospitalization, railroad regulation, conservation, and neutrality. Students would study the issues involved, define policy choices, and discover how people have chosen and will choose to resolve an issue through public discourse and action.

A two-year study of U.S. history and government (or, as cited earlier, a three-year world studies course with U.S. history) would enable students to delve more deeply into the "traditional" values of U.S.

society and the larger world around them and discover how these values have changed and influenced our lives. For example, American individualism continues to hold its own alongside an abiding sense of community, while in other areas of the world the reverse has been true. The conflict of those two values is found in literature, art, and daily life. In many ways, such values also determine people's choices about personal and social behavior.

No attempt should be made to cover the entire scope of world history. That study should focus on major economic, social, and political ideas (such as justice, equality, liberty, and capitalism) and major events that have influenced the development of world culture. The evolution of representative democracy (English, 1215 to present); migration of peoples (Islamic peoples); communication-technological development (ancient science to industrial revolutions to microchips); and regional, national, and global conflicts would be appropriate areas of investigation. The program should be developed to promote public policy (how people and governments respond to change) orientation and critical thinking.

The following questions could provide useful unit theses: What kinds of global, political, economic, and social policies have the European nations made and carried out since the 15th century? What effect did these policy choices have upon all areas of the world? What societal responses were made to the industrialization and intensive urbanization in the various areas in which it developed? Why were some areas of the world slow to develop? What effect did the advent of printing technology have upon the intellectual and cultural development of Europe and the rest of the world? How were various peoples or minority groups treated because of their religious beliefs or their race or sex? What effect does the advent of European unity have on the economies of the United States and the rest of the world?

The study of non-European cultures (representative studies from African, Asian, Middle Eastern, and Native American cultures) should include the perspectives of the indigenous peoples (Banks 1994). Major ideas such as environment, imperialism, cultural development, nationalism, industrialization (to include technological development), and other concepts should control the choice of content, which should include comparison and contrast connections to other cultures. Emphasis on universal values of justice, human life, and dignity should be stressed throughout all these studies.

Another possible program configuration has great potential for helping students integrate and apply knowledge. This design involves choosing points at which students are given the opportunity to examine in depth what they have already learned and to apply that learning to new and different situations. Between 7th and 9th grade, for example, when students struggle to build an identity and search for ways to deal with crucial personal relationships, there should be an opportunity for them to identify, clarify, and propose alternative solutions to personal decisions and public policy issues selected from all levels—local, state, regional, and national. The 12th grade is recommended for concentration on a similar pattern, addressing how personal decisions and public policy issues—drawn again from all levels of governmental concern—might also be interrelated. The program should provide direct training in public policy analysis; examine a variety of philosophical and ethical rationales; integrate the social sciences, humanities, science, and mathematics; encourage some kind of public or community service (tied into the formal study); and, as a result, help students see the benefits of the integrated nature of knowledge.

These two integrated learning units continue to stress the need for students to see the relationship between their learning and their continuing role in the broader society. Doing so exposes students to the realization that knowledge can be organized and interpreted in a variety of ways, depending on their world view and the world views of others. Change is the constant that they come to understand. The programs enhance the value of critical thinking for students and require the use of different methodologies from the various knowledge sources. By using these tools, students reinforce previous learning about developing, communicating, and negotiating their own personal policies as well as those of national or international import.

Year 13: Public Service

If citizenship education, defined as learning to take "the office of citizen," is as significant and important as the vast majority of American people believe it is, perhaps now is the time to revive an old but good idea: public or community service (Boyer and Levine 1981). Such service would make real the relationship between thought and action to promote the public good, helping individuals apply the knowledge they have gained and practice their reasoning skills. Before a student goes on to college to focus on self-enhancement, a period of time given in service to others might encourage a greater sense of community. Such a term of public service would also strengthen the commitment to the goals of society for those for whom getting a job after high school is the immediate goal.

No such program can be successful if limited to make-work projects or work simply created to fill the bill. Former President Jimmy Carter has publicized one kind of service: giving of time and skills to rebuild or provide housing for the poor, using donated materials. Local services to the elderly, needy children, and other groups are areas of possible service, as are public works, environmental improvements, and public surveys. Education services that involve teaching aides, tutoring, peer counseling, working with teenage groups, service to senior citizens, or serving on school board advisory groups are also creative, constructive uses of time. The kinds of projects generally of low budget priority in local and county areas—such as historical preservation (houses, objects, and records)—could also be accomplished through such a program.

A Look to the Future

Certain dominant trends have implications for social studies programs. Demographic data point to an increase in the number of elderly citizens in the United States and the proportion of minority students in our schools, and employment and migration patterns reflect changing economic conditions. The national debt, balance of international trade, unemployment, and growing global military development and sales are also adding to citizens "need to know." It is estimated that information is doubling every 24 months, and the half-life of most technical undergraduate degrees is about four years. Attempts to keep pace with societal changes often demand "researched" answers, and research, in turn, drives social change. Caught up in this whirlwind of change, learners and teachers are forced to ask: What knowledge is of most worth? Is learning how to learn most important? How can I become a better policymaker? Answers to these questions must be grounded in the notion that knowledge is created through discourse—connections between and among students, teachers, and information. This knowledge, however, is not value free. It is locked into the contextual limitations of the cultural setting, the bureaucratic structure of the school, the ideologies of the classroom actors, and information in the text.

Textbooks, other data sources, and the larger community are significant information sources from which social studies content can be drawn. But what criteria can be used to select the most useful content? The answer to this question is political—a decision based on the authority of individuals and groups steeped in tradition and the conventional wisdom of the profession. However, educators need to go beyond the conventional wisdom and address the abilities of seeing connections, using different logics, creating new knowledge, communicating with others, and making policy decisions when charting program development and improvement.

Students must understand the direct relationship between knowledge and power. Social studies must exercise this power by awakening imagination, stretching abilities, deepening understandings, empowering policymaking, and driving our sense of obligation to the larger communities of which we are a part. The ideal of *E Pluribus Unum* must be presented as a picture of the complex and diverse world in which we must live with some grace and cooperation, understanding that our personal well-being is always tied to the health of the community. In many ways, social studies educators must take curriculum leadership, not only in regard to educational theory and practice, but in the larger understanding of the relationship between education and freedom.

References

Banaszak, R.A., H.M. Hartoonian, and J.S. Leming. (1991). *New Horizons for Civic Education*. San Francisco: Foundation for Teaching Economics.

Banks, J. (1994). *Multiethnic Education: Theory and Practice*. 3rd ed. Boston: Allyn and Bacon.

Beane, J. (1990). *From Rhetoric to Reality: The Middle School Curriculum*. Columbus, Ohio: The National Middle School Association.

Beard, C.A. (1932). *A Charter for the Social Sciences*. New York: Charles Scribner's Sons.

Beard, C.A. (1934). *The Nature of the Social Sciences*. New York: Charles Scribner's Sons.

Bellah, R., et al. (1986). *Habits of the Heart*. New York: Harper and Row.

Boulding, K.E. (1985). *The World as a Total System*. Beverly Hills: Sage Publications, Inc.

Boyer, E., and A. Levine. (1981). *A Question of Common Learning*. Princeton, N.J.: Carnegie Foundation for the Advancement of Teaching.

Bradley Commission on History in the Schools. (1988). *Building a History Curriculum: Guidelines for Teaching History in the Schools*. Washington, D.C.: National Excellence Network.

Brady, M. (1989). *What's Worth Teaching?* Albany: State University of New York Press.

Bragaw, D. (March 1986a). "Excellence: A Professional Responsibility." *Social Education* 50: 214–219.

Bragaw, D., ed. (November/December 1986b). "Scope and Sequence: Alternatives for Social Studies." *Social Education* 50: 484–485.

Brooks, J.G., and M.G. Brooks. (1993). *In Search of Understanding: The Case for Constructivist Classrooms.* Alexandria, Va.: Association for Supervision and Curriculum Development.

Butts, R.F. (1989). *The Civic Mission in Educational Reform: Perspectives for the Public and the Profession.* Stanford, Calif.: Hoover Institution Press.

Cleveland, H. (1985). *The Knowledge Executive.* New York: Harper and Row.

Dewey, J. (1916). *Democracy and Education.* New York: Macmillan.

Dewey, J. (1927). *The Public and Its Problems.* New York: Henry Holt and Company.

Dewey, J. (1938). *Logic: The Theory of Inquiry.* New York: Henry Holt and Company.

Engle, S.H., and Anna Ochoa. (1988). *Education for Democratic Citizenship.* New York: Teachers College Press.

Ferguson, M. (1976). *The Aquarian Conspiracy.* Los Angeles: J.R. Tarcher Co.

Gardner, H. (November/December 1991). "The Unschooled Mind." *Teacher Magazine,* pp. 40–44.

George, P.S., and W.M. Alexander. (1993). *The Exemplary Middle School.* 2nd ed. Orlando, Fla.: Harcourt Brace Publishers.

George, P.S., C. Stevenson, J. Thomason, and J. Beane. (1992). *The Middle School and Beyond.* Alexandria, Va.: Association for Supervision and Curriculum Development.

Goodlad, J. (1984). *A Place Called School.* New York: McGraw-Hill.

Hunt, M.P., and L.E. Metcalf. (1968). *Teaching High School Social Studies: Problems in Reflective Thinking and Social Understanding.* 2nd ed. New York: Harper and Row.

National Commission on Social Studies in the Schools. (1989). *Charting a Course.* Washington, D.C.: Author.

National Council for the Social Studies. (1994). *Curriculum Standards for Social Studies. Bulletin 89.* Washington, D.C.: Author.

Newmann, F.M., and D. Oliver (1970). *Clarifying Public Controversy.* Boston: Little, Brown and Company.

Newmann, F., T.A. Bertoucci, and R.M. Landsness. (1975). *Education for Citizen Action: Challenge for Secondary Education.* Berkeley, Calif.: McCutchan.

Peirce, C.S. (1956). *Chance, Love and Logic.* New York: George Brazillier, Inc.

Raskin, M.G., and H.J. Bernstein. (1987). *New Ways of Knowing: The Sciences, Society, and Reconstructive Knowledge.* Totowa, N.J.: Rowman and Littlefield.

Ross, A., and K. Olsen. (1993). *The Way We Were, The Way We Can Be: A Vision for the Middle School.* Oak Creek, Ariz.: Susan Kovalik and Associates.

Saxe, D.W. (1994). *Social Studies for the Elementary Teacher.* Boston: Allyn and Bacon.

Stevenson, C., and J.F. Carr. (1993). *Integrated Studies in the Middle Grades: Dancing Through Walls.* New York: Teachers College Press.

Task Force for Global Education in the U.S. (1987). *The U.S. Prepares for Its Future.* New York: The American Forum.

Toepfer, C. (1990). *The Middle School Curriculum.* Columbus, Ohio: National Middle Schools Association.

Toepfer, C. (June 23, 1994). "Integrated Curriculum." Paper presented at the Annual Middle Grades Conference in Greenville, North Carolina.

Vars, G. (1987). *Interdisciplinary Teaching in the Middle Grades.* Columbus, Ohio: National Middle Schools Association.

Vygotsky, L.S. (1978). *Mind in Society: The Development of Higher Mental Processes.* Cambridge, Mass.: Harvard University Press.

Wronski, S.P., and D.H. Bragaw, eds. (1986). *Social Studies and Social Sciences: A Fifty-Year Perspective.* Washington, D.C.: National Council for the Social Studies.

Zangwill, I. (1975). *The Melting Pot: A Drama in Four Acts.* New and Revised Edition. Facsimile edition. LC 74-29532.

Social Studies Programs Incorporating Aspects of a Policy Approach

Suzanne Middle School
Walnut Valley Unified School District
525 Suzanne Road
Walnut, CA 91789

Shawnee Mission Unified School District 512
6649 Lamar
Shawnee Mission, KS 66202

School District of Waukesha
222 Maple Avenue
Waukesha, WI 53186

Iroquois Middle School
2495 Rosendale Road
Niskayuna, NY 12309

Kittredge Magnet School of High Achievers
2383 North Druid Hills Road, N.E.
Atlanta, GA 30329

Knox Elementary School
700 West Orchid Lane
Chandler, AZ 85224

Benevnue Middle School
Benevnue Road
Rocky Mount, NC 27801

This represents a sampling of Social Studies Programs of Excellence, recognized by the National Council for the Social Studies, 3501 Newark Street, N.W., Washington, DC 20016. The authors are grateful to NCSS for this service.

11

Technology Education

M. James Bensen

Technology Education is an educational program that has made the transition from what had previously been known as Industrial Arts (see Bensen 1988). Technology Education curriculums have made a dramatic change in the past two decades. Instead of loosely organized courses in such areas as woodworking, metalworking, and drafting, these curriculums are now usually advanced courses that draw their content from the rapidly changing comprehensive technology of the world. Although these curriculums vary by state and school system, Technology Education courses today usually are in such areas as Communication Systems, Manufacturing, Research and Development, Engineering, Entrepreneurship, Design, and Biotechnology.

Technology and Technology Education Defined

Because the concepts of technology and technology education are so closely related, a discrete definition for each will add clarity and precision for using these terms. Although "technology" has become a household word, it means different things to different people. The definitions provided here for these terms are broadly accepted by both the practitioners in the field of technology as well as those in education.

Technology. "Technology is a body of knowledge and the systematic application of resources to produce outcomes in response to human wants and needs" (Savage and Sterry 1990).

Technology Education. "A comprehensive, action-based educational program concerned with technical means, their evolution, utilization, and significance: with industry, its organization, personnel, systems, techniques, resources, and products, and their sociological impact" (International Technology Education Association [ITEA] 1985).

Technology differs from science and should not be simply viewed as applied science. Technology has its own methods, systems, and disciplines—as science does—and it is a major driver of change in this world, a source of much of our economic well-being, safety, and quality of life. Technology also holds the potential for destructive means, if put under the direction of people who choose to utilize it for their personal gain rather than for the common good. The model below (Figure 11.1) depicts the kind of scientific, technological, and technical work that people perform and the consequences resulting from their work. Scientific work relates to the science programs in our schools; technological work would provide the basis for technology education programs; and technical work would be what we call "vocational education" in our schools. This chapter describes the nature of programs that provide experiences in the disciplines, systems, process, and impact of technology.

FIGURE 11.1

Comparing Scientific, Technological, and Technical Work

Form of Work	Aims		Means		Consequences
Scientific	Motivated by a cognitive or theoretical interest	To know that . . .	Methods, tools, and skills characteristic of discovery	Guided by systematic rules of inquiry	Theoretical knowledge in the form of theories and laws
Technological	Motivated by a pragmatic or instrumental interest	To know how . . .	Methods, tools, and skills characteristic of invention	Guided by theoretic knowledge and by effectual practice	Instrumental knowledge in the form of systematized rules
Technical	Motivated by a practical or productive interest	To do or produce	Methods, tools, and skills characteristic of production	Guided by systems of prescribed rules or by rule-of-thumb	Things done or produced

Source: S. Kasperzyk, "A Technology: A Theoretical Base for Industrial Arts Education," unpublished doctoral diss., Michigan State University, 1973.

Goals, Content, and Standards

Goals

The goals of technology education are of general education intent, with a primary focus of achieving technological literacy. This broad, far-reaching scope of educational intent sets technology education programs apart from vocational education (preparation for work), educational technology (teaching media), or the narrow use of computers in our schools. ITEA outlines the goals of technology as follows:

1. Utilizing technology to solve problems or meet opportunities to satisfy human wants and needs.
2. Recognizing that problems and opportunities exist that relate to and often can be addressed by technology.
3. Identifying, selecting, and using resources to create technology for human purposes.
4. Identifying, selecting, and efficiently using appropriate technological knowledge, resources, and processes to satisfy human wants and needs.
5. Evaluating technological ventures according to their positive and negative, planned and unplanned, and immediate and delayed consequences (Savage and Sterry 1990, p. 20).

Content

The content of technology education programs is evolving rapidly across the country, with several schools of thought influencing the structure of the curriculum. Among the more prominent approaches taken in the design of these programs are the following:

1. Technological Systems. These programs, which are organized around human adaptive systems, are among the more frequent and prominent in technology education. As stated by DeVore (1992), these technical means enable people to (1) transform the resources of the earth into useful products; (2) transport themselves, raw materials, and finished products throughout the earth and into outer space as well; and (3) transmit, receive, store, retrieve, and use information in various forms in the operation and management of their technological enterprises (p. 1). These systems are then translated into technology education programs that include courses such as Communication Systems, Transportation Systems, and Production Systems. And it is now common in the curriculum to find, for example, the Production Systems course further divided into courses on Manufacturing Systems (produced in-plant) and Construction Systems (produced on-site).

This approach to program development utilizes the universal systems model, shown in Figure 11.2. The universal systems model of input, process, and output provides a "systematic" way of thinking; in technological processes, it provides focus, direction, and precision to conducting the activity. The input provides the intent of the activity, along with the resources to carry it out. The process provides the approach undertaken to achieve the intent and is either enhanced or restricted by the resources. The output is the satisfaction of the intent, using the process to meet optimum conditions through efficient practice. In the design of curriculum materials, the "universal system" is used effectively in communicating, producing, or transporting.

FIGURE 11.2
Universal Systems Model

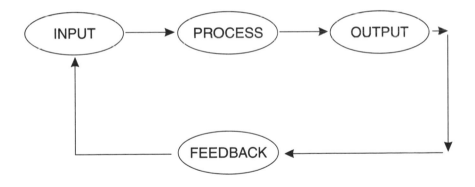

2. Design and Technology. These programs are gaining momentum, particularly at the early elementary grades. With a focus on design and the utilization of technology to provide experiential learning, Design and Technology programs are powerful motivators for learning. As identified by Todd and Hutchinson (1992), business and industry leaders are expressing a need for a new kind of employee—one who can adapt to changing technologies, work both independently and as part of a team, think critically, and manage resources. Todd and Hutchinson predict that these qualities may be key to our success as a nation in the high-tech, global community of the 1990s and beyond. Design-based technology education may be what is required to achieve this kind of future.

The focus of design-based technology education is on process. Such processes as innovation, entrepreneurship, design, and problem solving are often integrated into other subject areas of the curriculum. Todd and Hutchinson (1992) indicate that these hands-on experiences increase retention and strengthen the transfer of learning to other life situations.

3. Integrative Technology. Interest is growing in integrating the study of technology with other school subjects. Two goals of this movement toward integration are to increase learning and to provide a context for the more abstract elements of the school curriculum. The Math/Science/Technology approach is one example of an integrated program. Gauger's (1992) approach to integrating technology laboratories into the high school chemistry and physics courses in Oak Park, Illinois, has proven to be extremely effective in improving learning in those science classes. Kenneth Smith's program in Charles County, Maryland (ITEA 1989) offers another example of an integrated curriculum. Smith's program is based on problem solving and cuts across the traditional subjects of the school. He states that "helping students identify and select a technological area that interests them is the key to the entire program" (ITEA 1989, p. 37). Figure 11.3 shows how a common technological device serves as a vehicle for integrating scientific and mathematical concepts into the curriculum.

4. Engineering. Colleges and universities typically organize their engineering programs around the "disciplines" of technology, as contrasted to that of process or systems. Though most human endeavors are multidisciplined because work is done in society, the use of singular disciplines has been helpful for studying technical means. Technology programs emphasizing engineering have several advantages. Offering a K–12 program that would include such disciplines as mechanical, civil, and chemical engineering is likely to improve students' understanding of the role of these technology programs and increase societal support for them. Such programs also emphasize problem solving and provide a motivating learning environment for students (Bensen and Bensen 1992). Some recent K–12 engineering program designs by Thomas Lio at SUNY at Stoney Brook have caught the attention of teachers throughout the country and have resulted in highly successful courses (Lio 1992, 1993). For the past three years, teams of science and technology teachers from several states have been trained to implement these programs with very positive results, including a noticeable increase in the enrollment of college-bound students in the programs.

FIGURE 11.3

Integrating Technology

Topic	Parts	Scientific Concepts	Mathematical Concepts
Space Shuttle	Rocket Engines Wings/Tail Fuselage Wheels/Brakes Friction	Newton's Laws of Motion Bernoulli's Principle Aerodynamics Hydraulics	$F = M \times A$ Where F = Force M = Mass A = Acceleration
Telephone	Receiver Transmitter	Electromagnetic Induction Sound Waves/ Conversion of Energy Diaphragm Function/ Sound Waves	$I = \dfrac{E}{R}$ Where I = Constant E = Voltage R = Resistance
Steam Engine	Boiler Cylinder and Piston Cold Water Valve Beam	Kinetic Molecular Theory Evaporation Pressure Condensation Simple Machines/ Work/Energy	$P = \dfrac{F}{A}$ Where P = Pressure F = Force A = Area
Windmill	Sails Gears/Shaft Simple Machines Mechanical Advantage/Work/Force	Bernoulli's Principle Wheel and Axle	$MA = \dfrac{OF}{IF}$ Where MA = Mechanical Advantage OF = Output Force
Bicycle	Frame Pedals/Sprockets Wheels	Alloy Principles/ Metallurgy Simple Machines/Levers Wheel/Axle Mechanical Advantage/Work	$W = F \times D$ Where W = Work F = Force D = Distance

Source: Technology in Action, 1989.

Standards

Status. Standards for technology programs and facilities were developed and introduced to the field in 1985 (Dugger, Bame, and Pender 1985). These standards were designed to assist in the assessment of technology programs and included the following topics:

1. Philosophy
2. Instructional program
3. Student populations served
4. Instructional staff
5. Administration and supervision
6. Support systems
7. Instructional strategies
8. Public relations
9. Safety and health
10. Evaluation process

Although these standards were useful for designing overall programs, they were not designed for setting student performance levels. Hence, under ITEA's leadership, the background work for the development of a Technology Education Standards Project to assess student performance has been completed. At the time of this writing, funding for this project from the National Science Foundation seemed likely.

Benchmarks. The American Association for the Advancement of Science (AAAS), through its Project 2061, has developed benchmarks for the study of technology that will serve as a baseline for later work in the development of standards. *Benchmarks for Science Literacy* (1993) organizes these benchmarks around three areas: (1) Technology and Science, (2) Design and Systems, and (3) Issues in Technology. In addition, these benchmarks were generated by grade level. The sampling of these benchmarks here shows how they change both by area and by grade level:

TECHNOLOGY AND SCIENCE

Kindergarten through Grade 2

By the end of 2nd grade, students should know that

• Tools are used to do things better or more easily and to do some things that could not otherwise be done at all. In technology, tools are used to observe, measure, and make things.

Grades 3 through 5

By the end of 5th grade, students should know that

• Technology extends the ability of people to change the world: to cut, shape, put together materials; to move things from one place to another; and to reach further with their hands, voices, senses, and minds. The changes may be for survival needs, such as food, shelter, and defense, or communication and transportation, or to gain knowledge and express ideas.

Grades 6 through 8

By the end of 8th grade, students should know that

• Engineers, architects, and others who engage in design and technology use scientific knowledge to solve practical problems. But they usually take human values and limitations into account as well.

Grades 9 through 12

By the end of 12th grade, students should know that

• Technology usually affects society more directly than science because it solves practical problems and serves human needs (and may create new problems and needs). In contrast, science affects society mainly by stimulating and satisfying people's curiosity and occasionally by enlarging or challenging their views of what the world is like.

DESIGN AND SYSTEMS

Kindergarten through Grade 2

By the end of 2nd grade, students should know that

• People can use objects and ways of doing things to solve problems.

Grades 3 through 5

By the end of 5th grade, students should know that

• There is no perfect design. Designs that are best in one respect (safety or ease of use, for example) may be inferior in other ways (cost or appearance). Usually some feature must be sacrificed to get others. How such trade-offs are received depends upon which features are emphasized and which are down-played.

Grades 6 through 8

By the end of 8th grade, students should know that

• Design usually requires taking constraints into account. Some constraints, such as gravity or the properties of the materials to be used, are unavoidable. Other constraints, including economic, political, social, ethical, and aesthetic ones, limit choices.

Grades 9 through 12

By the end of 12th grade, students should know that

• In designing a device or process, thought should be given to how it will be manufactured, operated, maintained, replaced, and disposed of, and who will sell, operate, and take care of it. The costs associated with these functions may introduce more constraints on the design.

ISSUES IN TECHNOLOGY

Kindergarten through Grade 2

By the end of 2nd grade, students should know that

• When a group of people want to build something or try something new, they should try to figure out ahead of time how it might affect other people.

Grades 3 through 5

By the end of 5th grade, students should know that

• Any invention is likely to lead to other inventions. Once an invention exists, people are likely to think up ways of using it that were never imagined at first.

Grades 6 through 8

By the end of 8th grade, students should know that

• The human ability to shape the future comes from a capacity for generating knowledge and developing new technologies—and for communicating ideas to others.

Grades 9 through 12

By the end of 12th grade, students should know that

• Technological knowledge is not always as freely shared as scientific knowledge unrelated to technology. Some scientists and engineers are comfortable working in situations in which some secrecy is required, but others prefer not to do so. It is generally regarded as a matter of individual choice and ethics, not one of professional ethics (AAAS 1993, p. 57).

Influences on the Curriculum

In their efforts to implement technology education programs, educators face almost equally strong deterring and supporting influences.

Deterring Influences

Among the major influences that plague the implementation of technology education programs is the tradition that deems the study of "know-how" as being of lesser value than the traditional academic program. Anything that appears "practical" has been seen in the minds of traditional educators as "shop" and has been considered appropriate only for the less-able student. But in fact, a high percentage of very bright or "gifted" students who do not learn well by verbal or abstract approaches seem to find the more applied approach stimulating, motivating, and easier to understand.

A second deterrent to technology education programs is the idea that if it involves technology, it is vocational education. Although technology education can indeed help students explore careers, the objectives of these programs are not vocational in the traditional sense. Technology education contains many of the elements important for the rapidly changing and redesigned world of work, but it should not be limited to work preparation. A well-designed technology education program should prepare *all* students to live—and live well—in an increasingly technological culture.

A third deterring influence on technology education programs is that of equating "computers" with technology. Unfortunately, many educators still hold this extremely narrow view of technology, and many schools across the country use these two terms interchangeably. This confusion delays securing full support for comprehensive technology programs.

Supporting Influences

The power and force of technology today is self-evident. It is fueling rapid change and global competition as never before. In 1900, the knowledge base was doubling every 50 years; today it will double while a student is going through high school.

Thus, the study of technology is imperative for the well-being of our nation and for the common good of our people. The growing recognition that technology is the key resource for our future economic condition is helping to support technology programs in our schools.

Structure of the Curriculum

The study of technology takes many forms. Two features, however, are generally found: (1) the program is experientially based, and classes are taught in a laboratory setting; and (2) theory and problems are often presented in classrooms and resource centers; then students take these ideas and put them to work, either individually or in teams of problem solvers.

One of the more common curriculum structures in use is from the work of a task force of the International Technology Education Association, which was directed by Ernest Savage and Leonard Sterry, published in *A Conceptual Framework for Technology Education* (Savage and Sterry 1990). This model, represented in Figure 11.4, was generated through a national study and has served as a "consensus" curriculum structure in many states.

FIGURE 11.4

A Model Curriculum Structure

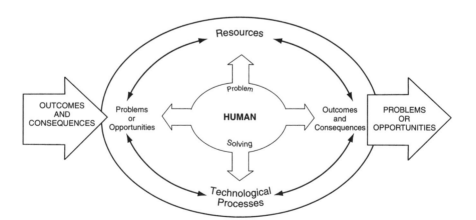

This model provides direction and reminds curriculum designers of the essentials of systems. By following this model, educators can provide a comprehensive program that is both content and process based. At the center of the model is the element of "human problem solving." The root issues feeding into the model—outcomes and consequences—are then identified as problems or opportunities. These are solved using resources and technological processes, which results in new outcomes and consequences. This model depicts a continuous, "closed-loop" process. When using this model in conjunction with a scope-and-sequence chart, educators have the framework for a comprehensive program design.

Program Scope and Sequence

Designed to meet the needs of students and also constrained by a school or school district's resources, technology education programs can and do take on a variety of scope-and-sequence structures. A common model is one where the curriculum is integrated with other subjects in the elementary grades, moves on to more specific offerings for the early adolescent, and ends up with unit courses in the senior high grades. Programs that offer experiences at the adult level are customized for the population. The scope-and-sequence chart shown here (see Figure 11.5) provides some structure to categories of instruction by level (Bensen 1988).

The Council for Technology Teacher Education *Yearbook* series (1952–1995) provides resources for programs that are designed for each particular level. Although the curriculum was referred to as "Industrial Arts" when this series was written, the content of this series provides significant insight into the philosophy and structure of K–12 programs, goal setting, readiness of learners, approaches to instruction, and the rationale for including content in the school curriculum (Lockette 1973, Householder 1972, Thrower and Weber 1974). The proceedings of a Technical Foundation of America symposium (ITEA 1992), and *Technology Education: An Action Plan for Minnesota* (Gilberti 1994) also provide additional concepts for curriculum design.

FIGURE 11.5

Level of Experience and Goal Emphasis: Preschool to Adult

	LEVEL OF EDUCATION				
	Preschool/ Elementary	Middle/ Jr. High	Early Senior High	Advanced Senior High	Adult Education
Educational Experiences	Integrated into the Curriculum Careers Tools Machines Processes Problem Solving	General Technology Industrial Enterprise	Communication Systems Transportation Systems Production Systems	Advanced Enterprise	Individualized courses to meet needs and interests
Goal Emphasis	Technology Awareness Industrial Awareness Career Awareness	Technology Orientation Industrial Insight Career Self-Concept Development and Exploration	Technology Exploration Industrial Understanding Career Cluster Exploration	Technology Utilization Industrial Interpretation Career Development and Beginning Specialization	Technology Assessment and Transfer Industrial Applications Career Reorientation and Leisure Pursuits

Program Delivery by Level

The delivery of programs by level of instruction takes into consideration students' needs and interests within the context of the integrity of the knowledge base of technology (see Figure 11.6). Programs at the elementary level are usually integrated into the curriculum to provide meaning and context for learning. When technology programs are integrated with real-world concepts, students find their formal instruction in such areas as math, science, and social studies more relevant and easier to understand.

For early adolescents, programs take on more of a general exploratory approach by offering separate courses. These courses may be more content based, such as a class entitled "Introduction to Technology." Or they may be more process-based learning experiences, in which students address a community need such as designing a playground for the local preschool or developing a plan for rerouting a highway around their city.

At the senior high level, unit courses are most often utilized to deliver the program. These are usually such separate courses as Communication, Manufacturing, Construction, and Transportation. Minnesota and Wisconsin offer an engineering course where the class functions as a design and development team. Students at different schools who are taking this same course often compete with each other to design, fabricate, and test a super-miles-per-gallon vehicle. The students' solutions must work within given criteria, such as using a common engine and alternative fuel; they test their vehicles on a track at a local university. Students' designs often produce vehicles that achieve over 200 miles per gallon.

Other effective delivery methods at the senior high level include such experiences as the Industrial Enterprise, Principles of Technology, and Research and Development. Programs at the senior high level can also include school-to-work initiatives such as Tech Prep and Youth Apprenticeships.

Large schools with many faculty members can usually offer courses in all levels of the sample scope-and-sequence chart. Small schools, which typically must limit their offerings, should provide educational experiences in Levels I–III as well as selected offerings in the Synthesis Level.

Alternative Assessments

The applied nature of technology education programs provides extensive opportunities for alternative assessment. The use of laboratory ratings, industry standards, and established certification tables (such as the integrity of welds) are excellent ways to bring relevance to assessment. In curriculums that are more design and process oriented, community experts can serve by offering critiques to students' solutions, judging competitive events, and examining portfolios.

When using enterprise activities—where students establish, organize, and operate a company—elements to assess are the quality of the organization, its economic success, and its ability to provide learning experiences. Of course, assessing how individual students acquire knowledge, skills, and attitudes follows patterns set in other educational programs.

Constructivism and Technology Education

The current interest in Constructivism in curriculum design and the educational theories of Piaget find an excellent fit with technology education. DeVries (1987) relates that Piaget's theory is constructivism—the process part of the account of cognitive and sociomoral development where action plays such an important role. Several key constructivist ideas find particular support in technology education:

FIGURE 11.6
Wisconsin Secondary School Technology Education Program Model

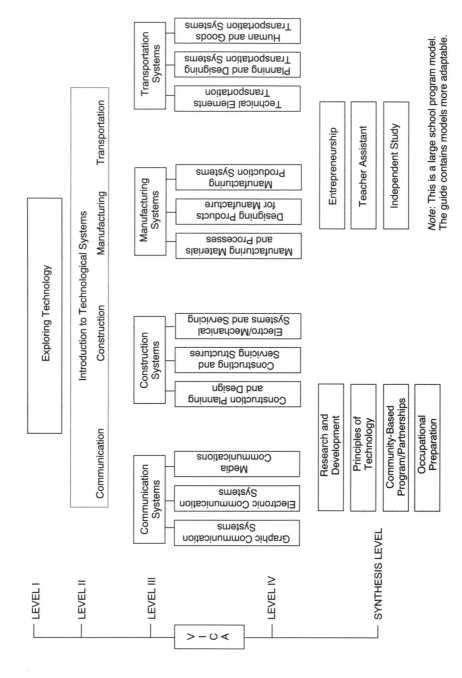

Note: This is a large school program model. The guide contains models more adaptable.

- *Teaching Classification.* The study of technology is rich in opportunities for teaching classification. In such classification areas as materials, processes, systems, and technical standards, the need to think logically, create structures, and develop cognitive frameworks is extensive.
- *Teaching Problem Solving.* Technology education challenges students from the start with opportunities for solving problems, designing solutions, inventing, prototyping, and reengineering.
- *Teaching of Games, Experimentation, and Cooperation.* A common approach in the teaching of technology education is to engage students in research and experimentation activities. Another very popular learning activity is one in which students participate in an enterprise to form a company, raise capital, and produce goods or render services to meet a particular need of society. The design of these enterprise activities often includes games, and cooperation is integral to the students' learning experience.

Edwards (1986) relates that Piaget's theory is based on the central idea that all knowledge is constructed, which is congruent with well-designed and well-delivered technology education programs. This is further collaborated by Piaget (1983), who believed that to present an adequate notion of learning, one must first explain how the learner manages to construct and invent, not merely how he repeats and copies. Hence, for technology education to meet the criteria of constructivism, it must move rapidly from the traditional teaching mode where the teacher demonstrates and the student imitates, to one where the teacher serves as a facilitator in a problem-solving and design-oriented learning environment. Technology education provides rich and extensive opportunities for meeting the criteria of good physical-knowledge activities as identified by DeVries (1987, p. 93): (1) the child must be able to produce the phenomena by his own action, (2) the child must be able to vary his action, (3) the reaction of the object must be observable, and (4) the reaction must be immediate. As learning environments move from the known to the unknown and foster progressivism in students' knowledge and capacity, technology education serves well.

Current Issues

One of the most pressing current issues in technology education is the shortage of adequately prepared technology education teachers. In the 1970s and '80s, many teacher education programs in technology education were closed because of low enrollments. Many university placement services are now reporting 5 to 10 openings for every qualified graduate in technology education. A substantial increase both in the number of good teacher education programs and well-prepared graduates from such programs is needed to meet this critical teacher shortage.

A second issue is the current duplication of effort in the development of new experience-based programs to reach the "forgotten half"—those youngsters who are not participating in the traditional college prep curriculum in high school and who are viewed as being ill prepared for meeting the challenges of the future (Halperin 1988). These programs have initially been designed around approaches such as "Tech-Prep," youth apprenticeships, and Education for Employment. Many leaders in this program movement are unaware that a well-designed Technology Education Program could suitably serve the forgotten half. At issue is the significant duplication of effort to reinvent curriculum that already exists and could meet these needs.

Resources for Curriculum Planning

Resources for technology education curriculum planning are abundant. Over 40 state education departments across the United States have developed curriculum guides on technology education. In addition, numerous individual schools have excellent resources that are available to others upon request. Publishers and laboratory suppliers are also providing contemporary resources for curriculum planning. ITEA (1914 Association Drive, Reston, VA 22091) has a large inventory of resource materials to assist educators in program improvements. The ITEA Annual Conference features seminars, expositions, technology festivals, demonstrations, and workshops designed to assist teachers and other curriculum designers. State technology education conferences also provide outstanding support for program upgrading and staff development.

For those who would like to know where to start in obtaining materials for improving their programs, contact the Technology Education Coordinator of your state's Department of Education. The "Other Resources" section at the end of this chapter includes the following states' contact information: Florida, Illinois, Iowa, Minnesota, New Jersey, New York, Virginia, and Wisconsin. The Industry and Technology Department at Ball State University (Muncie, Indiana) coordinates a curriculum resource center that has excellent materials. The Department of Technology and Society at the State University of New York, Stoney

Brook, has taken the lead in developing K–12 engineering materials. Programs developed by Mike Needen and Michael Jensen in Delta, Colorado, are drawing international attention, as are programs by Brad and Terry Thode, a husband-and-wife team of innovators in the Haley, Idaho, elementary and middle schools (see "Other Resources" section for complete contact information).

Summary

Technology education programs are undergoing major curriculum reform as educators seek new and improved approaches for designing and offering innovative learning programs for their students. In the future, formal standards, benchmarks, and outcome assessments may tend to restrict the thinking of creative technology educators. Although some of this may be inevitable, we must be careful to maintain the dynamic nature of technology. The future of society depends upon its adaptability; technology is one of the ways that society stays adaptable. Technology education programs must foster this dynamic change process for building a better tomorrow.

References

American Association for the Advancement of Science. (1993). *Benchmarks for Science Literacy.* New York: Oxford Press.

Bensen, M.J. (1988). "The Transition from Industrial Arts to Technology Education." *Content of the Curriculum* (1988 Yearbook), edited by R. Brandt. Alexandria, Va.: Association for Supervision and Curriculum Development.

Bensen, M.J., and T.M. Bensen. (1992). "Positioning and Marketing Technology Education: Joining Forces with the Establishment, Part I." *Interface.* Menomonie, Wisc.: Wisconsin Technology Education Association.

DeVore, P.W. (1992). "Introduction to Transportation Technology." In *Transportation Technology Education* (41st Yearbook, Council on Technology Teacher Education), edited by J.R. Wright and S.A. Komacek. Columbus, Ohio: Glencoe, Macmillan/McGraw-Hill.

DeVries, R. (1987). *Programs of Early Education: The Constructivist View.* New York: Longman.

Edwards, C.P. (1986). *Promoting Social and Moral Development in Young Children: Creative Approaches for the Classroom.* New York: The Teachers College Press.

Gauger, R. (March/April 1992). "Chem Tech and Physics Teach: The Integration of Science and Technology." *TIES.*

Gilberti, A. (1994). *Technology Education: An Action Plan.* St. Cloud: St. Cloud State University, Minnesota Technology Education Association.

Halperin, S. (November 1988). *The Forgotten Half, Pathways to Success for America's Youth and Young Families.* Final Report, Youth and America's Future: The William T. Grant Foundation Commission on Work, Family and Citizenship.

Householder, D.J., ed. (1972). *Industrial Arts for the Early Adolescent.* Bloomington, Ill.: McKnight.

· International Technology Education Association. (1985). *Technology Education in Action: Outstanding Programs.* Reston, Va.: Author.

International Technology Education Association. (1989). *Education in Action: Outstanding Programs.* Reston, Va.: Author.

International Technology Education Association. (1992). *Critical Issues in Technology Education.* Reston, Va.: Author.

Kasperzyk, S. (1973). "A Technology: A Theoretical Base for Industrial Arts Education." Unpublished doctoral diss., Michigan State University, East Lansing.

Lio, T.T. (1992). *Teacher Enhancement Workshops in Technological Literacy and Engineering Concepts.* Stoney Brook, N.Y.: State University of New York.

Lio, T.T. (1993). *Principles of Engineering: A National Initiative.* Stoney Brook, N.Y.: State University of New York.

Lockette, R.E., ed. (1973). Industrial Arts for the Senior High School. Bloomington, Ill.: McKnight.

Piaget, J. (1983). "Piaget's Theory." In *Handbook of Child Psychology,* 4th ed., Vol. 1, edited by P.H. Mussen. New York: John Wiley.

Savage, E., and L. Sterry. (1990). *A Conceptual Framework for Technology Education.* Reston, Va.: The International Technology Education Association.

Dugger, W.E., E.A. Bame, and C.A. Pender. (1985). *Standards for Technology Education Programs.* South Holland, Ill.: The Goodheart-Willcox Company, Inc.

Thrower, R.G., and R.D. Weber, eds. (1974). *Industrial Arts for the Elementary School.* Bloomington, Ill.: McKnight.

Todd, R., and P. Hutchinson. (January/February 1992). "Design and Technology: Good Practice and a New Paradigm." *TIES*: 5–10.

Additional Resources for Technology Education

Bensen, M.J. (1980). "Selecting Content for Technology Education." *Programs and Proceedings for Symposium '80: Technology Education.* Charleston, Ill.: Eastern Illinois University.

Technology Education: Principles of Engineering, Grades 9–12. (1990). Albany, N.Y.: The State Department of Education, Bureau of Technology Education Programs.

The Technology Education Curriculum, K–12. (1988). Richmond, Va.: Commonwealth of Virginia, Department of Education.

Waetjen, W.B. (1992). "Psychological Bases of Technology Education." *Technology and Human Behavior.* Reston, Va.: The International Technology Education Association.

Zilbert, E.E., and J.W. Mercer. (1992). *Technology Competence: Learner Goals for All Minnesotans.* (Report of the Legislative Task Force on Technology Competence). St. Paul, Minn.: State Council on Vocational Technical Education.

Other Resources

State Governments

Florida Department of Education
Division of Technology Education
243-L Collins Building
Tallahassee, FL 32399

Illinois State Board of Education/
 AVTE
Industrial Occupations
100 North First Street, C-421
Springfield, IL 62777-0001

Iowa Department of Education
Technology Education Division
Grimes State Office Building
Des Moines, IA 50319

Minnesota Department of Education
Industrial Technology Education
 Specialist
628 Capitol Square Building
St. Paul, MN 55101

New Jersey Department of Education
Technology Education Supervisor
255 West State Street, CN 500
Trenton, NJ 08625

New York State Department of
 Education
Supervisor for Technology Education
One Commerce Plaza
Albany, NY 12234

Virginia Department of Education
Technology Education Specialist
P.O. Box 6Q
Richmond, VA 23216

Wisconsin Department of Instruction
Technology Education Supervisor
125 South Webster Street
P.O. Box 7841
Madison, WI 53707

Schools and Universities

Department of Industry and
 Technology
Ball State University
Muncie, IN 47306

Mike Needen, Coordinator
Technology Education
Delta Public Schools
Delta, CO 81416

Director of Technology Education
School of Industry and Technology
University of Wisconsin-Stout
Menomonie, WI 54751

Brad Thode, Technology Instructor
Middle School
Haley, ID 83333

Terry Thode, Technology Instructor
Elementary School
Haley, ID 83333

Conclusion

Allan A. Glatthorn

My intent in this final chapter is to identify significant trends in the curriculum by analyzing both what the previous chapters have discussed and what they have not examined. Thus, this chapter is not simply a summary, but attempts to use the current literature on curriculum in general to complement the excellent analyses of the individual subjects included in this work. The focus is on the implications of this literature for curriculum leaders at the local level.

At the outset, it would be useful to put this book into perspective by explaining that the book represents a compendium of what I have termed the *recommended* curriculum (Glatthorn 1987)—that is, the curriculum recommended by experts in the field. I believe the authors of the chapters in this book have done an excellent job of delineating that recommended curriculum. However, the recommended curriculum is only one of six curriculums at work in the schools. The *written* curriculum is that represented in curriculum documents intended to guide what is taught; such documents are produced by state education departments, district curriculum offices, and schools. In the past, those written curriculums seem to have paid little attention to the recommendations of experts; the evidence now suggests that district leaders are more aware of such recommendations as the National Council of Teachers of Mathematics standards.

The *taught* curriculum is the curriculum delivered by the classroom teacher. The picture grows more complex here. Recent research indicates that teachers tend to ignore the recommended curriculum and pay only limited attention to the written curriculum, checking it occasionally to see what the district wants taught. Teachers are influenced far more by the *tested* curriculum, the curriculum embodied in state and district tests, and the *supported* curriculum, the curriculum embedded in textbooks and software. (See Glatthorn 1993 for a review of the factors influencing teacher planning.) Finally, there is a large gap between the taught curriculum and the *learned* curriculum, what students actually learn from the teacher's instruction. The learned curriculum, of course, is the bottom-line curriculum.

Thus, the question for local curriculum leaders as they read this text is a complex one: How should they use the recommendations of this work and others to develop written curriculum documents that will enable teachers to foster the learned curriculum? The answers to this question that I present here should be seen as flexible guidelines, since curriculum development is too complex to be reduced to a formulaic list of mandates.

Use the recommended curriculum as part of the knowledge base.

At the beginning of any project to develop a K–12 curriculum in a given field of study, curriculum leaders should carefully review the relevant chapter in this work and summarize the content recommendations found in this book. The knowledge base should also include other major components: content standards developed by professional groups; recommendations of other experts; research on effective teaching of that subject; and exemplary curriculum materials developed by major projects and organizations, such as the National Science Foundation in science.

The knowledge base has two major uses. It represents a set of benchmarks for evaluating locally produced guides. And it should form the basis of staff development provided to teachers, so that their recommendations are based on informed judgment.

Take due cognizance of emerging standards in the field.

As the authors of these chapters note, each subject area is developing or has developed specific standards for curriculum in that field. Note the distinction that Kendall and Marzano (1995) make here between *content standards* (what students should know and be able to do) and *curriculum standards* (descriptions of the instructional techniques and recommended learning activities). As leaders build the knowledge base, Kendall and Marzano recommend focusing on the content standards as the operative guidelines. They should also give special attention to the *benchmarks* provided by the experts; the benchmarks are the expected performances at various developmental levels, such as the end of grade 8.

The difficulty that both curriculum leaders and classroom teachers face is the large numbers of content standards and their related benchmarks. As Kendall and Marzano point out, if a district implemented all the standards and benchmarks recommended by subject experts, a student would have to demonstrate mastery of 1,541 benchmarks embedded within 157 standards, a total that represents the mastery of three benchmarks each week. The only reasonable way out of this dilemma is for leaders to critically review the standards and benchmarks and identify those that are most useful for their own district. As noted below, the large number of standards and benchmarks runs counter to the recommendation that curriculum emphasize depth, not coverage.

In making this decision, leaders may well keep in mind the number of benchmarks Kendall and Marzano recommend for each level: 75 for grades K–2; 125 for grades 3–5; 150 for grades for 6–8; and 250 for grades 9–12.

Pay close attention to state frameworks.

The task of curriculum development becomes even more complex with the development and dissemination of *state frameworks*. Curry and Temple (1992) identify two types of frameworks: "traditional frameworks," which are often rigid and prescriptive taxonomies of subject objectives, unrelated to other components of the system; and "progressive frameworks," which are less prescriptive and more likely to emphasize themes and concepts, and underscore the linkages between curriculum, instruction, and assessment. Massell and Fuhrman (1994) determined that as of late 1993, 15 states had already implemented curriculum frameworks, while 30 others were embarked upon the development of such materials. The fact that these state frameworks in many cases have become the foundation for state end-of-course tests means that local leaders must pay serious attention to them, whether they are traditional or progressive.

Despite the importance of state activity in curriculum frameworks and testing, this issue was largely ignored by the authors of the chapters in this book, except for the chapters on the arts and home economics. Perhaps the omission is the editor's responsibility, since authors were not specifically asked to address this issue.

Ensure that curriculum reflects a constructivist perspective.

Almost all the authors make explicit reference to the influence of constructivism on curriculum. While the theory is variously defined, in general, experts emphasize the following principles of constructivism: The learner is an active maker of meaning; learning at its best is socially constructed, as learners interact with each other; knowledge becomes generative as the learner applies it in the solving of contextualized and meaningful problems; learning at its best results in conceptual change; and optimal learning involves metacognition, reflecting about one's learning throughout the entire process. (See Brooks and Brooks 1993 for a more thorough discussion.)

One of the key implications of constructivism for the curriculum is that depth becomes much more important than coverage. If students are to locate knowledge, acquire learning strategies, and apply that knowledge and those strategies in solving complex problems, then obviously in-depth units are required. The excessive requirements of standards, benchmarks, and frameworks (three benchmarks a week) seem antithetical to the need for in-depth study based on constructivist principles.

Integrate with caution.

Several of the authors underscore the importance of cross-subject integration, which typically involves students in studying thematic units based on content from two or more separate subjects. As Vars (1991) notes, the research seems to support the effectiveness of such units. However, two cautions should be kept in mind. First, many of these integrated units are poorly designed and are not based on sound principles of learning, as Brophy and Alleman (1991) indicate. In their view, integration is a means, not an end unto itself. The other difficulty with too much integration is that constructivist problem solving requires in-depth subject matter knowledge, slighted in many integrated units.

Beware of the hyper-verbalization of the curriculum.

I use the term "hyper-verbalization" to signify the process of emphasizing verbal learning to the exclusion of other ways of knowing. All subject areas should strive for a balance in the ways of knowing. The chapters in this book on what are mistakenly termed "minor" subjects (i.e., the arts, home economics, and technology education) suggest that these important subjects are becoming increasingly conceptual and verbal in their orientations. The virtue of traditional approaches to these subjects was that they emphasized kinesthetic, musical, visual, and manual ways of knowing, thus providing rich opportunities, especially to students whose verbal skills were not strong. These courses need to continue to be grounded in concrete, meaningful learning experiences. The so-called "major" subjects need to heed this warning as well. Balance in the ways of knowing should be achieved within as well as across the subject matter areas.

Curriculum development is an ongoing process, not an event.

Perhaps the final lesson to be learned from this book is that curriculum development must be seen as a continuous process, one in which leaders plan for a cyclic review of all the subjects. Each of the chapters suggests a picture of these fields of study in the process of reconceptualization. Even in a field such as mathematics, where there seems to be a strong consensus, change is ongoing. The NCTM standards, which at the time seemed like a final pronouncement of what should be learned in mathematics, are currently being revised. English language arts, as Myers points out, seems to be a discipline in search of a definition.

Curriculum development at its best has always been a complex science and art. The message of this book is that it is getting more complex all the time.

References

Brooks, J.G., and M.G. Brooks. (1993). *In Search of Understanding: The Case for Constructivist Classrooms*. Alexandria, Va.: Association for Supervision and Curriculum Development.

Brophy, J., and J. Alleman. (1991). "A Caveat: Curriculum Integration Isn't Always a Good Idea." *Educational Leadership* 49, 2: 66.

Curry, B., and T. Temple. (1992). *Using Curriculum Frameworks for Systemic Reform*. Alexandria, Va.: Association for Supervision and Curriculum Development.

Glatthorn, A.A. (1987). *Curriculum Renewal*. Alexandria, Va.: Association for Supervision and Curriculum Development.

Glatthorn, A.A. (1993). *Learning Twice: An Introduction to the Methods of Teaching*. New York: Harper Collins.

Kendall, J.S., and R.J. Marzano. (1995). *The Systematic Identification and Articulation of Content Standards and Benchmarks: Update*. Aurora, Colo.: Mid-continent Regional Educational Laboratory.

Massell, D., and S. Fuhrman. (1994). *Ten Years of State Education Reform, 1983–1993*. New Brunswick, N.J.: Consortium for Policy Research in Education, Rutgers University.

Vars, G.F. (1991). "Integrated Curriculum in Historical Perspective." *Educational Leadership* 49, 2: 14–15.

About the Authors

Andrew Ahlgren is Associate Director of Project 2061 at the American Association for the Advancement of Science and Professor Emeritus of Curriculum and Instruction at the University of Minnesota. He is a principal contributor to *Science for All Americans* and *Benchmarks for Science Literacy.* He previously was project coordinator for Project Physics and authored numerous publications on research methods, student characteristics, and science and mathematics education, including *Cycles of Nature: Introduction to Biological Rhythms,* published by the National Science Teachers Association. Address: Project 2061, AAAS, 1333 H Street, Washington DC 20003.

M. James Bensen is President of Bemidji State University, having previously served as President of the Dunwoody Institute in Minneapolis. Prior to his work at Dunwoody, he was Dean of the School of Industry and Technology at the University of Wisconsin-Stout. He has held numerous offices in professional associations at the local, state, national, and international levels. Address: Bemidji State University, Deputy Hall, 1500 Birchmont Drive, N.E., Bemidji, MN 56601-2699.

Christine Blaber is Associate Director of the Center for School Health Programs at the Education Development Center, Newton, Massachusetts. In this role, she works with administrators, teachers, parents, and students to develop and support the implementation of an enhanced comprehensive school health education program at three middle schools in New York City. She serves as cofacilitator of the ASCD Comprehensive School Health Education Network and has worked as a classroom teacher and consultant in health education for many years. Address: EDC, 55 Chapel Street, Newton, MA 02160.

Donald H. Bragaw is Professor of Education in the School of Education at East Carolina University. Formerly President of the National Council for the Social Studies, he is the author of publications dealing with the history of social studies education; the relationship of culture and language; and the intersection of science, technology, and society. Address: 120 Gates Drive, Winterville, NC 28590.

Charles B. Corbin is a Professor of Exercise Science and Physical Education at Arizona State University. He is senior author of *Concepts of Physical Fitness* (8th ed.) and *Fitness for Life* (3rd ed.) with Ruth Lindsey. These are the leading college and high school texts in the area of physical fitness. He is a past president of the American Academy of Kinesiology and Physical Education and has published more than 30 books and 150 professional and research articles in the areas of exercise, fitness, and physical education. Address: Department of Exercise Science and Physical Education, Arizona State University, Box 870701, Tempe, AZ 85287-0701.

Allan A. Glatthorn is Professor of Education in the School of Education at East Carolina University. He is the author of *Developing the Quality Curriculum*, published by ASCD in 1994. He has written numerous professional books in the areas of curriculum and supervision and has consulted with more than two hundred school systems in the areas of curriculum development and teacher supervision. Address: Speight Building, East Carolina University, Greenville NC 27858.

Anna O. Graeber is an Associate Professor in the Department of Curriculum and Instruction in the College of Education at the University of Maryland, College Park. She is currently a member of the Editorial Panel of the *Journal for Research in Mathematics Education*. She has written numerous articles and chapters, many of which concern students' mathematical misconceptions, one of her special interests. Address: University of Maryland at College Park, Center for Mathematics Education, College Park, MD 20742.

Deborah Haber is Special Health Specialist at the Education Development Center, Newton, Massachusetts. In this role, she works with administrators, teachers, parents, and students to develop and support the implementation of an enhanced comprehensive school health education program at three middle schools in New York City. She currently serves as cofacilitator of the ASCD Comprehensive School Health Education Network and has worked as a classroom teacher and consultant in health education for many years. Address: EDC, 55 Chapel Street, Newton, MA 02160.

H. Michael Hartoonian is presently the State Supervisor of Social Studies Education for the State of Wisconsin; president-elect of the National Council for the Social Studies; and author of two books and numerous articles in the fields of ethics, economics, and social studies education. Most recently, he was a major contributor to the Social Studies Standards issued by the National Council for the Social Studies. Address: Graduate School, Hamline University, St. Paul, MN 55105.

Paul R. Lehman is Professor of Music and Senior Associate Dean of the School of Music at the University of Michigan, Ann Arbor. He has served as President of the Music Educators National Conference and recently chaired the task force that developed the national standards for K–12 instruction in music. He is the author of six books and more than one hundred articles and reviews concerned with curriculum, teacher education, and measurement and evaluation. Address: School of Music, University of Michigan, Ann Arbor, MI 48109-2085.

Myriam Met is Coordinator of Foreign Languages for the Montgomery County Public Schools in Rockville, Maryland. She serves on the Advisory Council for the National Standards in Foreign Language Education and is cochair of the College Board's Pacesetter Spanish Task Force. She has authored numerous articles in refereed professional journals and contributed chapters to many professional books. Address: Montgomery County Public Schools, Rockville, MD 20850.

Miles Myers is the Executive Director of the National Council of Teachers of English. He is the author of *Negotiating English and Literacy*, to be published in 1995. He has written numerous professional books and articles in the areas of literacy and assessment. Address: National Council of Teachers of English, Urbana, IL 61801.

Robert P. Pangrazi is a Professor of Exercise Science and Physical Education at Arizona State University. He is the author of numerous books used worldwide, including *Dynamic Physical Education for Elementary School Children,* (coauthored with Victor Dauer), which is now in its 11th edition. He is editor of a number of journals and has published extensively in the professional research literature. Address: Department of Exercise Science and Physical Education, Arizona State University, Box 870701, Tempe, AZ 85287-0701.

Sharon S. Redick is Associate Dean of Academic Programs in the College of Human Ecology at The Ohio State University. She is the editor of the 1996 Family and Consumer Sciences Teacher Education Yearbook, *Research in Family and Consumer Sciences Education.* She teaches graduate-level curriculum courses in Home Economics Education and is the author of three curriculum guides. She is currently chair of the American Association of Family and Consumer Sciences, Education and Technology Division. Address: Ohio State University, Home Economics Education, 206 Campbell Hall, 1787 Neil Avenue, Columbus OH 43210-1295.